"Friendship is one of the greatest glories and joys of life. Lamb addresses it helpfully, and his book is sure to speak to the yearnings of many."
OS GUINNESS, AUTHOR OF *LONG JOURNEY HOME*

"Richard's visionary and practical words mark the path to experiencing the intimacy we long for with God and others. This book has forever influenced the way I view my pursuit of God and my relationships with friends. I highly recommend it to you!"
MARK GAUTHIER, NATIONAL DIRECTOR,
U.S. CAMPUS MINISTRY, CAMPUS CRUSADE FOR CHRIST

"Weaving together powerful biblical insight, personal stories and the context of contemporary culture, Rich Lamb demonstrates the power of community under the leadership of Jesus. This book is a must-read for those who wish to experience the richness of the vertical relationship with God through the real-life horizontal friendships he has given us."
MARK ASHTON, ASSOCIATE EVANGELISM DIRECTOR,
WILLOW CREEK COMMUNITY CHURCH

"A ringing call to spiritual growth through mutual accountability in Christian community. Just the kind of help we need to overcome the ghastly individualism in American Christianity."
RONALD J. SIDER, PRESIDENT,
EVANGELICALS FOR SOCIAL ACTION

"*The Pursuit of God in the Company of Friends* offers a very practical read for those who want to see the gospel of Christ transform their relationships and their lives. A great resource for small-group discussion."
TOM SINE, FOUNDER, MUSTARD SEED ASSOCIATES

"As a pastor who has begun 'deprogramming' the church in order to build deeper neighborhood-centered communities of faith, I am thrilled to find Lamb's timely and on-target book. Readers will appreciate not only his thoroughness but also his personal commitment to pursuing God through the company of friends."
KEN FONG, SENIOR PASTOR,
EVERGREEN BAPTIST CHURCH OF LOS ANGELES

"Rich's clear work has rekindled my desire for a deepening company of friends in my own life. His honest stories and sharp, lively treatment of Scripture embolden me to take real steps in that direction. And I find myself hoping my friends read this book soon!"
DON EVERTS, AUTHOR OF *JESUS WITH DIRTY FEET*
AND *THE SMELL OF SIN*

"Through the centuries some very illuminating books on friendship have been written. Add to that list the unique treatment of the subject by Richard Lamb, *The Pursuit of God in the Company of Friends*. Addressed primarily to a young adult readership, it gives concrete, helpful counsel to all of us no matter where we are on the timeline. It will enrich our lives by deepening and enlarging those relationships with the fellow pilgrims we call friends."

VERNON C. GROUNDS, CHANCELLOR OF DENVER SEMINARY

"Individualism reigns supreme in our culture and has thoroughly permeated our Christian subculture; Richard Lamb's book offers a much-needed corrective. Especially helpful are the many practical suggestions for building friendships, such as listening, asking good questions, avoiding competition and finding reconciliation. I could imagine Lamb's book transforming the relationships (and therefore the lives) of a group on campus or in a church."

MARY ELLEN ASHCROFT, PROFESSOR OF ENGLISH, BETHEL COLLEGE, AUTHOR OF *TEMPTATIONS WOMEN FACE*

"Rich has terrific insights into the various Scriptures, which form the basis for findings in each chapter. He also has real-life illustrations liberally sprinkled throughout his flow of input. Rich has a passion about interdependence in the body. And finally, the book is very browsable. Any chapter can be read with profit apart from the whole of the book. It is clear that Rich is modeling for us throughout the whole book. He is himself one who is in the 'pursuit of God in the company of friends.'"

ROBERT CLINTON, PROFESSOR OF LEADERSHIP, FULLER THEOLOGICAL SEMINARY

"The emerging generation longs for true community yet struggles to know how to get there. Rich Lamb speaks to this longing by giving us biblical and personal pictures, stories, and practical ideas for making spiritual friendships and authentic community a reality. Caution: Not for the faint of heart!"

RICK RICHARDSON, AUTHOR OF *EVANGELISM OUTSIDE THE BOX*

"Rich Lamb's *The Pursuit of God in the Company of Friends* tells of the vital place spiritual friendships have played for him in knowing God. Deeply personal, very helpful. I have seen many books on friendship, and many on knowing God, but few that put them together so well."

LEIGHTON FORD, PRESIDENT OF LEIGHTON FORD MINISTRIES, AUTHOR OF *TRANSFORMING LEADERSHIP*

"Rich Lamb has given us not only a compelling invitation to deeper and more enduring friendships, but also a sumptuous feast of biblical insights, uncommon wisdom, winsome illustrations and practical skills. We throw around words like *grace, forgiveness, love, service* and *commitment,* but nowhere do we learn their deeper meaning better than in the company of true friends. This book charts a path to build those friendships and discover new life."

STEVE HAYNER, PROFESSOR OF EVANGELISM,
COLUMBIA THEOLOGICAL SEMINARY

"Rich's book powerfully touches on our shared longing to encounter God together in community. By weaving together the biblical story, his own personal story and practical wisdom, Rich charts a trustworthy path to the kinds of relationships and relating patterns that open us to life-changing experiences with God in the company of others."

RUTH HALEY BARTON, COFOUNDER,
THE TRANSFORMING CENTER,
AND AUTHOR OF *INVITATION TO SOLITUDE AND SILENCE*

"Rich Lamb gives us plenty of biblical constructs of what Christian community should involve and entail, then injects them with true, personal stories. Some of Rich's stories stretch our boundaries while others affirm the good things we are already doing. 'Yet deeper, yet broader' was the quiet encouragement I felt as I read. Genuine community and friendships take work; *The Pursuit of God in the Company of Friends* told me they're worth it."

PAUL TOKUNAGA, ASIAN AMERICAN MINISTRY COORDINATOR,
INTERVARSITY CHRISTIAN FELLOWSHIP

"Richard Lamb eloquently argues the crucial point that being friends and being intentional partners in the expansion of Jesus' kingdom are not only not at odds, they're inseparable. May many thousands of people freshly experience that most fulfilling kind of friendship as a result of this book."

DAVE SCHMELZER, PASTOR,
VINEYARD CHRISTIAN FELLOWSHIP OF CAMBRIDGE

"It is hard to imagine any topic more central to the heart of Christian faith and life than 'pursuing God in the company of friends.' Rich Lamb's message is deeply rooted in the gospel and nicely illustrated by real-life stories. Here is a gifted writer and insightful teacher serving up a powerful, attractive alternative to the dominant cultural ethos of 'pursuing self-interest by using others.'"

DAVID W. GILL, AUTHOR OF *BECOMING GOOD:
BUILDING MORAL CHARACTER*

"Guided by biblical principles and informed by his own ministry experiences, Rich Lamb has produced a wonderful work that challenges the reader to see discipleship as a communal endeavor. This is an excellent resource for those who serve today's emerging generation that expresses a deep yearning for spiritual formation as well as authentic community."

PETER CHA, ASSISTANT PROFESSOR OF PRACTICAL THEOLOGY, TRINITY EVANGELICAL DIVINITY SCHOOL

"For those with ears to hear, Richard Lamb offers an apprenticeship-in-print in what he calls 'a quest for the ultimate in the midst of the intimate.' Born out of years of ministry in the university and the church, the vision he sets forth is formed by the stories of Jesus and embodied in his own practices in the push and pull of life. *The Pursuit of God in the Company of Friends* is for all who long for the reality of God and of community, and who are willing to wonder why one so profoundly shapes the other."

STEVEN GARBER, FELLOW AND LILLY FACULTY SCHOLAR, CALVIN COLLEGE, AND AUTHOR OF *THE FABRIC OF FAITHFULNESS*

"*The Pursuit of God in the Company of Friends* is one of those books that comes at just the right time. It is clear that as our culture moves increasingly into a postmodern mindset, the whole question of Christianity as a community looms ever larger. How do we grow as people via Christian community? Richard Lamb tackles this important subject with rare insight based on a wealth of personal experience. His book combines biblical insights, classical sources, practical suggestions and, most importantly, numerous stories that bring alive these concepts for us."

RICHARD PEACE, ROBERT BOYD MUNGER PROFESSOR OF EVANGELISM AND SPIRITUAL FORMATION, FULLER THEOLOGICAL SEMINARY

"It is a happy fusion when an author writes on a topic because it is biblically important, applies it in a creative, fresh way without distorting or trivializing Scripture, and does so just at the time when contemporary society needs and values the subject. Rich Lamb does just this when he writes on friendship and community. He is insightful, incisive, honest and engaging. He is present in his own story neither as hero nor as villain, and certainly not as fool, but as an experienced friend."

WALTER L. LIEFELD, PROFESSOR EMERITUS OF NEW TESTAMENT, TRINITY EVANGELICAL DIVINITY SCHOOL

THE PURSUIT OF GOD

IN THE

COMPANY

OF FRIENDS

RICHARD LAMB

IVP Books

An imprint of InterVarsity Press
Downers Grove, Illinois

InterVarsity Press
P.O. Box 1400, Downers Grove, IL 60515-1426
World Wide Web: www.ivpress.com
E-mail: email@ivpress.com

InterVarsity Press® is the book-publishing division of InterVarsity Christian Fellowship/USA®, a movement
of students and faculty active on campus at hundreds of universities, colleges and schools of nursing in the
United States of America, and a member movement of the International Fellowship of Evangelical Students.
For information about local and regional activities, write Public Relations Dept., InterVarsity Christian
Fellowship/USA, 6400 Schroeder Rd., P.O. Box 7895, Madison, WI 53707-7895, or visit the IVCF website at
<www.intervarsity.org>.

Scripture quotations, unless otherwise noted, are from the New Revised Standard Version of the Bible,
copyright 1989 by the Division of Christian Education of the National Council of the Churches of Christ in
the USA. Used by permission. All rights reserved.

The personal stories in this book are retold by permission.

Cover design: Cindy Kiple
Cover image: Andrzej Burak/iStockphoto

ISBN 978-0-8308-3230-9

Printed in the United States of America ∞

Library of Congress Cataloging-in-Publication Data

Lamb, Richard, 1960-
    The pursuit of God in the company of friends / Richard Lamb.
      p. cm.
Includes bibliographical references.
    ISBN 0-8308-3230-0 (pbk.: alk. paper)
    1. Christian life. 2. Friendship—Religious aspects—Christianity.
I. Title.
    BV4647.F7L36 2003
    248.4—dc21

                                                                        2003010914

| P | 24 | 23 | 22 | 21 | 20 | 19 | 18 | 17 | 16 | 15 | 14 | 13 | 12 | 11 | 10 | 9 | 8 | 7 |
| Y | 26 | 25 | 24 | 23 | 22 | 21 | 20 | 19 | 18 | 17 | 16 | 15 | 14 | 13 | 12 | 11 | 10 | |

To my children, Mark and Becca.

This is indeed my deepest hope for you.

Contents

Introduction
The Transforming Power of Discipleship in Community

The University of California, Santa Cruz, is built into a redwood forest on the top of a hill, above the beaches and cliffs of Santa Cruz. One of my favorite scenic spots, the Cowell College courtyard, overlooks Monterey Bay. In the middle of the courtyard a mounted plaque proclaims the college motto: "The Pursuit of Truth in the Company of Friends." As breathtakingly beautiful as the campus is, the motto captivates me even more. It is the essence of what college should be—the quest for knowledge of things that truly matter, among beloved and valued friends. In Santa Cruz, this represents more than just a motto. The campus is structured—architecturally, academically, organizationally—around community and friendships.

So I have taken liberty with this idealistic campus motto to fashion the title of this book. I am not considering simply the academic pursuit of truth but the holistic pursuit of God. I take as the impetus for my task my own passion, not simply for "a truth" or some piece of the transcendent, but for the very heart of God. I want to experience God!

As you have picked up this book, I believe you are like me: (1) you were attracted to the phrase "the pursuit of God," (2) you liked the notion of "the company of friends" or (3) both. Consider, for example, the opposite phrase: "Doing Nothing in Particular Completely by Yourself." It's both purposeless and lonely. What captivates me about the Cowell College motto is that it brings together two basic drives you and I experience: the drive to do something important with our lives and the drive to spend our lives surrounded by people we enjoy. In these motivations lie the appeal of the common adventure, the fellowship of the quest.

What is meant by the phrase "the pursuit of God"? A pursuit is different from a hobby or a passing interest. A pursuit is actively sought, often in a disciplined, systematic way. Christians speak about "discipleship," which has similar connotations. But a pursuit implies a goal, a destination, the end of our quest. Our goal is nothing less than God himself. We want knowledge, not just of principles about God, but of the very nature of God. We want to know his sense of humor, his way of working in the world, the soft spot in his heart for each one of us.

The phrase "pursuit of God" is a double-entendre. It speaks both of *our* pursuit of God and *God's* pursuit of us as his lost and prodigal children. Of course, it is this latter sense of the pursuit of God that dominates the salvation story, from God's approach to Adam and Eve in the garden after they had sinned to the story of the people of Israel, from the exodus to the exile and return. It is also the dominant theme in the story of Jesus' pursuit of his disciples, calling them into relationship with him whether or not they were searching for him.[1]

An extended look at what I am calling "the company of friends" is crucial, never more than today, in a society obsessed with wealth. For millennia people have understood that the truly wealthy were people with deep friendships. But these kinds of friendships are like the stained-glass windows that adorn the cathedrals of Europe—they are certainly beautiful, but they take time and skill to create, such time and skill as is hard to come by these days. And they don't seem to fit easily into the contemporary architecture of our lives.

So a pastor cracks open the latest church structure book, complete with diagrams, flow charts and polling data, in order to get insight about how to motivate church members. A young professional woman seeks advice from a self-help book to know how to manage the tasks of her life and still have time to pursue satisfying relationships. A first-time dad feels unprepared to raise a child but has no idea where to turn for perspective.

In another era and context, these people and you and I would be able to draw on the wealth and resources of a community of family and friends that would give shape to our lives and to our pursuit of God. But as much as *community* has become a buzzword these days, a deep experience of community seems elusive. Our deeper poverty has left us without the relational resources to thrive, even as our technological wealth compounds. We have more and faster ways to communicate with one another, but insight, depth and intimacy grow ever more scarce.

This poverty leaves us less able to experience the power of the gospel. The language of Scripture seems less accessible to us. Its stories seem more distant. Its parables we judge to be less practical in our time. We find the structure of the Gospel stories less plausible, and so do people who examine our practice of our Master's teaching and find that the experience doesn't live up to the theory.

THE QUEST FOR THE ULTIMATE

In all of our culture's mad dash toward whatever is next, I believe God is what you and I are actually looking for. Not just ideas about God, not just the truth about God, but God himself. Whether we fully acknowledge it or not, we seek his presence and his power. We long to see the reality of his life and work available to us. But we want (and need) to find him with our friends. This journey is worth undertaking, and we want to share it with others. We want to participate in the quest for the ultimate in the context of the intimate. We want to know deeply and to be deeply known.

If what you want is friendship—deep, satisfying, purposeful, long-lasting friendship—I believe the only way to find it is to pursue God. If what you want is God—the certainty of his work in your life, the sense of his empowerment and blessing on your activity and pursuits—I believe that desire will bring you into contact and deeper relationship with a community of friends shaped by the same pursuit.

I am speaking of both a transcendent experience and a personal process. It is no less than the satisfaction of the two great impulses of our souls: upward and outward. A group of friends can come together to talk about God or even to pray. But we desire even more. We desire friendship with God in a way that touches all of our friendships. We desire knowledge of our friends in a way that touches even our understanding of our own souls. We desire involvement in something larger than we are, connected to others and fused to the heart of God.

Let me make this lofty image concrete: Jesus is the tangible incarnation of God, and his manner of inviting people into deep relationship with himself is the manner we have available to us today. Jesus gathered a group of people together, some good friends and brothers, some complete strangers and natural enemies, and eventually he told them that by their love for one another people would know that they had been touched and changed by God incarnate. In fact, this kind of friendship, inexplicable apart from God, was the apologetic by which he demonstrated his power to the world (John 13:35; 17:20-21). He told his disciples that their friendships would either make or break the mission of the church, his mission in the world.

What would it be like to pursue—and find—God in the company of friends? What would those friendships look like? The process we call *discipleship*, and the context we call *community*. Whether your deepest desire is for more of God, for deeper friendships or for both, join me as we explore together.

SPIRITUAL FRIENDSHIP

Aelred. Since then in friendship eternity blossoms, truth shines forth, and charity grows sweet, consider whether you ought to separate the name of wisdom from these three.

Ivo. What does this all add up to? Shall I say of friendship what John, the friend of Jesus, says of charity, "God is friendship"?

Aelred. That would be unusual, to be sure, nor does it have the sanction of the Scriptures. But still what is true of charity, I surely do not hesitate to grant to friendship, since "he that abides in friendship, abides in God, and God in him."

AELRED OF RIEVAULX

In these words, penned nearly 850 years ago, Aelred, the abbot of a Cistercian monastery in Rievaulx, a Norman village in Yorkshire, speaks in a dialogue format of the spiritual nature of friendship. Based in a long tradition, spiritual friendship nevertheless has a crucial role to play today. Spiritual friendship is built upon a willingness to talk of our hopes and doubts the way the first disciples, and disciples down through the centuries, have done. Yet too often we leave out of our conversation our deepest longings and fears about life and about God. Evidence of this is commonplace:

- A small group is quite verbal and active while its members are talking about the events of their lives. The group is a little less lively while discussing the passage of Scripture being examined. But the group becomes almost silent when the time comes for people to discuss the application of Scripture to their lives. Superficial or general responses are grudgingly given at the repeated invitation of the group leader.

- Even (and perhaps especially) with other believers, when asked, "How are you?" we respond automatically, "I'm just fine!" Even when we could reasonably believe people are sincerely interested in knowing, we have a hard time letting people in to know where the pain, disappointment and obstacles to progress in our lives have become faith stretching or overwhelming.

- Though we have a great desire to speak with our seeking or nonbelieving friends about our faith, it remains difficult to do so because we have no natural way of speaking about things closest to our hearts.

By contrast, spiritual friendship for almost all of us involves movement or growth of some kind. It means making choices to embrace values we may not have prized previously or to consciously work against the broader culture's assumptions and beliefs. We need at least a renewal, if not a conversion, a fresh wind of God's Spirit to help us to grow:

- *From individualism to community.* If it was ever possible to believe the Christian life could be lived within the confines of one's own private moral and doctrinal landscape, it seems difficult to believe it any longer. We become no longer willing to go to church and return home having the same superficial conversations week after week. We want to know and be known.

- *From privacy to openness.* Even small-group participation is no longer enough. We come to desire a small-group experience where people share, not simply a meal or a discussion, but their lives.

- *From superficiality to authenticity.* Even conversation about our lives is no longer enough. We desire a safe place among friends where we can talk about the realities of our lives. We want to honestly speak of those places where our faith seems not to be working or where our choices have not led us into what we had hoped they would. We also want to celebrate our successes and spiritual progress with humility.

- *From justification to sanctification.* We are not content merely to study Scripture; we are passionately committed to living what we study. We grow to understand that we are in a lifelong pursuit, and we know the journey will be more fruitful and more satisfying in the company of friends. We come to experience the transforming power of our discipleship in community.

For some of us, friendship itself is difficult; for others, making friendship spiritual is the hard part; for still others, making spiritual relationships authentic has been a stumbling block. This book is testimony to what is possible and an examination of what is attractive in the pursuit of God with our friends. Chapters one and two introduce the priority of friendship in the pursuit of God. In this process, people receive healing (chapter three), consolation and restoration (chapter four). People are enjoyed (chapters five and six) and practically served (chapter seven). People receive wise and welcome guidance (chapter eight), understanding (chapter nine) and forgiveness (chapter ten). They are celebrated, challenged and collaborated with (chapters eleven and twelve). They are called into service together in love (chapter thirteen). Chapter fourteen concludes the book with a look at the unique and eternal nature of friendship.

DISCIPLESHIP AND COMMUNITY IN THE GOSPELS

When I came to college, I joined the Christian fellowship on my campus. I knew it was the right thing to do, and I wanted to grow in my faith. Soon my staff leader, Greg, asked to take a walk with me. *For what?* I thought. I didn't know what to expect. Perhaps the conversation would be about God or the Bible or my prayer life—certainly something spiritual. Yet that first conversation focused on friendship. I didn't feel I particularly needed friends, and I expected little from the casual friendships I had made in the dorm. Greg suggested that it might be good for me to work at friendship.

I clearly remember being surprised at the topic of conversation. I came to realize later that Greg was in fact offering friendship, but more than that, he was offering to host me into friendships—friendships that would be centered on, among other common pursuits, a pursuit of God. Two of Greg's friends, Bill and Bob, later became my friends and are good friends to this day. I came to see that God cared about my friendships. I grew to see that he cared much more than I did.

In fact, even cursory glances through the Gospels confirm that the work Jesus did in the lives of his disciples occurred because the disciples were in relationship, not simply with him, but with one another. That manner of growth in spiritual depth—in the context of community—is not accidental. It is part of how people are built. We were created to seek God, and we were created to find him with others. Not only does this reflect the strategy of Jesus, but just as crucially, it reflects the design of God.

The word *discipleship* refers to learning that takes place through experience and under the authority of a master. Specifically, in Christian discipleship, we are looking at the Master and trying to learn from him. He shapes and guides us as we put our lives under his authority. This book is a look at Jesus as a teacher with the belief that his words and his model are authoritative and helpful for those of us who would be his followers. It is also a look at his circle of friends with a belief that essential elements of their life together are attractive and attainable for us. If we want to know God, we must be taught by Jesus. If we spend time with him, we'll find ourselves drawn in, attracted by his manner as much as by his message. Friendship, human and divine, is the lasting fruit.

ACKNOWLEDGMENTS

First of all, I acknowledge two things about myself: I am a natural teacher, but I am not a natural friend. My choice to leave behind my academic course of study (chemistry and later computer science) for the sake of a call to campus ministry was a move away from my technical expertise into a place of repeated failure and vulnerability. I never expected that I would still be pursuing a calling to student ministry twenty years after I first embarked upon it, in large part because I didn't consider myself a natural at the relational side of this ministry. In this I am grateful to God for his grace in my life. Occasionally I get glimpses of what I would be like had the company of friends not become a central theme and shaping influence of my life, and this renews my sense of gratitude.

Of course, a book—especially one on friendship—cannot be written in isolation, and I am particularly grateful to the people in my life who have taught me so much in this area. This is a partial list, but it includes people I think of when I look at the passages of Scripture I consider in the book: Al Anderson, Carrie Bare, Paul Byer, Curtis Chang, Andy Crouch, Daniel Fuller, Jennie Genske, Bill Glad, Paul Gutjahr, Brian Hamilton, Brian Housman, Sheila Kawaoka Grace, Charlie Knerr, Mark Phifer-Houseman, John Piper, Tom Pratt, Greg Read, Kevin Rhodes, Dave Schmelzer, Pete Sommer and Gene Thomas.

Two groups of friends have made critical contributions to my understanding and practice of the theme and insights of this book. When I first began student ministry, Steve Colby, Brian Hamilton and Seth Shapiro were students at U.C. Santa Cruz. The four of us ("The Schmooz-ers") met together regularly for prayer and honest discussion of our lives, and this experience began to shape how I understood friendship in the pursuit of God. Many years later I began to meet annually with a group of three other good friends and partners for prayer, support and account-ability in our personal, spiritual and ministry lives. This "Finishing Well" group includes Bill Glad, Kevin Rhodes and Mark Phifer-House-man. I am grateful to God for his work in me through these friendships.

Writing any book is a vulnerable experience. I wonder, *Will anyone read it? Will it be helpful?* Writing a book on the topic of friendship and spiritual growth is even more risky, as it deals with core personal issues. (Perhaps all authors tend to feel this way, but I did not feel this way about my first book, a computer programming textbook.) I am, there-fore, grateful for a wide company of friends who have been willing to read parts or the whole of the manuscript and give me faithful, honest feedback. They have both helped me to see what I could not see and encouraged me that my efforts have not been wasted. Thank you, my friends: Roger Anderson, Fred Bailey, Scott Baker, Janet Balajthy, Steve Barr, Jeff Bassette, Tom Boyle, Scott Brill, Clare Broyles, Jody Chang, Keith Cooper, Jordan Dea-Mattson, Garrett Girard, Bill Glad, Geoff Gordon, Pete Groeneveld, Bobby Gross, Paul Gutjahr, Alec Hill, Doug Hirzel, Susan Dante House, Brian Housman, Elizabeth Hoyt, Jason Jensen, Lisa Lamb, Erik Larsen, Anita Lee, Scot Lewis, Stace Lindsay, Elaine Lo, Donna Meier, Melinda Melone, Jennifer Morrow, Ming Nagasawa, Beth Neustadt, Laurie Niewoehner, Liz Nilsen, Charles Park, Mark Phifer-Houseman, Jason Poling, Dave Schmelzer, Melinda Tuan, Steve Tuttle, Lisa Ujifusa, Peter Vessenes, Steve Watson, Brian Wo.

I write this book as a twenty-year veteran of InterVarsity Christian Fel-lowship (IVCF) staff. I am grateful to my supervisors who have encour-aged me along the way. (I have had four since I began this project many years ago.) Thanks to John Ratichek, Doug Whallon, Janet Balajthy and Alec Hill for understanding my desire to write and its place in my min-istry with IVCF. I'm also grateful to my teammates and partners, with whom I've learned what I have to share. And as a supported missionary for the last two decades, I am grateful to everyone who has supported God's work through our ministry.

Finally, and of course, I'd like to acknowledge all the support my wife has given me toward the completion of this project. Lisa is a true partner and friend. Our relationship has both kept me growing with other friendships and been enriched by those friendships.

Friends in the Pursuit of God

Now friendship is nothing else than perfect agreement on all divine and human things, joined to kindliness and affection; and than this, wisdom alone being excepted, I am inclined to think that no better gift has been given to man by the immortal gods.

CICERO, *LAELIUS ON FRIENDSHIP*

The honeymoon was over. We were having our first fight. And I was losing.

Six months earlier, the courtship had begun. We began as a group of eight considering starting a new church in Cambridge, Massachusetts. While we were talking about the potential, we had shared enthusiasm and vision. We had shared dreams. We had decided to take the plunge.

The plunge consisted of, among other things, moving into apartments near each other. My wife and I (and our two kids) lived with our good friend Sandy, a single woman. Three single men lived next door. The other couple lived across the street. Four of us had lived in Cambridge for six years or so, while the others had just moved from the San Francisco Bay area. We were having our first meeting after the entire group was finally in town. And our first fight.

We had big plans. We all had a sense that God might be pleased to use this fledgling group to plant a church that could make a significant contribution to God's work in the wider Boston area. Yet our immediate hope was simply to have a meaningful experience with a small group of friends. We wanted to meet God with one another in a way that would give us hope that others would want to join us. But our first time out was not encouraging.

The issue was interpersonal, not strategic. One member had challenged another member of the group on his priorities. The Cambridge people arrayed behind our Cambridge team member, while the California contingent did the same for their fellow Californian. I was impatient, dismayed with the seemingly cavalier attitude of those who had just a few weeks before moved across the country. They seemed in no hurry, content to scout out the situation in Cambridge. Apparently they felt they needed to learn for themselves what I could have told them, indeed had already told them, in a few minutes' time. Though their commitment to the endeavor, illustrated by their cross-country move, should not have been in doubt, I spoke up, implying that I had *my doubts*, in a way that left little room for partnership or compromise.

Greg, who was for most of us in the room one of our best friends, broke it open when he said, "Rich, you're being stubborn. I want Dave to come to like you as much as I do, but you're making it hard. Whether this church gets planted or not will come down to this: can we become friends and love each other in ways that are attractive and real?"

That night it was me; over the next two years, each of us would get to a point where we would need to ask someone's, or the group's, forgiveness for our words or tone. It seems we came to a brink and walked away more often than any of us likes to remember. We cared a great deal about our vision and goals, and our experience often didn't match up with our ideals.

Our self-mocking group had as its mascots an unlikely pair of friends, Pinky and the Brain, two cartoon lab mice who nightly hatched delusional plans for taking over the world. Words from the television show's theme song, "One is a genius, the other's insane," gave the description of these two, and their antics amused us. But behind it was a metaphor—their friendship formed the axis of great vision. At the beginning of every show, Pinky would ask the Brain, "What are we going to do tonight, Brain?" Brain's routine reply would come, "The same thing we do every night, Pinky: try to take over the world." Like them, we too hoped that our coming together would eventually hatch a plan for broad (if not necessarily global) influence. The unlikelihood of two lab mice bringing their vision to reality seemed no greater than that of our small group coming together to make a difference in Boston. So we amused ourselves with less-than-flattering comparisons between Pinky and the Brain and our little band. And when we were at the point of fragmenting through our own conflict, these comparisons seemed especially apt. Greg's invitation to me that night was to recognize that a little stubbornness on my part was enough to unravel our grand plans.

Of course, the human story is often a story of the accomplishments of a few against all odds—and the few are usually allied as friends around a common experience or context. The founding friendships (and growing rivalries) of the United States (Washington, Franklin, Adams, Jefferson, Hamilton and Madison, among others) or the founding friendships of what became Silicon Valley (William Hewlett and David Packard, for example) tell a story of groups of people who came together to accomplish something amazing and profound—a fusion of personality, ambition, skills and dreams that made something unique happen.

The account of the founding of the Christian church is just such a story, having at its center Jesus Christ, the Son of God, unique in history. Nevertheless, the only structure he left in place for the propagation of a faith that would come to embrace a billion living people was a small group, a dozen people whose friendships would enable, embolden and empower them to live lives that "turned the world upside down" (see Acts 17:6).

The topic of friendship was a favorite of the Greek philosophers. They viewed friendship as a gift from the gods, finer than wealth and everything else except wisdom. Aristotle described qualities enjoyed by friends that continue to be apt and helpful today: friends (1) enjoy one another, (2) are useful to one another and (3) share a common commitment to "the good."[1] My purpose here is not to dwell on the philosophical underpinnings of these requirements but simply to note them and to point out that the first-century disciples of Jesus satisfied these requirements in obvious ways. Twenty-first-century disciples of Jesus are called on to do so as well. (Unfortunately, today, any broad understanding of friendship would probably include only the first requirement: "friends are those we take pleasure in being with."[2])

Jesus was both the human host of the small group he brought together and the divine object of its quest. This uniqueness can obscure the way that his strategy can be a practical model for us today. It is valuable to both wonder at our Lord's uniqueness as God incarnate and to learn from his strategy as a model host and friend.

So let us begin at what is properly the beginning: the inauguration of Jesus' ministry at the shores of the Jordan River. Let us see what we can learn from the process by which Jesus called people into relationship. The story we are going to look at first begins with John the Baptist pointing to Jesus and saying to his disciples, "Look, here is the Lamb of God!" (John 1:36). This is precisely what I hope to do, not only in this chapter but throughout the book. We will look at Jesus, at his invitation into friendship and his strategy for making and hosting friendships, focused together around the pursuit of God.

GOD IN PURSUIT OF FRIENDS (JOHN 1:35-51)

The phrase "God in pursuit of friends" just doesn't seem right, does it? Yet this is what the Gospel writers tell us: Jesus of Nazareth, God-become-human, spent his early time with people in moves of friendship, initiating with and even receiving initiatives from people in ways that would be familiar to us. As Eugene Peterson so attractively phrases John 1:14,

> The Word became flesh and blood,
> and moved into the neighborhood. (The Message)

Jesus wasn't so much being unapproachably divine as he was winning friends, people with whom he would share his life, friends for whom he would eventually give his life.

The scene in John 1 is filled with small details giving testimony to the shape and character of the friendships among the first disciples of Jesus. Though these friendships grew over the course of Jesus' time with them, their prehistory, displayed here, is worth noting. Andrew and John, the Gospel writer, had already been following John the Baptist when they heard him identify Jesus, "Look, here is the Lamb of God!" "Lamb of God" is a technical term meaning "the messiah," the anointed and expected one. John and Andrew were softhearted and receptive, and they realized there was no point in following a herald of the Messiah (John) once the Messiah himself walked by, so they literally began to follow Jesus as he walked along the road. Jesus turned around and asked, "What are you looking for?" (verse 38).

Good question. As disciples of John, they were indeed looking for something, something deep, significant. They were in pursuit of God himself. "Could this be the one?" was their unutterable question. But they were unable to speak about the hope that they had deepest in their hearts. Of course, the right answer to Jesus' simple question would be "God" or "the Lamb of God" or even "Well, *you*, we think." Instead they looked down at their feet. "Teacher, uh, . . . where are you staying?" Jesus then invited them to his wilderness campfire for dinner.

John did not describe the remainder of the day. But whatever they received during the next twelve hours, Andrew couldn't wait to go and find his brother, Simon, and tell him what he had discovered: "We have found the Messiah" (John 1:41). Andrew had come to believe. In turn, his brother and John's friend Simon was introduced to Jesus and began to follow.

"Jesus decided to go to Galilee" (John 1:43). Jesus, himself a Galilean, had been miles from home near the Jordan River getting baptized by John. There he met, of all people, several other Galileans whose homes were close to his own. He then decided to go to (that is, return to) Galilee. If Jesus were starting some kind of political movement, you might think he would try to expand his base. He already had Galilean representation, so perhaps he should have developed his Judean support and focused on the big city, Jerusalem. But instead he

returned to Galilee, only to recruit more Galileans—in fact, friends of the men he had already recruited. Of his twelve apostles, four were pairs of brothers and partners in the same fishing business. Jesus wasn't pursuing a representative demographic strategy; rather, he was building a group of men who would become deep and deeply purposeful friends.

Jesus sought and found Philip in the town of Bethsaida, the hometown of Simon Peter and Andrew. With Philip it was different from how it was with Andrew and John, in that Jesus took initiative to find him. Philip wasn't exactly looking for the Messiah. When everyone else was in the Jordan River valley responding to the strong teaching of John the Baptist, Philip was at home in Bethsaida minding the farm or tending his nets.

So with Jesus' finding of Philip we have another take on the phrase "the pursuit of God." With Philip, God was the pursuer. Later in Jesus' ministry, he told stories that illustrate this simply and succinctly:

> The kingdom of heaven is like treasure hidden in a field, which someone found and hid; then in his joy he goes and sells all that he has and buys that field.
>
> Again, the kingdom of heaven is like a merchant in search of fine pearls; on finding one pearl of great value, he went and sold all that he had and bought it. (Matthew 13:44-46)

Both men found something precious and went to extreme lengths to acquire it. But one was a seeker, in search of fine pearls, while the other merely stumbled upon his treasure. This makes sense of our own experience as well. Some disciples of Jesus are properly *seekers*—they were pursuing God when they came across Jesus. Others of us are *stumblers*. We were not at all looking for God (or perhaps, much of anything) when God came across our path and surprised us by the joy of being found by him.

"We have found him about whom Moses in the law and also the prophets wrote, Jesus son of Joseph from Nazareth" (John 1:45). Philip said, "We have found." I like this about Philip. In fact, we could ask Philip, "Who found whom?" Jesus found Philip, but the impact on

Philip was a sense of "Eureka! I found it." He took a risk in saying they had found the Messiah; he was being refreshingly noncynical, almost naive in his enthusiasm. He displayed a vulnerability rare among male friends. Nathaniel responded, "Can anything good come out of Nazareth?" (verse 46)—ready with wit and cynicism to rib his friend on his naive settling on "the One."

This kind of response is familiar to me. I was with my high school friends several years after we had finished college. I mentioned my romantic interest in a young woman, Lisa Washington, who was going off to study at seminary. I had a sense she might be "the one" for me, and so I offered her name and story in reply to the predictable question "Is there someone special?" But I was living in California and she was moving to New Jersey for seminary studies, which normally take three years. The matter didn't look favorable. My friends kidded me as Nathaniel kidded Philip. The likelihood of my hopes becoming reality wasn't high. (Although against all odds and to my amazement, they did: Lisa eventually agreed to become my wife.)

Imagine if Philip had said, "I've met the girl of my dreams. She is the daughter of Joseph of Nazareth." Nathaniel might have responded in exactly the same way, "Can anything good come out of Nazareth?" What a typical male response to a vulnerable plea for shared excitement! Nathaniel grew up in Cana, ten miles from Nazareth—it's not like he was Mr. Cosmopolitan. He undoubtedly shared with anyone from Nazareth the rural Galilean accent. Perhaps Philip and Nathaniel had a long-standing friendship with a familiar pattern of naiveté and sarcasm.

Philip said to Nathaniel, "*We* have found," implying some familiar group, a gang of friends, a "we" with whom Nathaniel would be familiar. Philip, Andrew and Peter all grew up together in this small town in Galilee, friends who played kickball together in grade school and who talked together about girls in high school (or at least their first-century Palestine equivalents).

Nathaniel's sarcastic response to Philip gives just a bit of the texture of these friendships—Nathaniel was a little more his own man, unyielding to easy persuasion, but once convinced, firm in his convictions. Hence, when Jesus met Nathaniel, he declared, "Here is truly an Israelite in whom there is no deceit!" (John 1:47). Nathaniel was puzzled; how did Jesus know him? Jesus simply indicated that he could see things others could not, both deep in the heart and when physically remote. Jesus said to Nathaniel, in effect, "I've had my eye on you." He showed it by his knowledge of Nathaniel under the fig tree. This was apparently unprecedented for Nathaniel, who was the first to kneel before Jesus in worship and declare his identity as God and King.

So a pattern emerges. Jesus didn't get very far with John and Andrew before Andrew ran off to bring Peter. He didn't know Peter and Andrew long before he went and found their friend Philip. And he didn't know Philip long before he "saw" and called Philip's friend Nathaniel. Jesus brought together a group of friends who were to become better friends. These friendships came to have Jesus in the center and life with God as their focus.

Why did Jesus bring together this group? Because (among other things) people need each other in order to find God. This fledgling group illustrates the two manners of approach to God already suggested—seekers and stumblers. *Stumblers* need seekers to help them not be complacent. Philip and Nathaniel could have remained at home, never knowing that the Creator God of the universe was in their hometown. *Seekers* need stumblers to help them to be attentive to reality and to cease seeking when confronted with God himself. It was Nathaniel, a stumbler, late on the scene with Jesus, who was the first to declare himself in worship to the Messiah.

At the end of the scene with Nathaniel, Jesus said, "You will see greater things than these" (John 1:50). Jesus made a promise to Nathaniel, one he makes to each of us who actively pursue God. Some identify with stumbling into a relationship with Jesus; others are on a search. Some find that belief comes easily; for others, action comes quickly once they struggle through belief. Some of us, having begun as stumblers, now find we are in a seeking mode, while for others of us, the reverse may be the case. Jesus brought together a group of friends—men who had known each other for a long time and yet who were different from each other in ways familiar to us.

Jesus invites us into a company of diverse friends because we need each other. He invites us to join this company that is together in their pursuit of God, to learn from and grow to love each other in that pursuit. And we may find, as the disciples did, that in the midst of this pursuit of God we find ourselves swallowed up in the pursuing, wooing, deeply satisfying love of God himself, as he reveals himself in the life and person, the words and works, of Jesus.

EXPECT UNLIKELY FRIENDSHIPS

When they first began to work together, Gilles and Doug were politically and socially polar opposites. Doug was a clean-shaven Republican from a semi-rural California town, the son of a father who worked in a nuclear defense lab. Gilles was a long-haired, bearded radical, the son of a pastor who had been a radical activist. Gilles grew up in Africa and felt anything but patriotic toward the United States. Doug and Gilles did not trust one another nor respect each other's convictions, but at that time, we agreed together that God had put them on the same ministry team and could, just possibly, be at work in their relationship. After four years of much work, forgiveness and growing love, at Gilles's wedding Doug stood with him as best man.

The fact that many of Jesus' closest disciples were fishermen, partners and friends obscures for us that Jesus also called people with very different backgrounds into relationship with him and one another. Matthew was a tax collector; Simon (not Peter) was a Zealot (Matthew 9:9; 10:3; Luke 6:15). These two individuals spanned the political spectrum for the Jews of the day. The Zealots despised tax collectors more than anyone. Tax collectors were in cooperation with the Romans, while the Zealots were committed to an overthrow of the Romans and a return of Judea to home rule. Jesus called both of these men into his group of twelve disciples, illustrating that what bound them together was much greater than the political differences that certainly would otherwise have kept them apart.

Jesus' choice of two men who were polar opposites reflects spiritual, not political, principles. In Ephesians the apostle Paul commented on the theological reality of the greatest distinction between people in Paul's day, that of Jew and Gentile. At the heart of Paul's description of God's reconciling work, he wrote, "In Christ Jesus you who once were far off have been brought near by the blood of Christ. For he is our peace; in his flesh he has made both groups into one and has broken down the dividing wall, that is, the hostility between us. He has abolished the law with its commandments and ordinances, that he might create in himself one new humanity in place of the two, thus making peace" (Ephesians 2:13-15).

Obviously, dividing walls of hostility still separate a variety of groups today, with tensions rampant between men and women, between people of different ethnic or social backgrounds, even between Republicans and Democrats. These all exist within the body of Christ. Few of these tensions are as explosive as that between Matthew the Roman collaborator and Simon the (Zionist) Zealot, and yet the group Jesus fashioned brought these two together. A crucial mark of the gospel taking root in people's lives is that these dividing walls begin to come down.

The first time I met Bill, during my freshman year in college, we couldn't have been more different. In high school Bill had lettered in three sports each of his four years. My only high school involvements were band and debate. No letters at all. If we had attended the same high school, each of us could easily have found reasons to look down on the other. Bill was attractive, muscled, funny and socially confident. I, uh, . . . was not. (Bill was confident; I was merely arrogant.) We were at our year-end college fellowship retreat when Bill was asked to share his story and to speak a little from Scripture. I resented Bill for receiving this plum assignment instead of me. I had attended most of the fellowship meetings all year, while Bill had not, and he had only relatively recently become a Christian, whereas I had been one for over a decade.

Eventually Bill and I did become friends. We began to enjoy one another with some mutual friends. In our junior year we took classes and studied together, and so we began to be useful to one another. As student leaders in the Christian fellowship, and after college when we both went into ministry, we grew in our common commitment to "the good." After over two decades of friendship, despite thousands of miles separating us geographically, we continue to see each other annually (with a small group of men who have known one another since our college days) and speak with each other regularly throughout the year.

I have a good friend, Francis, who at the time I met him was a "street person." He is a follower of Jesus; he is also paranoid schizophrenic and he talks to himself all the time. He was living in a tent when I first met him, about eighteen years ago, living on the $338 per month he received from the government because of his disability. At that time I gave him some wood that he used as platform for his tent. Since then our friendship has grown. Along with my wife, I have brought some small measure of stability and community into his life; Francis, in turn, has brought a lot of humor, affection and serendipitous wisdom into my life. I have challenged Francis in areas of accountability and discipline; his presence in my life has caused me to grow in compassion and humble dependence on God.

A few months after my wife and I moved from Santa Cruz to Boston, Francis also moved out to Boston. (His financial situation had changed dramatically—both of his parents had died since I had first met him and he had inherited a trust fund, administered by a cautious lawyer.) He moved to maintain our friendship; he said Santa Cruz wasn't the same without us. Every time Francis was with me, others around were curious: "Who is this man? Why is he here?" Yet Francis shared several holiday dinners with large gatherings in our home, and it was obvious that my friendship with Francis did not easily fit into the rest of our relationships. I would vouch for my friend, describing this friendship as both a result of my faith and a part of my ongoing growth as a disciple of Jesus.

Often I expect too little from God in the area of friendships. I do not expect that people who are fairly different from one another can become good friends. Yet Jesus' words in John 13:35 are most clearly proven true when these kinds of friendships happen: "By this everyone will know that you are my disciples, if you have love for one another." When black and white, Republicans and radicals, economists and artists become friends, then the world will see the undeniable power of God at work.

THREE IMAGES OF COMMUNITY AND DISCIPLESHIP

Why does God choose to use a group of people whose pursuit of him involves an often tortuous path of friendship with one another? Why does God work in this way? When I went away to college, a youth leader spoke of the image of a burning ember, separated from other embers, that would quickly grow cold. This man challenged me to join a church or college fellowship that would keep my love for God burning hot. This image has been seared into the minds of many before me and since.

The Renaissance genius Michelangelo won a commission from the Florentine elders to work on a huge block of marble, *il Duccio*, a flawed and miscut mass of stone. Other Florentine sculptors assumed the block would break under the strain of the huge gouge in its side. Yet in his mind's eye Michelangelo was able to see in the stone a fourteen-foot tall image of David, the shepherd boy-man who had killed lions and bears with his bare hands. After four years of painstaking carving, he was able to release the beautiful image of David from the piece of flawed marble, turning the block rejected by others into the most striking sculpture in Florence.

When I hear teaching or read books about Christian discipleship, it seems we are to be people in search of our God-ordained Michelangelo, who sees in us raw material waiting to be crafted into mighty men and women of God. If only the right person were to apply his or her chisel to chip away all that is not Christian maturity! We would finally come to resemble a breathtaking work of art others would recognize as "Disciple."

I've had lots of people invest hours in helping me to mature as one in pursuit of God, but in general it has come in diffuse, indirect ways, through a variety of means. I honor my parents, Sunday school teachers, mentors and friends who have taken an interest in my growth as a person and as a follower of Jesus. These people and the millions like them are a great gift to people anywhere trying to grow into devoted followers of Jesus. And yet I cannot identify who that single Michelangelo would be in my own life.

Also, as one who has been in Christian ministry to college students for over twenty years, I find that I don't identify closely with this image of a discipling Michelangelo. I don't easily see the final product from beneath the raw block of immature personality and undeveloped gifts. I don't usually know what is extra stone and what is essential to the particular sculpture. If I were to apply my chisel, I would feel all too likely to slip and chop off someone's nose. I have spent many years investing my life in young Christians, yet the image of a sculptor-teacher does not match my experience.

Let me suggest another image depicting how rough, ordinary rocks become things of beauty and great value. In order to fashion smooth gemstones from ordinary gravel-sized rocks, one uses a lapidary tumbler. One puts the stones in the tumbler, adds a little grit and water, and then closes the lid and turns the machine on—for days and weeks, until the rough rocks become polished stones fit for setting. Of course, the finer the raw material, the more beautiful the final gem, but it is difficult to imagine at the outset exactly what will become of the material that is placed inside the tumbler.

I have come to see that Jesus' own maturing strategy was more like polishing gems in a rock tumbler. He made disciples in community. The process, over time, involves the stones rubbing up against and falling on one another: conflict, reconciliation, communication, learning to work together and challenge one another ("iron sharpening iron," as in Proverbs 27:17). As I land on and chip away at the other stones, I myself am polished and changed, as are they. The longer I am in God's tumbler of community, the more I take on the shape of the gem God intends me to be.

I am in several tumblers simultaneously. I am in the tumbler of my family and am both a shaping influencer of my family members as well as one shaped, polished and occasionally humbled by my wife and kids. I am also in a tumbler experience in the various teams I serve on in my work—we understand our roles not simply as functionaries for the organization but as people who are being shaped and influenced by our relationships with one another. I am in a tumbler experience in my church, in a small group and in the other relationships I enjoy there. And I am in a slowly rotating tumbler of the set of friends with whom I enjoy fifteen or twenty years or more of history in our relationships. Though I see them less, I value them more, and they speak to me and indelibly shape my life through the impact of their own.

The tumbler image implies a concrete context. It is not simply the unavoidable process of maturity in a Christian; rather, it is a set of relationships in which God can bring about his purposes in the life of the individual.

The tumbler image, like any image, is an incomplete model, for it implies that spiritual maturity is all about crushing and wearing away, rather than also about building up. In fact, healthy communities in which people are close enough to rub against one another offer a great deal of mutual encouragement and building up of one another. Love, which is at the root of this process, is fundamentally positive and creative, not destructive.

Not therefore content with any of these images alone, I want to blend the last two, those of a sculptor and of a tumbler, because as beautiful as the gemstones turn out to be, the sculpture of David standing in the Accadamia in Florence, Italy, is infinitely more striking. I believe God is at work in each of us, individually and specifically, to bring us to striking maturity and stature, closer (in spiritual terms) to a fourteen-foot-tall statue than a one-inch gemstone. This seems to be similar to the image Paul was using in Ephesians 4:11-13, where he wrote, "The gifts he

[Christ] gave were that some would be apostles, some prophets, some evangelists, some pastors and teachers, to equip the saints for the work of ministry, for building up the body of Christ, until all of us come to the unity of the faith and of the knowledge of the Son of God, to maturity, to the measure of the full stature of Christ." "The full stature of Christ"—however amazing that sounds, at least we can say Paul had a large vision of what and who we are to become.

Yet the carving tools are in God's hands, not those of our pastor, our teacher or even our spouse (as much as he or she would like the chance to chisel away). The influence these leaders and our friends have in us is the influence of people who are with us in life, in the tumbler of the joint pursuit of God, in which God will make us into precisely the people he wants us to become. And God desires for a great many people to be involved in the process.

Therefore (to return to the burning ember image), I need friends not simply to keep my love for God warm but also to refine my love for God. Friendship is not simply defensive, maintaining faith, but proactive, growing faith as well. Friendship in community serves not simply to provide other individual embers burning brightly for God near me. Rather, friendship in community stokes and superheats the love for God in my heart. It is in this context that my ability to live by God's priorities—to love God, his Word, his people and his purposes for this planet—comes first and most clearly into focus.

I need different people in my life, not just others who love God, but also people who love him differently than I do. I need people who relate to God as seekers and stumblers, skeptics and believers, leaders and followers, radicals and loyalists. And when I attend my small group and think (as I often do), *These people aren't like me,* I need to follow up that reflex with a response not quite so reflexive: *Thank God they aren't!*

And so, happily, the call to pursue God in the company of friends is not simply a necessary defensive reaction to the challenge of burning brightly for God in a dim, cold world. Rather, it offers much more (as we will continue to see), and fundamentally it multiplies our joy. Jesus informed his disciples, "I have said these things to you so that my joy may be in you, and that your joy may be complete. This is my commandment, that you love one another as I have loved you" (John 15:11-12). Jesus linked his joy in us to our love for one another. Thank God that he doesn't often call us to follow him alone! Our fickle interest in friendship pales in comparison to his unwavering commitment to it.

◆ ◆ ◆

Those of us in the "Pinky and the Brain" church-planting team soon came to see that we needed one another. We faced a cataclysm—a central figure in our group, deciding to refocus his life, dropped out. We found that we needed each other much more than we had known. Outsiders would say that they saw great promise in us. People told us that they prayed for our group and received much in the way of promise and encouragement. This was not always obvious to us, especially after we had been meeting for two years and still didn't resemble a church.

Leadership and vision were definitely a part of it. All of us wanted to be church planters, but none of us particularly wanted to be head pastor, until through the affirmation of the group, the extraordinary gifts of a single individual—Dave—were identified and called out. Because of the way the church began, this wasn't destined to be a one-man show. Each of us was needed—none of us had perfect clarity as to where we were going or how we were going to get there. Yet, with the confidence of the team, Dave stepped up to lead, with remarkable results. The story of this group, and the church that it became, is the story of a company of emerging friends in the pursuit of God.

FOR REFLECTION

Each chapter concludes with a set of questions to consider. Please don't skip this section. You may not find every question helpful, but the only way to benefit from the Scripture study and stories in each chapter is to reflect on your own life—your relationships with God and your friends.

The questions will serve as a brief summary of the themes of the chapter. If you are using this book in a small-group setting, perhaps you will want to examine together one of the Scriptures in each chapter. Consider the reflection questions as starting points for your discussion and prayer together.

1. Inventory your friendships. Consider ways you make choices either to give priority to deepening friendships or to allow barriers to slow their growth and significance.

2. You may find it familiar to pray for your friends and their needs. But consider praying for your friendships themselves, especially for their quality and significance.

3. Think about the people in your life who relate to God differently than you do. Try to identify ways that these people help you grow in your understanding of and love for God. Also try to identify ways that your friendships help you grow as a lover of others. What are these friends good at that you need to learn?

4. Take some time to inventory your friendship patterns along race and ethnicity lines. How can you make choices to broaden your circle of friends?

5. How do you see yourself in the context of a tumbler, being changed (hopefully for the better) by the sometimes uncomfortable and painful process of rubbing up against the people with whom you are in pursuit of God? Take time to thank God for your fellow tumbler stones.

The Hospitality of God

Before you eat or drink anything, consider carefully who you eat or drink with rather than what you eat or drink: for feeding without a friend is the life of a lion or a wolf.

EPICURUS, PRINCIPAL DOCTRINES

My friend Geoff Gordon tells this story of how he got engaged:

Planning your engagement these days is almost as complicated as planning your wedding. Val and I had been talking about getting married for a while, and I wanted the proposal to feel like more than just a formality. I wanted her to feel honored, adored and surprised. More to the point, the bar for getting engaged had been set precariously high by my friends. Not only did Val deserve my creative best, but also my honor was at stake.

Val is a big fan of parks. She loves swing sets and slides. She also loves history and Italian food. It was obvious—the North End in Boston was the perfect setting. The place oozes with romance.

Here was my plan: I would tell her we were going to meet friends for dinner in the North End. While we were waiting for our friends, we would go for a walk and "happen upon" a park with swing sets. Then we would climb on the jungle gym that looks like a castle, where I would "spontaneously" announce that I was tired of waiting. Why not get engaged right there and then? She would laugh, at which point I would pull out the ring, slip it on her finger and declare my eternal love. Perfecto. As an added bit of romantic flair, I told my friend, "Will, go to the park a little bit before we are scheduled to arrive, and decorate the sidewalk and the jungle gym with luminarias." (Luminarias are constructed by putting candles inside of sand-filled paper bags. You see them lining sidewalks at Christmastime.) It was a good plan.

Sunday night, we arrived at the restaurant and I winked at the maitre d', a coconspirator. Our friends, Brian and Jennie, had not yet arrived. What a surprise! (They were not really coming, of course.) So I suggested a walk while we waited for them.

It was a beautiful evening and, just as planned, we happened upon a park with a pair of luminarias outside the gate. *Good*, I thought. *Will's had time to set up.* "Hey, a park. You love parks," I said to Val. "And look at that. Aren't those luminarias?"

As we stepped through the gate, I could see a figure crouching on the sidewalk not twenty feet ahead of us. It was Will, and he was just setting down the third glowing lunch bag. He had thirty more to go. Miraculously, Val didn't see him, and I suddenly realized that I really had to pee. "Let's find a restroom," I said, doing a quick about-face. We found a restroom and I stalled for time. Then we headed back.

By the time we returned to the park, everything was set up beautifully. Hallelujah! It was all very romantic, and the jungle gym with the drawbridge was lit up like a birthday cake. So far, so good.

"Val, let's climb around on that castle," I suggested. My heart was racing. This was it. The big moment. T minus thirty seconds.

We were holding hands and Val was looking beautiful when suddenly something was not right. We heard screaming: "He's running up that hill! Get him, he's running!" It seems my luminaria-lighting friend Will was running away from the police as fast as he could go.

Next there were lights and sirens. The scene went into slow motion and Val began to look scared. A big red truck appeared in front of the park. Five men in raincoats filed out, climbed onto my castle and stomped out the luminarias with black rubber boots.

I was frozen. I thought, *They think Will set this park on fire. . . . Does this mean the wedding is off?*

Val noticed how I was transfixed by the firemen. She tugged on my arm and said, "Let's go. I don't want to get in trouble. Besides, Brian and Jennie should be at the restaurant by now."

Meanwhile, I was desperately thinking, *We can't go back to the restaurant unengaged. Should I get down on my knee right here? Am I going to get arrested? I have no Plan B.* I submitted—we walked out of the park in silence.

Now my fear was that the maitre d' was going to rush out and congratulate us on our nonexistent engagement. What should I do? Should I propose on the sidewalk before we got to the restaurant? Too random. Should I propose in the restaurant? Too cliché. Somebody help me!

We entered the restaurant, and fortunately the maitre d' didn't see us. I peeked inside the dining room. To buy some time, I said, "I don't think Brian and Jennie are here yet."

Then Val, as if prompted by an angel, said, "Do you want to go back?"

My eyes widened with a flash of hope. At last here was the window I could leap through and flee this house fire of confusion. "Yes," I said gratefully. I could have kissed her. There would be no Plan B.

We strolled back to the park and I noted that Will's car was gone. The fire truck was gone as well. I told Val that I *really* wanted to go on that jungle gym. And so we did. Finally the moment seemed right and I told her I thought we should get engaged there. As expected, she thought I was kidding. Even when I get down on my knee, she still didn't believe me. I pulled out the ring. I was nervous and so I slipped it on over her glove. On the wrong hand. I said, "I love you. Will you marry me?" At this point I had nothing eloquent to go with the question.

Val was in disbelief. "What are you doing?" she asked. "Are you serious? Here? Now?"

I told her I *was* serious. But she still was not getting it. It was time to fill in the gaps. I stood up, hugged her and, near tears, cried out, "Baby, they put out my fires!" At which point my heretofore perplexed and slightly annoyed girlfriend widened her eyes and let out the loudest bellow of laughter I have ever heard. Ever. And I had to ask, "Is that a yes?"

Now that the smoke has cleared, I have to admit that things turned out better than I ever could have planned. Good family stories are like treasured heirlooms. Best of all, I got the girl. I think she felt honored and adored. Anyway, my friends were impressed.[1]

Hospitality involves making a welcoming space for relationships to grow. And relationships need different kinds of space in which to flourish. First, they need *physical space*, a place where they actually happen, where people meet or can be comfortable together. Geoff decided that a small park with a castle playground in the North End of Boston was the perfect location for a proposal. Relationships also need *temporal space*, that is, time and planning, and *social space*, or creativity and vision for helping people be at ease in new settings. Geoff went to great lengths to plan every detail so that this evening would be memorable for Val, seizing upon luminaria as the crowning touch that would set the right mood. Relationships additionally need *emotional space*, room for thoughtfulness and intentionality to go beyond superficiality. Geoff planned his verbal strategy for taking his relationship with his girlfriend to new depth and commitment, including his feigned spontaneity and impatience at the external delay. And finally relationships need *spiritual space*, as when we ask God for wisdom regarding how to care for a friend or greater love with which to deepen our friendships. Perhaps Geoff should have prayed a little more for wisdom regarding his chosen plan. On the other hand, he did "get the girl," as he put it, and she felt honored and adored.

Hospitality involves all of these ways of making space for relationships. We first meet the hospitality of God in the creation story, where we read that God prepared a garden and gave Adam and Eve every advantage for their new life to be creative and fruitful. But in the work of Jesus we see the human side of divine hospitality: Jesus welcomed people into relationship not only with himself but also with one another. He served as host, making space and attending to the details in order to enrich the relational experience of his guests.

JESUS: THE LIFE OF THE PARTY (JOHN 2:1-11)

One time my wife and I were hosting a party for over a hundred college students, members of the local IVCF fellowship and their friends. The crowd was large, the music loud, the chaos growing, and yet I knew most of the people in our home. That is, until two young men walked into the house, apparently looking for a different kind of party. I greeted them warmly as they walked by, but they kept moving, as if on a quest. A few moments later they returned, having scoped out the scene. One leaned toward me and asked hopefully, "So, uh, where is the booze?" I tried to explain to him that this was a Christian fellowship party, and while we were not serving alcohol, they were welcome to any of the snacks and drinks we were offering. At that point, with no discernible change in expression and as if on cue, they turned and kept going right back the way they had come and out the door. Apparently these guys had formed the equation "Party means booze. No booze means no party."

Apparently, according to the story we read in John 2, Mary the mother of Jesus thought the same way.

The Gospel writer John told us of only seven of Jesus' miracles, not counting the resurrection.[2] John admitted that he had thousands of miracles from which to choose (John 20:30; 21:25); each miracle he included, then, must represent something significant for it to have made it into the list of the top seven. In this story Jesus used his cosmic power—the same power that spoke the universe into existence—to keep a party going, "the first of his signs" (John 2:11). At first blush it seems a waste of a miracle, or at least a waste of the *first* of his signs. John used Jesus' miracles as signs to point to Jesus' supremacy over the Pharisees' interpretation of the law, Jesus' supremacy over Moses (who gave temporary bread, while Jesus is the bread from heaven) and Jesus' supremacy and power over the natural world and even over death. But here, in showing us the ease with which Jesus turned water into wine, he illustrated Jesus' esteem for relationships: marriage and friendships.

We find Jesus, Peter, Andrew, James and John, Philip and Nathaniel all at the party when the wine ran out. Oddly, Jesus was not at this event to teach, to call disciples, to save anyone's life or to heal any ill people. Nothing that happened at the party was recorded until the crisis erupted that generated the drama. Mary approached her son: "They have no wine" (John 2:3).

Now, you have to wonder why she said this. Was Jesus prone to solving little household problems in this fashion? "Jeeeeesus, we're out of milk again!" "Jesus, hon, your dad has a craving for figs, but they're no longer in season."

No; in fact, it seems that Jesus was not used to solving little household emergencies. He said, "My hour has not yet come" (John 2:4). Jesus knew that he *would* have an "hour," and at that point this kind of thing might be fair game (he made bread in a similar fashion once his hour had come). But he was concerned about timing, pacing and impact. He wasn't impatient to reveal himself.

To be honest, it doesn't strike me as an emergency. No lives were at stake; no theological issues (healing on the Sabbath, for example) hung in the balance. Simply, it seems the party could not go on without more wine.

Yet Mary didn't take a "Not now" from Jesus. Instead Mary spoke to the servants: "Do whatever he tells you" (John 2:5). Here we have a very human glimpse of Mary and her relationship to Jesus. She may indeed have given birth to the Lord God, but to Jesus she was still "Mom." He did what his mom requested.

The wedding feast was a celebration of a relationship crowned with honor and God's blessing. Jesus came to this feast not only as guest but also as host. Jesus blessed this marriage the way he blesses friendships that are oriented toward the pursuit of God. It is a picture of some of the surprising gifts Jesus brings into our friendships: social lubrication, help, the unexpected, abundance, quality and himself.[3]

Jesus eases social interaction. Mary said, "They have run out of wine." We tend not to think this is the kind of thing Jesus cares about. Sure, if we're having difficulty understanding the Bible, we'd turn to Jesus. Or if someone were depressed, we might go before God in prayer. But running out of wine at a party?

The wine at a party can represent the need people have to get over their natural insecurities, their tendencies to be self-conscious and to think too much about what others might be thinking of them. We need help like this especially when relationships are beginning. Jesus offers us, among other things, the inner resources to get beyond our fears in relationships. Jesus' presence in our lives can help us even to become better conversationalists, to be more interested in other people than we would be without his help.

I have a confession to make: I am a recovering nerd. I was a chemistry major in college. Before I joined InterVarsity staff, I taught computer programming at Stanford University. I do math in my head. And typically for most nerds, I found that although I excelled at understanding numbers, I lagged at understanding people. In high school and college I avoided unscripted social settings—parties, dances, hanging out with people without an agenda. Scripted social settings, on the other hand, were easier for me. These included table games, movies, academic class discussions and Bible studies. I was most insecure when it seemed that anything could happen and when my verbal participation would need to be impromptu.

I have found that God's perspective on relationships helps me to become less self-conscious, as I am more concerned with trying to get to know other people than with trying to impress them, judge them or simply avoid being troubled by them. I came to believe that God had a purpose for me in unscripted settings, and so I began to expect that I could even grow to enjoy them. While I haven't become an extrovert, I find I am able to have hope that these times can be relationally fruitful, and so I am much more willing to take risks. God was able to help me do what others turn to alcohol for—to loosen up and enter into the party.

Jesus helps us overcome barriers to friendship. Jesus' powerful help at the wedding seems to have kept the party from meeting an untimely end. Similarly, the help Jesus brings us may be the resources to move ahead in friendships when we encounter resistance. Inviting Jesus into our friendships may bring about greater clarity on how to release time for relationships to grow.

A recent college graduate, Peter, joined our weekly Thursday evening small group. He worked as a consultant and commuted from Boston to Delaware every Monday morning, returning from his four-day week of late nights on Thursday afternoon. However, he would occasionally miss his shuttle back to Boston in time for his small group because of the demands of his job. Even when he did make his small-group meeting, he would often come in so exhausted that his time at the meeting was useless to him. Peter was eager for his relationships to grow and gladly gave priority to consistent participation in the small group. Repeatedly Peter asserted that small group, in fact, was the highlight of his week. But eventually it became clear that in order to grow in his relationships in the church, he needed not only more time but also more energy and more consistency. Jesus provided the clarity about what he needed to do as well as additional motivation and joy at being able to make the change. Peter gave notice at his consultancy, quit his job and was relieved and released in many ways that enabled him to grow in relationships with God and with his friends.

Of course, the point is not that we should all quit our jobs in order to be available for relationships; Peter's situation was pretty extreme and his level of dissatisfaction desperate. But Peter sought help from the group in the form of prayer for relief, for guidance, for courage in his conversations with his boss and for faith to trust God with his future. The group was both a motivator for Peter to make the lifestyle change as well as a means for him to navigate it successfully.

Early on in the life of our church plant in Cambridge, we noticed that while singles and young couples were joining our small groups, the number of parents with young kids lagged. We tried several small-group structures (with and without kids), but nothing worked well until we held a book study with energetic child care provided at the church. Boundaries in marriage and in parenting was a topic in which all of the parents recognized they needed help.[4] We gathered about fifteen couples, together with their children. We then broke the group down further into single-sex discussion and prayer groups for part of the time. Finally, we found a means by which people who were open to grow in relationships had enough support and motivation to come together and do that.

Deepening friendships has perhaps never been simple, but universal busyness amid the complexity of work and family life these days makes it especially difficult. With motivation, we can overcome these barriers, and God can give us resources and creativity to do it. Perhaps the biggest barrier is simply the lack of expectation that relationships can ever be different and deeper than they are.

Jesus brings the unexpected. Jesus' decision to bring timely help at the Cana wedding could have been carried out in a variety of ways. I suppose the people had empty wine containers that Jesus could have miraculously refilled. But Jesus didn't make use of the conventional containers at his disposal; rather, he used the twenty-five-gallon ceremonial washing pots. These pots were used to help Jews complete ritual cleansing, and for Jesus to use them in this way would have meant defiling them. For us, it would be a little like deciding to use the Communion set as shot glasses for a party. No one could have anticipated the means and the scope of Jesus' solution to the problem.

Our little Cambridge church-planting team struggled to work together—we had some strong personalities with different ideas about where we were going and how we'd get there. But as I mentioned before, about the time things were getting desperate, one of our number announced that his life was heading in a different direction, and in a few weeks he was gone from our team, our church and our city. The tension around this decision strained each of our marriages and friendships on the team. We never would have chosen this pathway to establishing ourselves as a team, but the event catalyzed teamwork, partnership and prayer like nothing had before. Within a month of his leaving, we had our first public worship service, with forty in attendance. Six months later, we held an Easter service with nearly 150 people in the room. God used the unexpected, as disappointing and painful as it was at the time, to bring us forward as a team of friends and partners.

Jesus brings abundance. Jesus made the equivalent of eight hundred bottles of wine! Jesus ushers in a life of abundance, as he said, "I came that they [his followers] may have life, and have it abundantly" (John 10:10).

I have seen God bring so many friendships into my life that I no longer think as I once did. When I left college, I honestly thought I was leaving behind the best friendships I would ever have. Not that in general I lacked faith for God to work in my life. But these friendships were unique, or so I thought. Over the next few years, however, I experienced a flowering of my friendships and ministry partnerships. Of course, most notably among them was my friendship and partnership with Lisa, the woman who became my wife. Then we left Santa Cruz for Boston, and I was sure we were leaving behind a garden of community and friendships for a relative desert. The transition was hard and took nearly two years, but after that it was clear that God once again had given us more than we could have expected or thought to ask. More friends, partners, housemates, even baby-sitters; more new relationships, engagements, weddings. Then, finally, even the children of friends—playmates of every age for our own two children.

A few years ago we again experienced a transition as we joined the group I mentioned at the beginning of the book. Eight of us set out to be friends in the common pursuit of God. We left behind a church community that we enjoyed in many ways, one that could well serve a young family. We joined a group of people who loved our kids but didn't share our life situation. For the first two years, our children were the only two kids in our church. However, the abundance God had given to my wife and me he soon extended to our kids as well—we had fifty or more children in the church community of people who were trying to pursue God and become friends together. The small group of eight had grown into a large New England church of five hundred adults in just four years.

Jesus offers quality. Oddly, the steward was surprised not about the existence of the extra cache of wine but at its high quality. Wow! They saved the best for last!

Jesus brings us into the highest quality friendships available. The best aspects of any friendships (between believers or not) exist because of God's general blessing of human friendship and relationships. Yet we all are aware of the pain present in any close relationship, pain often proportional to the intimacy of the relationship. God in our midst makes this pain not only bearable but redemptive, and so he makes whatever is good in our friendships that much better. Whatever is bad and destructive is pruned away, over time, through allowing Jesus to be ever more present in our lives and relationships.

At this writing, my wife and I have been married for over sixteen years. Several summers ago, while on vacation and feeling travel stressed, we argued. We said some of the most hurtful words we've ever spoken to each other. The fight rattled us, but it focused us in a way that broke our complacency about our relationship. It prompted us to look at entrenched relational patterns. We recognized that we had allowed some bad habits to creep into our communication since we had become parents. For example, as conscientious parents, we were consistent in trying to spend time with our young kids before bedtime, reading and singing to them and praying with them. But we had been failing to make any consistent extended attempts to speak with one another at the end of that routine, each of us often reverting to work, study or reading alone. Trying to address this, Lisa would often take initiative with me, but it always felt to her as if she were interrupting my work or reading. This further exacerbated patterns of impatience on my part as well as frustration and a feeling of being ignored or not valued on her part. We sought the help of friends and people we trusted to give us insight. It was a humbling, uncertain process, but Jesus' words and hope gave us the ability to forgive and persevere.

Since then the difference in our relationship has been remarkable. We made some changes to our nightly routine, and we both became more attentive to our own unhelpful relational patterns. We might have hoped simply to get back to the quality of life and relationship we had before our children were born, but Jesus brought us through to a stronger relationship than before.

Jesus offers himself. Jesus brought all these blessings to the wedding because he himself was there. He didn't just send a gift; he was fully present. Jesus doesn't simply bring good gifts to us or even a promise of abundance; he brings himself. All of who he is comes with his presence in the midst of our friendships. Jesus is, in fact, the resource to build and keep friends. Jesus hosts us into an experience of unexpected, high-quality abundance.

One way to view the resources that Jesus brings into our friendships is to view them as resources that particularly help us during different stages of our relationships. These resources help us to deepen our relationships, whether we are just beginning and need curiosity or we are deeply involved and need the ability to forgive and seek forgiveness. Each of these resources offers us the ability to move beyond barriers that keep our friendships from growing and thriving. Table 1 summarizes these ways Jesus blesses and fosters relationships.

A LOOK AT MARY

In this scene in John 2, Mary shows us how to get the benefits of the presence of Jesus in our lives. She is an apt model because she obviously knew how to enjoy her friends while in Jesus' presence (she prevented an untimely end to the wedding feast) and knew how to bring Jesus into the midst of her celebration. She celebrated her friends and received Jesus' help to do so. What's her secret?

Table 1. Resources Jesus Brings into Our Friendships

Jesus Offers Us	Essential Quality	The Antidote To	Stage in the Relationship
Help to be socially at ease	Curiosity, self-confidence	Self-focus, self-consciousness	Introductory
Help to overcome barriers	Commitment, initiative	Lack of time, superficiality	Going deeper
The unexpected	Flexibility, responsiveness	Crisis, external struggle	The point of testing: Will this relationship make it?
Abundance	Hope, expectation	Scarcity, fear, anxiety	Transitions and new beginnings
High quality	Forgiveness and reconciliation	Sin that comes with intimacy and depth	Depth has already been achieved
Himself	All of the above	All of the above	All of the above

Mary displayed three attitudes and actions that made all the difference: expectation, invitation and obedience. We can learn from all three. First, Mary expected that Jesus could help. In the area of friendships, we often don't expect Jesus will or can do anything. We may pray for healing for a friend or for our friends' salvation, but do we expect that Jesus will bring into our lives the resources (energy, time, wisdom) to be a better friend? Second, Mary issued an invitation by bringing the problem to Jesus. How can we grow in our reflex to go to Jesus in prayer, not simply for our friends but for our friendships? Third, Mary displayed her obedience when she emphasized the importance of not second-guessing Jesus, saying, "Do whatever he tells you" (John 2:5). He may tell us to do weird things, but this is how we'll see the hand of God in our life and relationships. Often obedience to Jesus will disrupt our plans or put us in a vulnerable place with our friends, yet through our obedience we will see God at work.

My sophomore year in college, I had a room of my own in a small residence, Whitman House. We ate great food cooked by a chef from Germany, Mr. Druhn. The chef and I shared a passion for red meat. Dinner was served at 6:00 p.m., not during a ninety-minute window as in the dorms. Sometimes I unavoidably came late to dinner, and on several such occasions I arrived to find that Mr. Druhn had saved my dinner for me, still hot, including select servings of meat. I benefited greatly by being the chef's favorite carnivore in the house. But during that year, a friend of mine, Al, a senior in the campus Christian fellowship I was involved with, suggested that I might move back into the dorms for the following year. He challenged me to return to a place where I could have more opportunities for friendships with students in the Christian fellowship and could take advantage of ministry opportunities through leading a Bible study in the dorm. Al made a compelling case, and he offered me friendship and partnership for the following year to make the move successful and worthwhile.

So that's what I did. Everybody in Whitman House thought I was crazy. Indeed it looked like self-inflicted social malpractice. In the housing lottery, I received a sophomore roommate who was more likely to try to pick up a girl than a book, easily distractible and distracting. I was back eating dorm food—I had lost twelve pounds eating the stuff during my freshman year. Yet I became available for relationships like I had never been before. I came to see that the coziness of my Whitman House experience left me both unavailable for friendship and unmotivated to extend myself beyond my superficial relationships.

All the key relationships I developed during college were built during that junior year. Bob, a fellow chemistry major and member of the Christian fellowship, became a friend as we studied together. Our senior year, we led a Bible study together. We became friends, as eventually did our wives, and more recently our kids have become friends during joint vacations and visits.

If we go through life with the expectation that Jesus can help and that he brings high-quality resources into our lives, then we'll turn to him and invite him into our friendships. But to unlock that power and the abundance he offers, we must do what he tells us to do.

For me, obedience to Jesus' words has meant humbling myself to acknowledge that I have acted in anger rather than properly communicating that I was hurt. One of the downsides of midnight access to e-mail is that you can write before you have a chance to rethink what you are doing. I have had to laboriously patch up relationships more than once because of my use of "time saving" e-mail.

Obedience has also meant reordering my priorities. We live in southern California now, and not Cambridge, Massachusetts, in part because of a desire to honor our parents. This reordering of priorities meant that we left familiar friends and church to move across the country, again with the expectation that God would bless new relationships. Of course, sometimes God's call and a reordering of priorities may take us away from parents, as it has done for my wife and me at other times in our lives.

Obedience has also meant opening up our home to people living with us. My wife and I have lived with about fifty people since we were married, not including short-term guests in our home. Often they have been people we know well, but sometimes they have been new friends with a housing need we could meet.

Obedience may even affect our television viewing. At one point I became hooked on *The West Wing*, a television show aired on Wednesday nights. But then I joined a new small group that met on Wednesday nights. I tried to tape a couple of shows, but our VCR stopped working. I made a choice not to be distracted by unduly orienting my life around a television show, and God blessed the relationships made possible by that decision.

We face turning points all the time where the question is, do we expect God to be present in our lives in a way that will make a difference in our relationships? our marriages? our families? our friendships at school, work or church? our friendships with people who don't know God? Jesus offers all of who he is to host us into deeper, more satisfying relationships with people for their sakes, for our sakes, for the sake of the kingdom. Are we willing to hear the call of God in our lives such that we are available to people? Mary understood the secret of receiving the blessing of Jesus in friendships: do what he tells us to do, no matter how crazy it seems.

THE HOSPITALITY OF TIME ALONE WITH GOD

Friends pursue God together, but those friendships and that pursuit are nourished by time alone with God. It is as simple as that. Mary knew how to gain access to the power of Jesus to bless her friends—she went directly to him and made her request.

This book focuses on the communal and relational side of our pursuit of God. But fundamentally the pursuit of God involves a relationship, and a relationship involves time and communication. The invitation of this book is to make two moves simultaneously: (1) to move with our friends to grow toward God, and (2) to move in our relationship with God to grow in our friendships. These two moves maintain the hierarchy present in the Ten Commandments or in Jesus' great commandments: our first calling is to love God, and our second is to love others. But as we'll see, these loves reinforce one another.

Much of this will involve effort and intentionality toward our friends. The story at the beginning of the chapter showed Geoff preparing in many ways to create space for his relationship to move to a deeper level of commitment. Here I want to speak of the need to prepare spiritual space for our relationships to grow. Henri Nouwen, speaking to people concerned with making their relationships meaningful and authentic, wrote, "I am deeply convinced that gentleness, tenderness, peacefulness . . . are nurtured in solitude. Without solitude we begin to cling to each other; we begin to worry about what we think and feel about each other; we quickly become suspicious of one another or irritated with each other; and we begin . . . to scrutinize each other with a tiring hypersensitivity."[5]

A pursuit of God that involves no prayer will become a fiction. Either it is no longer a "pursuit"—it becomes stagnant and empty—or it is no longer God we are pursuing but one of his gifts. Indeed, for many, the corporate nature of the quest to find God can distract from the object of the quest.

Renée was a dedicated member of her college Christian fellowship. She came into the fellowship, and into faith, because of a personal tragedy. After an accident, people in the fellowship rallied to serve and pray for her, and eventually she was healed. Yet soon after graduation, Renée seemed to lose her moorings and she walked away from faith in God. In reality, she had been more connected to her friends through their tangible acts of service than to the God who motivated their love.

Elizabeth, a former IVCF staff partner, had enlisted my wife and me as prayer partners for her three-week itinerant mission trip in Spain. I committed to pray daily for her and wanted to encourage her with my prayers, but I knew she'd never receive any letters while on her brief trip. So I began sending her daily post cards to her home address. The text of each post card was my written prayer for her each day, based on my knowledge of the rough outlines of her trip. When she returned home, she was able to read all of my prayers for her, and we could celebrate together the work God had done to answer prayers for her, her team and their ministry.

Friendship in the pursuit of God involves not only speaking to our friends about God but also speaking to God about our friends. Without a growing relationship with God, involvement in any group of friends will make us susceptible to cynicism, pride, petty jealousy and impatience. It is our ability to receive clarity and conviction from God in prayer that will keep our hearts soft toward our friends and able to love and serve them when it seems inconvenient to do so.

God is big on relationships. They are central to any great theme in the Bible. They are central in the life, teaching and death of Jesus. God himself is relational. God's purpose for all creation and his means of accomplishing that purpose are relational. His strategies, tactics, priorities and plans are relational. His hopes, intentions and callings to his followers are relational. We are his followers and children, and he is shaping us to be more like our Father and our Lord.

FOR REFLECTION

1. God-inspired hospitality may involve many things. Think about the ways your resources are, or could become, available for the purpose of helping relationships to grow.

   - *Physical space:* a clean, neat living room, dining room or kitchen; a guest room or game room

   - *Time:* initiative to set aside time to encourage relationships to form

   - *Social space:* thinking about what would help people be at ease as they are forming new relationships, such as through snacks, games, and so on

   - *Emotional space:* asking appropriate questions in group settings that open people up or take the discussion to a deeper level; offering hugs, tears, affirmation, encouragement

   - *Spiritual space:* spending the time in prayer and reflection to discern deeper needs in people, helping them enter more fully into relationships with others

2. Sometimes we may find that our lives embody choices to give priority to things over people, or tasks over relationships, in ways that leave us with little room for God to answer our prayers for deeper friendships. Take a few minutes to inventory the barriers in your life that might need to come down. Don't ask God for wisdom about any nec-

essary changes unless you have committed to doing what you hear him saying!

- *Living situation:* time availability with spouse and family or housemates

- *Work:* hours, intensity, relational availability on the job, relational availability outside the job

- *Church involvement and small group:* superficial contact with people or expectations for relational depth

- *Time:* the nature of free time; how entertainment time and money are used

- *Location:* deciding among competing priorities, such as commute time, church choice, affordability

Each of these choices identifies factors that make friendships easier or more difficult to pursue.

3. Pray for your friends, for eyes to see them as God does and for ears to hear God teaching you how better to pray for them.

3

The Healing Touch of God

Take up your bed. Carry the very mat that once carried you. Change places,
so that what was the proof of your sickness may now give testimony to your
soundness. Your bed of pain becomes the sign of healing, its very weight the
measure of the strength that has been restored to you.

PETER CHRYSOLOGUS, *ON THE HEALING OF THE PARALYTIC*

The casual conversation trailed off as people in the small group
sensed that the evening meeting was soon to begin. Then the doorbell
rang—a sure sign of a visitor, since group members knew simply to walk
in. I opened the door to my home to invite the young woman in.
Therese, a young teacher, had received information about the small
group at church the previous Sunday and was there to check it out.
Therese was quiet but seemed to enjoy the evening and came back for
the next several weeks, though she rarely spoke.

Then one evening Therese requested prayer for a friend of hers who
was dying at a young age. As the group gathered around Therese, the
hearts of the group members were present to pray, not simply for
Therese's friend, but also for Therese's evident pain. During the prayer,
Therese confessed her own enduring sense of shame, due in part to her
struggle with maintaining a healthy approach toward food. The prayer
time shifted focus once again, more specifically addressing Therese's inner sense of shame and condemnation over the failures and disappointments of the past. As the group proclaimed their concern for and
solidarity with Therese, something began to happen. Where her shame
had kept her quiet and on the periphery of the small group, her sense of

need had brought her to the center (literally, as the group gathered around her to pray). As several people proclaimed an end to shame in Jesus' name, Therese understood something about the gospel—the touch of God often comes in the company of friends. In fact, the touch of God makes deep friendship possible in the first place. Therese attained a deeper level of intimacy and trust with our group that evening.

◆ ◆ ◆

Heather had to decide how to answer the question the small-group leader had asked ten minutes into their first time together as a small group. Should she be honest or give the safe, predictable answers the other women in her small group seemed to be giving? Characteristically blunt, she blurted out, "Well, *you*, Leanne, and to be honest, the three of you as well." The question: "What are your biggest fears as you begin this summer project?"

Heather had long prayed about and pondered whether to participate in a summer-long project in Yellowstone National Park. The relational evangelism project was set against the backdrop of the stunning natural beauty of the park. But as project participants, Heather and the others would work long days on the food crew or housekeeping staff. She was deeply motivated to be there, but she expected the other participants, especially her small-group members, to be like Christian students she had known—superficial and untrustworthy.

Leanne, Heather's small-group leader, was prepared for Heather's answer, or at least didn't seem flustered by it. Rather than resent Heather's bluntness, Leanne served and listened to Heather well over the next few weeks. The women in her small group became close friends as they experienced similar challenges and struggled with similar fears. Heather found she could talk honestly about God and her own hopes and concerns, and she received compassion from the others. Their prayer times became daily highlights for Heather and the rest of the women in the group.

Heather came to Yellowstone to seek God, thinking that progress would come in spite of the other people on the project and in her small group. Instead God touched her, healing some of the wounds of the past, and gave her a company of friends and a renewed vision of how God works in such friendships.

God ministers grace to his people through the gift of friendship. We will come to see that friends are both a source and a destination of the healing process, ushering people to Jesus for his touch and receiving them back from him into wholeness and health.

HEALING AND FRIENDS (MARK 1:40–2:17)

This passage includes a series of three stories in which the relational circles of the people who met Jesus played an increasingly prominent role. In each of these three stories, Jesus touched a man in a way that changed the man's life.

The first story (Mark 1:40-45) involves a leper, an outcast whose life had been defined by his leprosy. This man's ailment was seen as both physical and spiritual, making him unclean and unfit for social interaction. He likely had no remaining friends. His approach to Jesus, humble but hopeful, was perhaps his only chance at knowing anything other than desolation and alienation.

Jesus responded with pity and healed the leper. He touched a man who may not have been touched for years, validating the leper's healing and modeling full acceptance of the former outcast. Yet it was Jesus' words, not his touch, that healed the man. Strictly speaking, Jesus' touch was an extra—Jesus did more than the man had asked for. He addressed the emotional needs of the man for connection, not simply his physical need for healing. But it didn't stop there.

Jesus then spoke to the man sternly—an odd reaction. If we had been watching, we might have been more than a little offended by Jesus' tone of voice. Jesus commanded that the man do what the law required for reentry into society. He was not looking for publicity for himself—just the opposite, in fact. He called the man to offer a sacrifice as a proof, not of Jesus' power, but of the man's healing, so he could be declared free of leprosy. Jesus' remaining concern was that the man be able to re-enter the social and relational network of his community.

The story of the leper is not the only time in the Gospels when Jesus' healing touch propelled people back into a society that had rejected them. Jesus' touch in the Samaritan woman's life brought her from the outside of her community to its center (John 4:28-30, 39-42). Likewise, Jesus healed the demoniac and sent him back to his friends (Mark 5:18-20). In both cases, people who had been alienated and rejected were given mission, purpose and new hope for relationships in their community.

A contemporary example of the leper might involve anyone who struggles with insecurity, social awkwardness or fear of rejection. This person might believe that his or her personality or other traits drive people away. Jesus' touch comes in some personal and powerful way, removing alienation from others and from God. Rather than feeling self-conscious and full of self-pity, the person comes to believe that he or she has something to offer to others, and this person's experience of friendship and community begins to grow.

The next scene in Mark is the story of the paralyzed man brought to Jesus by his friends (2:1-12). Whereas the leper came to Jesus on his own, the paralytic could not do so. His friends had to bring him on a stretcher. They were not able to squeeze themselves into the home where Jesus was teaching and healing people, so they abandoned decorum and took advantage of the flimsiness of the building's roof, taking it apart to let their friend down. Having demanded Jesus' attention in this way, they ultimately received what they wanted. "When Jesus saw their faith," Jesus spoke words of healing (verse 5). What did Jesus see? People who would stop at nothing to bring their friend to Jesus for healing.

The faith of friends may save. This is startling for people who, like me, are used to thinking of saving faith as an individual choice. Of course there is no reason to assume that the paralytic man didn't share in the faith of his friends. Yet it was the plurality of faith, not the single instance of it, that Jesus noticed and rewarded. Hence, the faith of friends may save—a sufficient reason in itself to pursue friends in the company of God (and vice versa).

A contemporary instance of the healing of the paralytic may begin with someone who struggles with bitterness, regret or despair, perhaps due to past sin or relational breakdown. The paralyzed person may feel unable to approach God on his or her own. Friends see what is happening and step in to pray, encourage or exhort this person to seek God's work and believe him for healing. The result is that this person comes face to face with a patient and compassionate Jesus, receiving forgiveness for the past and healing of the deceptions that kept him or her from seeking God in the first place.

For some, healing will bring us more into contact with friends. It may force us out of a hermitlike existence independent of the resources of other people. Jesus' healing may come in the form of a stern call to give priority to friendships that, for one reason or another, we have let slip away or atrophy. For others, the healing touch of Jesus comes into our lives only because we have greatly relied on friendships that brought us into new or deepened contact with Jesus. Jesus' healing results in a greater ability to walk under our own power, bringing us along in our friendships from needy dependence to a potential for partnership and interdependence.

The third story in this sequence is that of Levi, also known as Matthew, the Gospel writer (Mark 2:13-17). Levi was a tax collector, an outcast in respectable society, but unlike the leper, he had made a choice to be such. Levi probably was not a tremendously religious man—he would have been overtly unwelcome in devout society, and the disdain was probably somewhat mutual.

Jesus met Levi at his tax booth and said simply, "Follow me" (verse 14). Who knows why Levi followed Jesus? Had he heard his teaching before? Was it Jesus' air of authority? Or did Mark leave out part of the story to get to the good part? Whatever the reason, Levi followed Jesus . . . all the way to Levi's own house, where he threw a party in Jesus' honor, inviting all of his tax collector (read "sinner") friends, prostitutes and other extremities of humanity in turn-of-the-era Palestine. But Jesus was present in their midst, eating and drinking, laughing and talking with Levi and his friends.

A contemporary Levi would be one who is alienated from religion, who feels he would not be welcome in a church. Our Levi of today would probably say he wouldn't want to go to heaven, because none of his friends will be there. But Jesus gets his attention by breaking the stereotypes of how God works and with whom. Jesus' touch travels deep into Levi's being, affirming him and assuring him of acceptance and love by God.

Mark, the master editor and scribe of Peter, had access to countless stories of Jesus, including remarkable healings and miracles. He included these three scenes, strung together without interruption, to communicate something of the strategy of Jesus, summed up in Jesus' response to the Pharisees: "Those who are well have no need of a physician, but those who are sick; I have come to call not the righteous but sinners" (Mark 2:17). To the sick, Jesus served as a physician, healing leprosy and paralysis. But to the sin-sick, Jesus served as a Savior, calling the leper back to believing society, forgiving the sins of the paralytic and accepting Levi and his friends into the intimacy of table fellowship. Levi, while receiving no physical healing for any ailment, also received the healing touch of God in his life, simply through the acceptance, attention and love of Jesus. This touch also changed Levi's life—its nature, its purpose, its course.

GOD'S TOUCH AND OUR FRIENDS

Looking back on it, it's clear that I was in culture shock. However, at the time I would have justified my reaction on theological grounds.

My wife and I had traveled with a group of seven Harvard IVCF students to Malaysia, joining another sixteen students and staffworkers from Stanford to spend a summer with a church-planting church in Kuala Lumpur. We wanted to be inspired and to gain vision for evangelism, missions and the ministry of the Holy Spirit. We were there, in part, to get zapped by God. The church we were visiting was a charismatic church, where speaking in tongues, falling over (being "slain in the Spirit"), prophecy and powerful healings were expected regularly. We were being prepared to help lead youth rallies and ministry events at some of the young church outreaches in towns around Kuala Lumpur.

As it turned out, the Malaysian culture was a fairly easy cultural exchange for us, though the experience was not without its moments. The language (the common worship language was English for this congregation), the food (tasty and plentiful) and the culture of the church (educated young professionals in Kuala Lumpur) made our transition smoother than it might have been. On the other hand, the theological framework of the teachers in the church (Pentecostalism, with a focus on material blessing) left me in the dust. Of course, it was culture shock (mostly), but because I was enjoying the food and speaking the language, I didn't recognize it.

The team from Harvard had been encouraged to learn as much as we could from our interactions with members of the Malaysian church. To their credit, the team members all had pretty good attitudes. As the team coleader, I lagged. While the others entered in and tried to join whatever was happening, I made sarcastic comments about the teaching and the simplistic focus on speaking in tongues. My attitude began to affect the group.

One free afternoon I was alone, reading, when some student members of the team came and invited me to join them and the others. The entire team had been talking, and then praying, about how my attitude was affecting them. Their concern was first for themselves, for their ability to learn from the experience in Malaysia and from the people in the church. Yet their concern quickly came around to me, focusing on my heart and my ability to appreciate and receive from the experience. Beneath my concern for theology, as we dug a little deeper, was an insecurity that previously I would not have been able to confess—I was afraid that God's power, love and presence would be strongly felt by others but not by me. I was afraid that God would withhold a tangible experience of his power from me. Now *that* was something that everyone on the team could understand and have compassion for.

Their strong words and call to pray for my attitude softened my heart, and I was able to repent of my sarcasm and resistance and be more receptive during the rest of the trip. This change, in turn, helped everyone on the team have a better experience in Malaysia.

This is one example of a paralytic-type encounter with Jesus: my friends brought me into contact with Jesus at a time when I wasn't able to go to him on my own. They prayed for my attitude—the thing that needed healing but would be a barrier to my seeking him. As if paralyzed, I couldn't go to God for what I needed, precisely because my lack stood in the way.

These three encounters with Jesus are paradigmatic for all of us. When we feel isolated from people, Jesus' healing touch sends us back to our friends. Our healing isn't complete until relationships are restored. When we feel alienated from God, friends bring us into contact with Jesus' healing touch. The faith of friends may save.

Jesus is a physician who heals our wounds and diseases, and he is a Savior who saves us from our alienation. Following Jesus is a personal choice and a corporate experience.

Sometimes we are like the leper in Mark 1—our insecurity and fear keep us from believing God can do anything in our relationships with others, but God's power enters our life in a way that requires movement toward our friends. Sometimes we are like Levi in Mark 2—our expectation of rejection from God keeps us from approaching him, but he seeks us out and surprises us with an embrace so wide that it encompasses not only ourselves but our friends as well. And sometimes we are like the paralytic—God performs healing work in our lives when we are brought to him by our friends. Figure 1 illustrates how these three scenes depict the nature of God's healing work in its relation to our friends. Each scene involves movement in some way, touching our lives and deepening our relationships. Table 2 summarizes these scenes and familiar ways we see them lived out today.

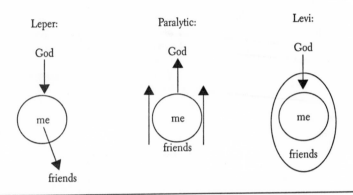

Figure 1. Three images of the healing touch of God

In the first chapter I introduced the image of the lapidary tumbler as a parable of the way people are changed by community. The role of friendships in the healing process is one of the ways that God uses the tumbler experience for our refinement and growth. Amazingly, he is able to use rough, unpolished stones in the tumbler for our mutual polishing process; people who themselves need healing are able to be instrumental in our own healing.

In the two stories that began this chapter, fear and shame threatened to keep Heather and Therese at a distance in the groups of which they were a part. However, God used other members of their groups not only to counteract the fear and shame, allowing them to open up, but also to begin to heal the underlying wounds.

This is why churches use small groups. It doesn't take a pastor to offer a prayer for healing or a word of encouragement or emotional support. In fact, the halting but sincere prayer of a friend may comfort even more than the smooth and measured tones of a professional.

Table 2. The Healing Touch of God Today

The Character: And contemporary manifestations	Opening State: What do I believe?	Dramatic Action: Who does what?	Final State: What is the result?
Leper: Insecurity, past rejection, disabilities, ethnic barriers, social awkwardness, fear, no resources to develop friendships	I am alienated from people and from God. I believe that immutable aspects of who I am drive people away.	Jesus touches my life in a personal and powerful way; he enables me to return to friends and community.	I no longer believe I am ugly and rejected. I have a compelling story to tell and something real to offer my friends.
Paralytic: Bitterness, regret, despair, physical and emotional limitations, sin	I am unable to go to God on my own. "Where was God when that happened to me?"	My friends bring me to Jesus. They pray when I don't have faith; they are patient with my questions; they encourage me to seek God's work in my life.	Face to face with Jesus, I am forgiven, healed and grateful. Jesus is patient with my need and he honors my friends in coming to him.
Levi: Alienation from religion, judgment, legalism, self-doubt, resentment of hypocrisy	I believe I must make a choice between my friends (whom I admire) and God (represented by religious people I can't stand).	Jesus gets my attention by breaking my preconceptions of how and with whom he works.	Jesus' touch deeply affirms me. I am no longer trying to fit in, as his presence in my life assures me I do. He'll even accept my friends.

FOR REFLECTION

1. Which of the three figures from Mark 1—2 do you relate to most closely lately? How has Jesus' touch affected how you relate to your friends?

2. What is one thing you could do about your condition?

3. How have your friends helped you to receive the healing touch of God?

4. How have you been involved in God's healing touch in your friends' lives?

4

Life, Death and Love Among Friends

In words which can still bring tears to the eyes, St. Augustine describes the desolation in which the death of his friend Nebridius plunged him (Confessions IV, 10). Then he draws a moral. This is what comes, he says, of giving one's heart to anything but God. All human beings pass away. Do not let your happiness depend on something you may lose. If love is to be a blessing, not a misery, it must be for the only Beloved who will never pass away.

Of course this is excellent sense. . . . Of all arguments against love none makes so strong an appeal to my nature as "Careful! This might lead you to suffering!"

To my nature, my temperament, yes. Not to my conscience. When I respond to that appeal I seem to myself to be a thousand miles away from Christ. . . .

There is no escape along the lines St. Augustine suggests. Nor along any other lines. There is no safe investment. To love at all is to be vulnerable. Love anything, and your heart will certainly be wrung and possibly broken. If you want to make sure of keeping it intact, you must give your heart to no one, not even to an animal. Wrap it carefully round with hobbies and little luxuries; avoid all entanglements; lock it up safe in the casket or coffin of your selfishness. But in that casket—safe, dark, motionless, airless—it will change. It will not be broken; it will become unbreakable, impenetrable, irredeemable. The alternative to tragedy, or at least to the risk of tragedy, is damnation. The only place outside Heaven where you can be perfectly safe from all the dangers and perturbations of love is Hell.

C. S. LEWIS, THE FOUR LOVES

Now a certain man was ill, Lazarus of Bethany, the village of Mary and her sister Martha. Mary was the one who anointed the Lord with perfume and wiped his feet with her hair; her brother Lazarus was ill. So the sisters sent a message to Jesus, 'Lord, he whom you love is ill.'

JOHN 11:1-3

Apart from the twelve disciples, Mary and Martha are probably best known as friends of Jesus. They spent time with him; they were supporters of his; he even stayed in their home. Martha was the typical older sister, the responsible one, while Mary was the young and idealistic dreamer. But they both loved Jesus in their own ways and were loved in return. They were economically dependent on their brother, Lazarus, also single. Lazarus was tragically stricken with a fatal illness early in life. He left behind unmarried sisters with a possibly uncertain financial future.

So they sent for Jesus. They didn't even mention Lazarus by name. I think they assumed that Jesus would come in haste. They likely imagined a quiet, private healing. "Keep it discreet, Jesus, but 'he whom you love' (you know who we mean) is ill."

> But when Jesus heard it, he said, "This illness does not lead to death; rather it is for God's glory, so that the Son of God may be glorified through it." Accordingly, though Jesus loved Martha and her sister and Lazarus, after having heard that Lazarus was ill, he stayed two days longer in the place where he was.
>
> Then after this he said to the disciples, "Let us go to Judea again. . . . Our friend Lazarus has fallen asleep, but I am going there to awaken him." (John 11:4-7, 11)

Perhaps it seems from the text that although Jesus' love for Lazarus would have compelled him to go as soon as he was able, other pressing concerns delayed him. Some translators deal with the text in this fashion. And yet John's Gospel mentions nothing about what he did in the meantime. No pressing concern, no healing, no sermon given. The next thing of significance that happened was Jesus going to be with Mary and Martha. The text indicates that he waited two days precisely *because* he loved Mary and Martha and Lazarus. He called Lazarus "friend," and not only *his* friend but theirs together. Somehow his waiting two days extended love for those sisters and was an act of friendship to Lazarus.

We must ask these crucial questions: Why did he wait for two days? How was this an act of love and friendship?

THE GOD WHO WEEPS (JOHN 11:17-38)

Jesus waited for two days and then went. Lazarus had been dead for four days by the time he arrived, so Lazarus didn't die because Jesus was dilly-dallying. In fact, Lazarus probably died within hours after Mary and Martha sent for Jesus.

"Martha said to Jesus, 'Lord, if you had been here, my brother would not have died. But even now I know that God will give you whatever you ask of him'" (11:21-22). John's narration of his Gospel story sometimes seems to omit normal conversational details. Maybe Martha met Jesus with softer pleasantries first: "How was your trip? So good of you to come. Oh, by the way, if you had been here my brother would not have died."

I actually imagine that John's narration, spare as it is, in this case is complete. Jesus arrived and Martha saw him and the first thing Martha thought to say was "Lord, if you had been here, my brother would not have died." Shortly afterward, when her sister, Mary, met Jesus, the first words out of her mouth were exactly the same: "Lord, if you had been here, my brother would not have died" (11:32).

Strange coincidence? I think not! I think Mary and Martha had been rehearsing this line for four days, saying to each other, "If Jesus had only been here . . ." and "Where was Jesus?" They had seen Jesus heal dozens of people, most of them complete strangers. They had assumed that Jesus would be at Lazurus's bedside, giving Lazarus the familiar and intimate touch of life and health. Their disappointment at his death issued in the refrain that we hear them both utter in this scene.

My wife and I have two healthy children, a boy and a girl. We have deeply faithful, believing friends whose two pregnancies closely followed our own. We walked through both difficult pregnancies with them. Their little boy was born with a hole in his heart and spent much of his first year in the hospital. Their second pregnancy was difficult from the beginning, and after only twenty-five weeks, the placenta detached and their daughter was born, only to die a day later. Where was God? Today our friends have something of an answer to the question, but in the midst of the pain and disappointment, it was difficult to say anything without sounding trite or naive. Indeed at that point our role was not to have explanations but to weep with them.

Where was God? Where was Jesus? Why would he let us down in this way? I think that's what had been ringing in the hearts and minds of Mary and Martha—it's the first thing they said when they saw him.

In the first scene between Jesus and Martha, Jesus said to her right away, "Your brother will rise again" (John 11:23). Martha replied, "I know that he will rise again in the resurrection on the last day" (verse 24).

Often in John's Gospel, Jesus said something metaphorical or figurative that people took literally. He said to a woman sitting at the side of a well, "If you drink of the water that I provide, you will never thirst." She responded, "I sure would love that water, then I wouldn't have to come to this hot well in the middle of the day" (see John 4:10-15). That's not exactly what he meant. He said a little later to the disciples, "I have food you don't know anything about." What he meant was: I get so excited by seeing the work of God in people that I forget even to eat. But the disciples thought, "Who brought him food?" (see John 4:32-33).

Repeatedly, Jesus said something metaphorical and the people took it literally, missing the point. Here the opposite happened. Jesus said, "Your brother will rise again," meaning it would happen in a few minutes. To this Martha replied, "I know that he will rise again in the resurrection on the last day." He spoke regarding what was about to happen and she spoke of eternity.

Next Jesus tried a different tack, asking Martha about her faith. Martha believed that Jesus was the Savior of the world. That was easy for Martha—that was her theology. Yet Jesus was asking, "Do you believe I am *your* Savior?" Martha hadn't actually experienced Jesus as *her* Savior. Jesus hadn't actually saved her *lately*. Here we have our first hints as to how Jesus was loving Martha and Mary even by waiting before coming to them. Martha was going to witness Jesus' power as she never had before.

Martha then went back and called her sister, Mary. Martha knew that Mary had a special relationship with Jesus. "Mary, the teacher wants to talk to you; you have a way with him. You talk to him; I think he'll understand you." Mary came out and knelt at Jesus' feet—a familiar place for Mary (see Luke 10:39; John 12:3). And where Martha engaged in theological struggle with Jesus, Mary just wept. And, in fact, Mary did get through to Jesus. Jesus wept. He was greatly disturbed.

Now, when I first read this story, I had a hard time understanding why Jesus cried. He knew the end of the story. Death wasn't the final scene. He knew what was going to happen and yet didn't rush on to meet it. Halfway between the incomprehensible sorrow of the now and the indescribable joy of the soon, he lingered and wept.

Why did Jesus weep here? Because he saw the scene as it was then, not as it was going to be ten minutes later. He felt the power of the emotions, and he was present in the midst of them. He was not looking on at a distance like a boy watching his ant farm. Jesus was present, surprisingly so. He entered into the emotions of Mary, even though he knew Mary's weeping was going to turn into joy. He was not above it or apart from it. Jesus made the choice St. Augustine regretted—and "St. Lewis" recommended—to set his heart on a mortal creature and let it risk pain.

So the image we have of Jesus—preresurrection, weeping—answers that unanswered question: where was God? He was there at our bedside, weeping with us. Though he knows the end from the beginning, though he holds the future in his hands, still he feels with us the pain of our losses and disappointments, at the time we are experiencing them. While it even may provide the bedrock of our faith to know of God's sovereignty, the picture here is of a God who cares and cries.

LIFE OUT OF DEATH

Jesus said, "Take away the stone." Martha, the sister of the dead man, said
to him, "Lord, already there is a stench because he has been dead four days."
Jesus said to her, "Did I not tell you that if you believed, you would see
the glory of God?" So they took away the stone. And Jesus looked upward and
said, "Father, I thank you for having heard me. I knew that you always hear
me, but I have said this for the sake of the crowd standing here, so that
they may believe that you sent me." When he had said this, he cried with a loud
voice, "Lazarus, come out!" The dead man came out, his hands and feet
bound with strips of cloth, and his face wrapped in a cloth. Jesus said to them,
"Unbind him, and let him go."

Many of the Jews therefore, who had come with Mary and had seen what
Jesus did, believed in him.

JOHN 11:39-45

If we had been able to ask Martha, "Do you believe Jesus can heal your
brother?" she would have said, "Of course; that's why we sent for him."
I also think that if Jesus had shown up the day Lazarus died, Martha
might have ushered Jesus into the room and said, "Jesus, is there anything you can do?" She may have heard (although it wasn't widely
known at the time) of how Jesus had healed a little girl who had died
moments before he arrived on the scene. However, someone who has
been in the tomb for four days is not just "mostly dead"—perhaps Jesus
could deal with that. No, Martha objected, four days dead is totally,
stinkingly dead!

Yet this is the very thing that Jesus wanted to give Martha: a picture
of his power—the power to bring back what she most wanted when she
had no faith or hope wild enough to even imagine it. He affirmed to
Martha that if she believed, then she would taste the overflow of his
blessing to transform her life. And that's exactly what happened.

"Lazarus, come out!" I like verse 44: "The dead man came out." In
other words, the man formerly known as dead came out. Fear, hope and
joy flooded into the hearts of Mary and Martha, mixing with the sorrow

already there before driving it out to stay. For people who are not fans of Jesus, this would be terrifying. The moment the dead man began to breathe, the entire crowd stopped breathing—until they broke out in rejoicing. Remember, Lazarus was still bound like a mummy; his legs would have been bound together tightly and his motion was still restricted. As Lazarus slowly performed the ex-dead-man's shuffle out of the cave, Jesus had the complete attention of the crowd. What immortal words did Jesus speak at the peak of this dramatic climax? "Unbind him, and let him go."

Jesus had in his words the power and authority to bring Lazarus back from the dead, but he chose to ask for help for Lazarus, still hindered by the bindings and rags of his death. It was the power of God that brought Lazarus back to life, but it was the hands of his friends who took off the constraints of death. Jesus could raise Lazarus by his power; why not do something much easier like release his bandages? Because Lazarus's friends had their role to play.

It remains the same today. It is God's power, only and alone, that can bring anyone back to life from the point of death, physically or spiritually. However, Jesus continues to use friends to welcome us back from the land of the dead. Our friends get their hands dirty taking off the smelly clothes of death and the tight constraints of bondage in order to free us for the real life God has for us.

I have several friends who lately have been undergoing treatment for cancer. These are consummate servants, upon whom many have leaned for wisdom and support. Through their healing process they have had the tables turned, needing to rely on friends to usher them back from (near) death to life in tangible ways.

Jesus became more than simply a good theory for Martha. He was not just the Savior of the world; he was now *her* Savior. He validated her theory and enhanced her faith as she received his love for her through the gift of her resurrected brother.

Likewise for us, Jesus becomes our Savior in a real sense when we face death and then feel his resurrection power. Often this happens with our friends around to welcome us back from the land of the dead with grace and patience. We can undergo death and a friend-filled release in many ways, but I am going to mention two as examples. One has to do with our high opinion of ourselves, while the other has to do with our plans for the future.

I grew up in a strong Christian home and was not at all exposed to pornography. It was difficult for me to relate to male friends who would occasionally share about their struggle with pornography addiction or temptation. Yet a few years ago I began to receive e-mail notices for pornographic websites, and my curiosity (and the ease and hiddenness of the access) got the better of me. I found that I too was susceptible to the lure of pornography. While I certainly would have acknowledged my own sexual struggle, I hadn't felt the power of temptation in this way before.

What died for me was my own (by comparison) high opinion of myself, made worse by the fact that I worked as a responsible staff supervisor for a Christian ministry. In fact, the only way I could get past the cycle of hiddenness and shame was to speak about it, first to my wife and my supervisor within InterVarsity and then with friends and others who knew me. This meant I had to let others see the messy, sinful side of me. Speaking with others both helped me not remain alone in my sin and gave me the discipline to turn away. I suffered the death of my own sense of invulnerability and then witnessed God's resurrection power through, in part, letting others in. This death and resurrection gave me, as it did for Martha in John 11, a fresh knowledge of the powerful saving work of Jesus in my life.[1]

Another, earlier period in my life illustrates how we sometimes experience death in our plans for the future. My junior year in college, my world was rocked in two ways simultaneously. My girlfriend, Kris, decided to end our relationship. At the same time, my plans to get a master's degree in economics while achieving a bachelor's degree in chemistry, all in four years, hinged on continuing the blistering pace I had set my first two years in college. They also required that I perform exceptionally well in the graduate-level econometrics course I was taking. I had always excelled in math, but finally I met my match. I dropped my course (the first time ever) and with it my plans for graduate work in economics.

These changes left me feeling adrift relationally and academically. I passed only two courses that quarter (six units, having averaged twenty units per quarter the previous two years). That and being without a girlfriend depressed me, especially because I had assumed that Kris was "the one." Yet this death opened me up to some new things that God began to do in my life. Newly needy because of these recent disappointments, I opened up to other friends about my life in ways that deepened our friendships and directed me toward God. Friends saw me in my death clothes and were compassionate in helping to remove them. Furthermore, freed from my twin preoccupations of academic and romantic intensity, I had much more time to develop these encouraging friendships.

In both of these situations I soaked in the love of God through the enrichment that came from friendships deepened by my trauma and loss. Whether the death we experience is of another person or of our own sense of identity, direction or place, with the touch of Jesus out of death comes new life, hope and fearlessness. If at this time we turn to our friends (and if we have such friends), there we find God's power and compassion available to us.

Finally, my focus on other ways we can meet death is not meant to trivialize the reality that many face the actual loss of loved ones and close friends. I know that I write as a member of a privileged socioeconomic community for whom tragedy and suffering are mostly distant concepts, not daily realities. The death I can talk about is metaphorical, not physical, and imagined, not imminent. A woman wrote to me of her friend whose two girls were raped and murdered, their bodies dumped in the desert. The gospel can be said to have power only when it has power to speak into a situation like this, to give hope when the situation is truly hopeless. But again and again in the Gospels and in this world, the people of God gather around to welcome back from death to life those who desperately need and gladly receive the resurrection power of Jesus. This is a messy, heartbreaking enterprise. But we cannot avoid this risk, as Lewis said, without peril to our souls.

FOR REFLECTION

1. How have you seen God at work to bring life out of death in your friendships and family relationships?

2. What are some of the things that may need to die in your life so that you can witness the power of God at work on your behalf? Are you aware of any painful death in any area of your life lately?

3. How might Jesus want your friends to be involved in your healing and restoration? What would it take to invite them into the process?

4. How might you or your company of friends release the power of the gospel into situations of tragedy amid poverty?

5

Presence and Intimacy in the Company of Friends

Here we are, you and I, and I hope a third, Christ, is in our midst. There is no one now to disturb us; there is no one to break in upon our friendly chat, no man's prattle or noise of any kind will creep into this pleasant solitude. Come now, beloved, open your heart, and pour into these friendly ears whatsoever you will, and let us accept gracefully the boon of this place, time, and leisure.

AELRED OF RIEVAULX, *SPIRITUAL FRIENDSHIP*

Recently on the radio I heard a poem written by an eighth grader from a middle school in Newton, Massachusetts, mourning the loss of her four friends who died when their school bus driver lost control of the vehicle on a field trip in Canada. The poem expressed common sentiments of grief, wonder, ache and loss. The poem climaxed with the poet's wish that she could exchange her life for theirs.

Speaking of his love for his disciples, Jesus said, "No one has greater love than this, to lay down one's life for one's friends" (John 15:13). One of the foundational principles of an army's success, we are told, is unit cohesion. That is so because, in the heat of battle, it is not a soldier's willingness to die for his country that is crucial, but rather that soldier's willingness to risk his life for his friends.

Yet because the life of a soldier is so remote for most of us, few of us have heartfelt access to either the heroism of extraordinary courage or the urgency of the infantry grunt who risks his life to pull his wounded friend to safety. How are these attachments formed? How are these sentiments aroused?

Perhaps, as you read the Gospels, the simple, compelling truths of Jesus' preached message ring so clearly that you could easily imagine being right there with Peter when he declared to the Lord, "I will lay down my life for you" (John 13:37). (Of course, that sentiment, uttered the night before Jesus' death, proved to be more than Peter was able to deliver.) As compelling as I find those truths to be, and as much as I have wanted to live by the gospel, I find I am rather less lofty in my motivations. Yet I am never more likely to risk my life for the gospel, or to choose to live for Jesus, than when I am around friends who feel the same way.

So how did Jesus do it? How did he bring together a group of disciples who would be willing literally to live and die for his cause?

One crucial aspect of Jesus' strategy can be summarized by a single word: *time*. Time with purpose. Quantity time. Quality time. There is no replacing it. Shortcuts don't exist. The military and police do it the same way. Comrades and partners facing deadly situations have already spent hours and hours together in routine drills and practice.

To pursue a relationship with Jesus, we must spend time with Jesus. To enjoy friendship the way Jesus did, we must spend time with other followers.

Often Jesus' model of building community is obscured for us by the simple fact that Jesus is God and we are not. Jesus had a divine claim on his disciples' time and decisions and entire lives, while we today cannot properly make such a claim on other believers. We must ask the question, how is Jesus a model for us?

One of the keys to answering this question lies in an analysis of how Jesus spent time with his disciples. As we search through the Gospels, we can make two broad observations. First, Jesus gave priority to his disciples' relationships with him because he was their only Lord and Savior. He was their source of spiritual power, authority and even life itself. This is a unique relationship between Christ and every true disciple of his, and it cannot be replaced by that of any friend or teacher. Second, like any good human leader, Jesus spent time with his disciples because he enjoyed and loved the people who had been given to his care and training. Jesus knew that much of the content of his teaching was going to be validated by the quality of life he and the disciples enjoyed together. Therefore, Jesus was both unique Savior and model teacher and friend.

Jesus enjoyed time with his disciples and he spent that time in a variety of ways, simply because he liked them. Here Jesus is a perfect model of a skilled friend who knew how to offer his friendship through hospitality and shared adventure.

CONCENTRIC CIRCLES OF RELATIONSHIP (MARK 3:7-19)

Jesus called his followers first of all to be with him. Yet what it meant to be with Jesus was different for different people who followed him. Jesus offered himself—his life, his time, his intimacy—more to some people than to others. This was not haphazard, random or capricious but rather was according to his plan. He loved the many, in some ways, by focusing on the few. We can see an outline of this perspective in Mark 3, describing the occasion when Jesus appointed his twelve disciples.

It is as if Mark imagined a map as he wrote this passage—it is geographically detailed. (See figure 2.) Mark gave us a satellite-camera view of what was happening, starting at a high altitude above Galilee. Mark described large crowds streaming toward Lake Galilee in order to hear Jesus and, if possible, to be healed. These people were coming from down south, in Judea and Jerusalem and as far as Idumea. From the north, both Jews and Gentiles came from Tyre and Sidon, nearly two days' journey away. To the east, they came from beyond the Jordan River. People came from all over Palestine.

As the magnification increases and the scope of our picture decreases, we see those who pressed in around Jesus, "the many," trying to receive healing from their diseases. These people had done more than hear of Jesus; they had actually received a touch, a look, a personal, though brief, show of mercy from Jesus.

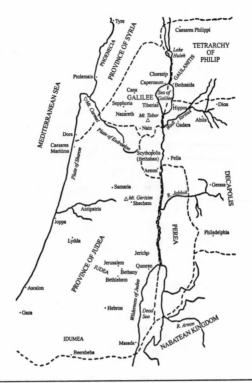

Figure 2. Palestine in Jesus' day

Then the magnification is amplified even more, and we see Jesus on the top of a mountain, calling "those whom he wanted" to join him for a retreat from the confusion and demands of the crowds (Mark 3:13). These were the company of men and women who were known as his followers. Our attention is drawn not to a mass of crushing bodies but rather to recognizable (though unnamed) faces. Perhaps these numbered as many as seventy (Luke 10:1)—people Jesus knew personally, ones he wanted to be with him. He took the initiative to invite them to spend time with him in a more relaxed setting.

Again Mark turns up the magnification another notch, and even the large crowd of followers fades into the background, as he focuses on "the twelve" whom Jesus appointed to specific tasks and with a call to be with him (Mark 3:16). These twelve were not just a nameless set of friends; these were the named set of disciples—each with a role and a destiny, a cofounder with Jesus of the early church (and one as the betrayer of the Son of God).

And then finally the magnification is turned up one final time, and Mark reminds us that even within the Twelve there was an inner circle: Peter, James and John, whom Jesus renamed with fitting and intimate nicknames. These three received the most intimate look into the life of Christ. They alone viewed the transfiguration and the resurrection of Jairus's daughter. Along with Andrew, they heard Jesus' prophecies about the destruction of the temple and the fall of Jerusalem. These three received from Jesus the harshest rebukes when their headstrong ideas clashed directly with his perfect understanding of his destiny, and theirs as well (Matthew 14:31; Mark 8:31-33; 9:38-39; 10:35-45; 14:26-31; Luke 9:54-56). In many ways, these three received special prominence in the Gospel accounts (John 13:21-26; 19:25-27; 21:15-24).

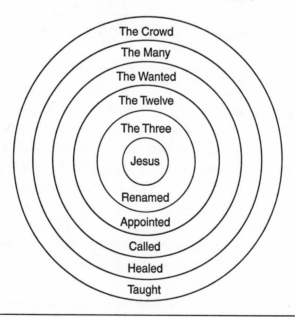

Figure 3. Jesus' concentric circles of relationships

These, then, are the concentric circles of relationship as revealed to us in this passage of Mark: Jesus taught the multitude; he healed the "many"; he called those "whom he wanted"; he appointed the Twelve; and he renamed the three. Greater depth and texture in the relationship characterizes each group as the circles are drawn tighter.

It may be hard to observe this pattern without thinking about elitism. Why did Jesus "want" some people but not others? Were some excluded from Jesus' inner circle simply because he didn't like them? Why did Jesus appear so exclusive?

Jesus' purpose included more than simply healing and feeding people. He took many opportunities to show mercy to people, to give them food and comfort when they were like sheep without a shepherd, to minister healing late into the night when they thronged about the door. Yet his purpose involved drawing together a people who would become his presence in the world after he left. This people, the body of Christ, the gathered church, would continue to feed and to heal in Jesus' name. Similarly, their ultimate purpose would go beyond the feeding and healing. They would continue to be God's people, reconciled to God and reconcilers of others by the same name.

So Jesus spent his time giving of himself to a small number of people. His disciples' lives would be so powerfully transformed that they could replicate and multiply his work in many more lives. In this sense the strategy of Jesus was not exclusive. He always responded to the crowds, even the Pharisees. He called them to himself and called them to repent. To anyone who asked questions, he gave answers.

However, Jesus' strategy to reach the multitudes in Palestine, and ultimately in the world, was to leave behind a small band of committed men and women.[1] In order to instill deeply in others the values and convictions by which he lived, he had to focus on a few. As we look at the Gospel accounts, at the end it seems that his mission had failed: the disciples left him and lacked any boldness to carry on after he died. Yet as he predicted, the Holy Spirit came and emboldened them and reminded them of all they had learned from Jesus. Then they were able to preach with the boldness characteristic of Jesus himself. As many people responded in faith to Peter in one day as were fed in ignorance by Jesus on the hills of Galilee.[2]

OUR CIRCLES OF RELATIONSHIP

What Jesus gave to Peter, James and John was much different from what he gave to members of the crowd on the day he fed the five thousand. It would have been foolish to give the depth of personal insight or intimacy reserved for his inner core of disciples to a random listener that day. The crowd needed what it received from Jesus and was ready for no more. We all have the "crowds" in our lives, acquaintances or other people who will never come to know us deeply but who still might receive the bread of compassion or sympathy or generosity from us. This could happen during a conversation on a plane or bus, on a busy street as we stop and help someone, or after church when we meet a visitor.

We each recognize "those whom we want," a smaller group of people who are friends, whose company we enjoy and with whom we have familiarity. Where a morsel of compassion might not do it, God's ministry through us might take the form of an evening of hospitality or a generous loan of money in a time of financial crisis. These are the people with whom we live out our faith. These may be a small group from church or a men's or women's prayer group.

Furthermore, we also need to have the most intimate group, perhaps only two or three people, in whose lives we are called to be vitally active and extravagantly loving. Our company of friends will include a larger group, but these few will be the ones who affirm and even clarify our identity—they are the ones who, in one way or another, will give us our nicknames. It will be from them and from our friendships together that we will most closely know who we are and how God has made us.

It may just be us, but my wife and I have found that life with children is more complex than life without them. Participating in a church small group is one area in which having children made things more complex. One of the ways we tried to handle this was to invite another couple, David and Susan, with two kids near in age to ours, to help us lead the small group we hosted. During the shared dinner, our kids would play quite well together, and then they all went to bed at the same time, coinciding roughly with the beginning of the worship and discussion portion of our evening together. (We set up little beds in an extra room in the house for David and Susan's children.) The four of us led that group, in one form or another, over the next eighteen months. Our own small group saw growth, subdivision and then further growth. Although we grew in friendships with everyone in the group through the time we spent together, we grew in friendship most with David and Susan. While we planned and prayed together for our group, we found we all had similar concerns and struggles (time together as a couple, wisdom regarding parenting and sibling issues, a heart for missions and eagerness to see the church grow in that area). Most crucially, they cared about the same people we did. We became friends as we led together.

It is one thing to notice the structure of Jesus' relationships; it is quite another to experience the same. Why don't our relationships follow this pattern? In part I think it is because we tend to have unhelpful assumptions about how life and friendships are supposed to work. These assumptions hinder our taking initiative with people in ways that would genuinely build relationships and deeper connection.

The egalitarian urge. "Everyone in my small group should receive the same, small amount of time and attention. If I initiate with someone, I must do it for everyone. If we have a dinner, we should invite everyone. If I begin to care here, then I will need to care everywhere."

When we recognize and embrace the concentric-circle pattern, we no longer lament the fact that we haven't gotten to know everyone in the small group equally well. Nor do we feel guilty that, while we like people in our group, we enjoy a few even more. This is precisely the pattern Jesus set up—he called his closest disciples to be best friends with one another.

The reciprocity meter. "I cannot take initiative with a friend until that friend reciprocates the initiative I have already taken. My initiative should be proportional and balanced."

Relationships measured by the reciprocity meter will necessarily sink to the lowest common denominator. It feels vulnerable for me to take more initiative in a relationship than has been reciprocated, but that is how relationships often take off. We need to recognize that some people don't have the same thresholds or energy for initial effort in relationship. Eventually, either the initiative will become mutual and a deeper relationship will emerge or it will become clear that it is not going to develop.

The day-off syndrome. "I take initiative and exert effort in my job all day long, all week long. I don't want to have to work on the weekend in relationships that don't happen naturally."

Often, fifteen minutes before my small group meeting begins, I feel a tinge of ambivalence. "I'm tired; perhaps I'll skip tonight." I rarely give in to this urge, because usually soon after arriving at the gathering, I am glad I didn't give in. I find I receive more of what I really need than I might have anticipated. When we make relational avoidance choices on the basis of our immediate energy levels, we are like kids choosing to eat candy or fast food for their hunger rather than any balanced nutritional snack. It may mollify in the short term, but it will not fulfill our deeper needs. At the end of an evening in front of the TV, we will have less energy for life and relationships than we would have by pulling our bodies up off the couch and joining a group of people pursuing God together.

The ideal time myth. "Now is not a good time for me, but later (next week, next month, at a different stage in my life) I will have more time to initiate or respond to the initiative of others."

If I don't set aside time now for relationships, and build up a pattern of giving priority to them, I will never get to the point where I have lots of time and know how to use that time well to build relationships. It would be tragic to arrive at retirement and have lots of time for relationships but have no energy or skills with which to build them.

Each of these assumptions has the same result: it inhibits our ability to take initiative with people or to respond well to the initiative we receive from others. By embracing these assumptions and believing the lies, we will lead lonely and isolated lives with shallow relationships. How do we counteract the dampening effect of these assumptions? By debunking them and reflecting on alternative realities.

Recently I received a phone call a few minutes before we were to sit down to dinner. William, a member of our church small group, was calling with an invitation to join him right then in taking his kids on a hike. Summer's blistering heat had taken its toll on his two boys, and he wanted to give his wife a break from them. Internally, my first response to the invitation was "This is not a good time to go. We still have to eat dinner, and then it will be time to quiet down for the evening." Fundamentally, I was ready to be done for the day, rather than to gear up for the effort of a hike. But I realized that this was the first such invitation from William I had ever had, and I definitely wanted to encourage that kind of initiative, so I said, "Give us half an hour." We ate our meal and then my kids and I joined William and his kids on an hour-long hike. Our kids enjoyed their time together, and William and I were able to catch up after not seeing each other for several weeks because of vacations. Chances are good that if I had said what I originally thought to say, further initiative from William would have been long in coming.

Table 3 summarizes with contemporary examples how we can make choices to be available to a variety of people in challenging but appropriate ways.

One time a few years ago a leader in my church came to me and asked if we could talk. He had noticed patterns in my life and wanted to ask me if I thought I had a drivenness that could be described as "workaholism." His approach was humble and tentative, and the attention he paid me and concern he showed me were not at all unwelcome. But at the end of our conversation, I was not persuaded. Frankly, I just didn't feel well known or well understood by him. Of course, I talked over the conversation and the questions it raised with my wife, Lisa, and she was no more persuaded than I was. But how could I know whether we were both just guilty of self-deception and rationalization? I called several friends, people who have been in my life for twenty years. So I spoke with Mark, Kevin and Bill about the comments of this leader, whom they all knew and respected.

In the end, my closest friends agreed that the assessment didn't ring true to them. Mark said it best: "Rich, you aren't a workaholic; you're a playaholic. It's just that your work is play for you!" This summary helped

Table 3. Our Concentric Circles of Relationship

Who (Mark 3)	What We Do	Examples
The Crowd: people we don't know, with names we never learn	We serve people we don't even know, sometimes anonymously, at a distance.	• Give money to an aid or missions organization. • Donate labor to help build a Habitat for Humanity house. • Paint a youth center.
The Many: people who come across our path with a need we can meet	We give a moment's kindness to people in our lives. We may learn their name, but it is often a single encounter. We serve in some occasional, nonrecurring way.	• Pray for a stranger because of a prayer request. • Volunteer to teach a lesson at a vacation Bible school. • Stop to give roadside assistance to someone.
The Wanted: the people we pray for	We retain interest in the lives of people we see often or with whom we communicate regularly. They may not know one another.	• Make a long-distance phone call to connect with an old friend. • Follow up on a friend's e-mail request for prayer with a note asking how it has gone. • Pray for the couple at church who had a miscarriage.
The Twelve: the people we pray with	We meet with a small group regularly and are in one another's homes. We look out for each other and work at deepening relationships.	• Engage in weekly sharing and prayer as part of a small group. • Offer hospitality to another during stressful times or undertake thoughtful acts of service.
The Three: the few people who tell us who we are, helping us know our identity in God	We have more intimate times with a few people, or just one-to-one, available to each other sometimes more often than once per week.	• Vacation together or attend a family camp or conference together. • Drop anything at a time of crisis in order to respond. • Gather with a few people at work who also seek God.

me to understand myself, my weakness and my strength, and the way forward in my own growth. My good friend Mark helped me to understand the muddle of me. While the church leader was observing something that was indeed an issue, it was my friends who were able to clarify and spell it out in ways that were affirming and yet challenging. My orientation to my work is *not* obsessive, fearful, damaging to my family or destructive to other relationships. Yet the original comment from the church leader provoked an insight, addressing an imbalance and perhaps a subtler form of addiction.

This is what we should expect to receive from our most intimate friends. Our closest friends tell us who we are. They affirm us and cajole us with affection and humor. They can nickname us "Sons of Thunder" and we accept it because we know it is true and because we know it is spoken in love. They will ratify or reject personality inventories and the conclusions that come out of them. Without these closest friends, we are like people without mirrors—we'll lose the ability to know what we look like, and soon it will be hard to go out in public without drawing stares.

Jesus Enjoyed His Disciples

The overwhelming evidence from the Gospel accounts demonstrates that Jesus enjoyed eating and drinking with his disciples. He enjoyed spending time with them. He lavished himself upon them, and he was glad to do it. The fact is, he wasn't always teaching them—he did not always take charge to advance his agenda or indoctrinate his neophytes. Much of his time with his followers was simply "social time," "relational time," "quantity time." He enjoyed his disciples, and they grew to become his close friends.

As we learn in Luke 22:15-16, Jesus told his disciples that he had "eagerly desired" to eat the Passover meal with them. It was not simply a functional occasion for him, but one filled with emotion, sadness and anguish. At this time Jesus desired to be with his closest earthly friends.

Jesus addressed his disciples with the term that had become a reality: *friends*. He said, "I do not call you servants any longer, because the servant does not know what the master is doing; but I have called you friends, because I have made known to you everything that I have heard from my Father" (John 15:15). Jesus had no secrets—he had included the disciples in on his entire plan. They were trusted friends, not minor operatives working on a need-to-know basis. These young disciples had become friends and partners in the ministry, and so he knew he could tell them everything he had received from his Father.

Certainly Jesus was intentional with the use of his time, but he also had room for the simple enjoyment of friendship. He was a master at making disciples, but that included genuine friendship with those same disciples. He loved being with them. He looked forward to it, he valued it and he left the planet with the intention of coming back so that he and his friends could be together again. Jesus was not concerned that every minute of his precious time be spent communicating deep spiritual truth. In fact, this is part of the deeper gospel truth that he intended to communicate: the Creator God of the universe wants to party with his human creation. Through Jesus' revelry with the disciples and other "sinners," we see a foreshadowing of the eternal divine celebration, where we will enjoy the heaven-shaking music of God-inspired praise and will feast at the table hosted by the Lamb.

TIME WELL SPENT

It can be easy to waste opportunities we have to be with people in the busyness of our lives. Often I find that times that are supposed to be relational end up being wasted on me because, at that point, I am not thinking about the relational value of the opportunity as much as simply navigating it comfortably. Whether I am entertaining in my home (and likely to be overly focused on the details of the meal) or at a church event, I can spend my time without seeing any obvious return.

The notion of *investing* time, in contrast to merely *spending* it, has to do with the intentionality involved with making strategic choices regarding how and in what contexts I will pursue relational time with people. If I know that certain settings are not likely to further deepen relationships with people, I may still choose to spend time in those ways, but I will be looking for avenues that are more likely to help me deepen my relationships. This doesn't have to feel like work, but it will involve thinking ahead. Here are some suggestions.

1. *Invest time in people where they live and work.* Jesus spent time with his disciples in the context of their daily life. He became acquainted with their parents and siblings. From that vantage point, he could see how the families treated one another and how they welcomed guests. He was willing to enjoy the hospitality of others and knew how to spend time at a party, and he communicated value and acceptance when he was willing to go into their homes (Mark 1:29; 2:15; Luke 7:36; 10:38; 14:1; John 12:1). Here Jesus is a model for us.

Something happens in my relationships with people when I have been in their home, noticing and appreciating the artwork or photos on the wall, the books on the shelves or the sports gear in the garage. The same thing happens when I have met them at their workplace, seen their office or cubicle and their posted comic strips, met some of the people they work with, eaten lunch in their company cafeteria or the local deli. An intangible metamorphosis happens at two levels. First, it changes the nature of the time we have together. Our conversation is marked, in part, by my attention to their life and surroundings. I communicate that their home or work setting is important to me. I am able to empathize with them in the challenges they face or to honor them for who they are and what they do. Second, this kind of experience changes, not only the time we have together, but also the nature of our relationship. Because I have entered into their world a little, I know them through more than just the words that pass between us.

Of course, the value of this investment is multiplied when getting to know someone in the context of their relational home—the spouse, children, roommates or family who live with them. It is possible to learn much about people through a little time in their own home, as well as to learn about some of the issues and challenges that they face in that setting.

Beyond all that I can learn, simply being together in a comfortable environment nourishes a relationship. Eating is a ritual of fellowship throughout Scripture, and food is a rich biblical metaphor. Real life happens at mealtimes. Prayer, laughter, exchange of ideas and honest sharing all occur around the table. My wife and I work with students from various ethnic and cultural backgrounds, and food and meals have much to do with culture. Furthermore, our own culture holds increasingly perverted views about food: bulimia, anorexia and binge eating are common, and fewer families eat together regularly. For many, eating together can be healing and redemptive. Being with people in their home settings, eating meals with them, enjoying casual time with them all serve one purpose—they are opportunities to grow in love and affection for the people whom God has placed in our lives.

A single friend, upon reading what I've written here, wrote to me, "It's interesting thinking about all this as a single with married friends—I've spent extensive time in other people's worlds with very little engagement from any in my world." As a married person with many single friends, I know that I have hosted people into my home much more than I have taken time to enter theirs. This initiative is appreciated, but we still need to look for ways for the reverse to take place also.

2. *Allow people to see how you live.* Paul spoke to the Ephesian elders, after the end of his three years of service to and among them, "You yourselves know how I lived among you the entire time from the first day that I set foot in Asia, serving the Lord with all humility and with tears, enduring the trials that came to me through the plots of the Jews. I did not shrink from doing anything helpful, proclaiming the message to you and teaching you publicly and from house to house" (Acts 20:18-20). Because of the nature of Paul's apostolic work in Ephesus, the people there saw how he lived. He was in their homes, in part because he made his home with them. Of course this was true of Jesus with the disciples—they didn't just meet him at 7:00 p.m. on Friday nights at the synagogue.

When we invite people into our home, either we can do it with the intent of allowing people to see how we live or we can do it with the intent of obscuring for people an accurate picture of how we live. Our efforts at hospitality can be directed at revealing who we are when we are at home or at maintaining a façade of order, calm and normality that can be sustained for only short periods of time. We may feel that obscuring for people how we live will help them to be comfortable, and if we live like slobs, we are probably right. But when our efforts of hospitality are oriented around creating a false picture of our life, surroundings and relationships, then hospitality will require a lot of effort and will yield less fruit relationally—we are effectively keeping people at a distance.

Of course, our friendships will be closer and more satisfying and true if we actually let people see us when we are most at home. We also will be more apt to be willing to invite people into our homes if we are comfortable with them getting an accurate picture of our lives.

When I first met Stanley, he was a member of the leadership team for the InterVarsity campus fellowship I was serving. Stanley, an African American, had grown up in downtown Boston in an African American church. While we loved the same Lord and read the same Bible (though not the same version), we found that we spoke of our experience of God fairly differently, and it took a while to build up enough trust for us to view each other as friends.

Over several years Stanley and I worked together and built our relationship. When Stanley graduated from college, he volunteered some of his time with InterVarsity through its Black Campus Ministry. I followed his growth as he contemplated engagement to Tacita, and I continued to stay in touch with Stanley and Tacita as they established their new life together in Boston. Several times they have been in our home, sharing a meal with our family. Often, with our kids around, time with Stanley and Tacita seemed disjointed, and we were easily distracted by our kids' antics. During a recent visit, though, we were able to look back over the years of our relationships and how God had worked. Stanley and Tacita both mentioned the simple value of seeing us love and parent our children. As distracting as our kids' behavior seemed to us, it was our response to them that made as big an impression as anything else we said. Stanley, a teacher, spoke of the importance of consistency in parenting as in teaching. Likewise, as a parent, I could encourage Stanley by speaking of the ways that I have seen my children's teachers be crucial for their intellectual and social maturing. While what brought us together was never "parenting issues" or help in that area, Stanley and Tacita enjoyed and benefited much from seeing a broader picture of our family life in the setting of our home.

3. *Invest "prime time" in people.* Jesus spent his prime time with his closest friends. During the week before his death, he intensified his time with his disciples and then longed for the opportunity to spend the Passover meal with his disciple-friends. For me, becoming friends with people has involved spending summers, vacations, holidays, weekends, evenings or other prime time with them.

Prime time communicates something that a sixty-minute appointment in the middle of a weekday afternoon does not. The time frame in which something happens often determines or contributes to (1) whether it feels like work or play, (2) whether it feels open-ended or boxed in, (3) whether there is room for spontaneity or must be planned, and (4) whether it is just another appointment or the highlight of the day. When I spend time that is normally considered part of an average workday, somehow it feels like work. But when I am willing to spend my Saturday evening with a few friends or my small group, then it is more clear that I consider this cherished play time. Meetings with people that occur at the end of the day or that are scheduled simply for a lazy weekend afternoon can be open-ended, can involve spontaneity and can communicate something different from the 7:30 a.m. breakfast meeting. I often tell people that I have been looking forward to my time with them all day.

This is not to say that I spend all of my prime time with friends or that the only time I spend with friends is prime time. My wife and I understand the need to set aside time for other people, but we also spend much prime time together, and for the same reason—any friendship, especially a marriage relationship, requires prime, open-ended, cherished time.

If time is the currency of relationships, offering prime time is like picking up the check. We know what and who we value by how we spend our time, especially that which is most precious to us. Time is the chief change mechanism in the tumbler of community. No small-group experience, no friendship, has indelible impact immediately, and lasting relationships are built over years full of hours.

We need to look for ways to share significant parts of ourselves with the people with whom we are pursuing God. Building deep friendships will look different in different contexts, but it will probably involve time spent on one another's home turf, an openness to invite people into our lives and the willingness to spend even prime time to deepen the friendship. How can we find time to build friendships in this way in an Internet age when time slips away at megahertz speed? Jesus found one way, a strategy that is available even to us today. We'll look at it in the next chapter.

FOR REFLECTION

1. Think about the concentric circles of your relationships. What group of people are your traveling companions in the pursuit of God? Who are the few with whom you are eager to share most intimately? What can you do to order your life around a greater focus on a few for the sake of the many?

2. How do you enjoy spending time with people? How can that be a means to pursue relational depth?

3. How do you spend time with people where they live and work?

4. When people are in your home, do you give them a chance to see how you live, or are you trying to hide that? How can you open up your life for people to see?

5. What is prime time for you? In what ways can you allocate prime time for the deepening of friendships? What bold steps could you make with your weekends, evenings or vacation days?

On the Road in the Company of Friends

Friends are as companions on a journey, who ought to aid each other to persevere in the road to a happier life.

PYTHAGORAS (582-507 B.C.)

If you want to go fast, go alone.
If you want to go far, go together.

AFRICAN PROVERB

I didn't know it then, but it was the end of my final summer as a single man. All I knew was that we were seeking manly adventure. My friends Steve, Brian and Seth and I were planning a three-week trip at the end of the summer. Our original plan was to travel up through Central America via public buses from Costa Rica or Nicaragua back to California. My supervisor with InterVarsity (these were IVCF students and I was their staffworker) wisely advised against this. After all, this was the mid-1980s, when people in Central America were being shot for wearing blue jeans, the uniform of the guerrillas.

So instead of dodging bullets in Latin American hot spots (as fun as that would have been), we took a trip from California to New York City, and then from there south and back west, visiting inner-city ministries and Christian communities around the East Coast and the South. With a full itinerary and seven or eight hosting ministries expecting us, the four of us piled into a car and looped around the country. I remember our repeated complaints of the slight "pangs of unfullness" we suffered when we would need to stop for our next meal—it seemed we were always eating something. Though visits to major American cities were not new for any of us, the areas we saw, such as the Bowery in New York, opened our eyes to the reality of urban poverty and homelessness, as well as the medical and social issues that attend such conditions. The missions and the people of the ministries we visited encouraged and inspired us. We spent much time in the car debriefing what we had seen. Every day we were challenged by what God was doing in city ministries, and we were excited to consider our own futures together. Every day our relationships with one another deepened. After it was all over, the four of us chose to live together the following year. Together, we continued to grow in our understanding of community and ministry.

JESUS AND FRIENDS ON THE ROAD

One of the ways Jesus spent time with his disciples was to take them on trips through Palestine, teaching, preaching and healing along the way. This gave Jesus a maximum of time with the disciples in semi-isolated and sometimes stressful situations. Jesus did not set up camp in Nazareth or Capernaum or, more strategically, Jerusalem and begin to preach to those who showed up to see him. Rather, he took his message to the people in the countryside and villages. And he took his disciples with him. Jesus and his disciples took road trips together.

The first indication that Jesus invited his disciples to join him on a road trip appears in Mark 1:38: "Let us go on to the neighboring towns; . . . for that is what I came out to do." Peter came looking for Jesus, interrupting his time of prayer, assuming that Jesus was planning to do more of what he'd been doing the previous night—healing people. Perhaps Peter assumed that he and Jesus would set up a country clinic, Jesus doing the doctoring while Peter ran the front office. But at this point the disciples learned for the first time that Jesus meant that they would literally follow him, that he would be traveling and that they were expected to come with him. They didn't stop moving until he ascended to heaven.

Here is a sample itinerary from the book of Mark, tracking Jesus' movements with his disciples:

- *Mark 3:13-19:* Jesus went on a mountain retreat with his friends to appoint his twelve disciples.

- *Mark 5:1-20:* Jesus and his disciples crossed the Sea of Galilee (Jesus calmed the storm) and they visited Gerasa, where he healed the man with the Legion of demons.

- *Mark 7:24-37:* Jesus moved north, to Tyre and Sidon, then back to the southeast, to the Decapolis, where he healed, taught and fed Gentiles, no doubt to the chagrin of the disciples.

- *Mark 8:10:* Jesus and his disciples met up with the Pharisees in Dalmanutha (wherever that was).

- *Mark 8:27:* Jesus and his disciples journeyed to the villages of Caesarea Philippi, where Peter called Jesus "Christ" (and Jesus called Peter "Satan").

- *Mark 10:1:* Jesus went to Judea for the first time since his baptism in Mark's Gospel.

Through this kind of itinerant ministry, Jesus was able to focus on the Twelve while also preaching the good news throughout Palestine and even beyond the areas where the Jews lived. Most of the high points of Jesus' time with his disciples, including of course the Passover meal the night before he was killed, took place outside of their hometowns and most familiar settings.

Let us return to the image of the lapidary tumbler changing rough stones into polished gems. Jesus' strategy for developing rough Galileans into apostles who could propagate his mission and his ministry involved a similar process—gathering a group and applying motion over time. Jesus kept his disciples moving, using road trips with the inevitable grit of conflict and reconciliation, serendipity and reflection. This movement produced many of the key teaching moments for his disciples. Jesus did all this in a society where the average person never traveled more than one hundred miles from the place of his or her birth. The same principle can be applied today.

ROAD TRIPS TODAY

Road trips accomplish much in a short time. No small-group meeting is so long that we cannot, if we so choose, maintain decorum and composure in such a way that people never really get to know us. When our relationships are circumscribed by wearing our "Sunday best" (whether on Sunday mornings or on Wednesday evenings), people will not be able to see us as we are. Road trips push our physical and social limits, whether it's the cramped and crowded quarters, the lack of our favorite foods to eat or the heightened expectations of a retreat weekend. We often find that we get to know people more in a weekend than we would in six months of weekly meetings. When I have seen your bedhead and you know what awful cereal I eat for breakfast, when we have worked together preparing dinner for twenty and have played cards together entirely too late into the evening, then we may have begun to catch a flavor of authentic life together. When we log hours together like that, we have the right to expect that we will listen attentively to one another's shared prayer requests and that we will care about the fears and insecurities we tenderly reveal.

The advantage of the road trip has long been identified by those in youth and college student ministry. Summer camps, weekend conferences and other trips away all have the benefit of getting people out of comfortable surroundings and patterns. Road trips of this kind offer experiences that broaden and deepen people's learning and their relationships. I am convinced that this needs to become a more standard form of friendship building if we want to take seriously the model of Jesus and grow in our friendships with God at the center.

One year, while I was on staff with InterVarsity in Santa Cruz, California, I was to be working with a large senior leadership group of nine students, organized in two teams. The challenge of so many relationships required something bold, so we decided to begin our time together by traveling for a couple of weeks at the end of the summer. The nine students and three staffworkers piled into three cars and drove eighteen hundred miles north, through Oregon and Washington and on to British Columbia and Vancouver Island. We stopped overnight at inner-city and InterVarsity ministries we knew about along the way. We saw each other's sin; repentance and reconciliation abounded. We needed to work together; people's gifts emerged. After two weeks of life on the road, we were glad to rest before new student outreach began. But our mobile bonding experience proved formative for a successful year of ministry as teammates.

In my ministry to college students, I have traveled with groups across the country and to Africa, Europe, Central America, Asia and the Caribbean. Different trips have different stated purposes: a crosscultural missions project, an inner-city exposure, an evangelism project, vacation. But all these trips have one purpose in common: to develop relationships in the context of a variety of experiences and stressful situations.

A classic "road trip"—an evangelism, work or missions project in some other locality and culture—is one of the best ways to build relationships, build a team and grow in mutual love and servanthood. In an unfamiliar culture, people learn dependence on God (most importantly) and also on their partners, who sometimes literally help them make it through the trip alive.

Unfortunately, many assume that adults in churches cannot gain the kind of value from road trips that students in campus ministries receive. Of course, a thirty-five-year-old parent of young children will have a trickier time arranging for this kind of a trip than a fifteen-year-old on summer break. Yet I am convinced that for people for whom time is scarcer, our need to get away and build relationships with purpose is that much greater.

More churches are sponsoring one- or two-week missions projects to the inner city or Mexico or some other proximate and needy area. We need to see these as opportunities not simply for teenagers. In some ways, the opportunity could even be wasted on them if the adults in the church never learn the kinds of things that can be learned on road trips like this.

Several summers ago, about ten adults from our church joined about twenty college students for a fifteen-day trip to Honduras to join with relief workers and a local church in some construction projects in the aftermath of Hurricane Mitch. For about half the adults, the trip was a first-time mission experience. Though the trip began as a chance to serve students, each of the nonstudents contributed in a key way and ended the trip indelibly changed.

Dena, a doctor, had long desired to serve with her medical training in a Third World setting. As the oldest member of the team (with children the ages of the students), she could easily have decided she didn't belong. Yet because of her training and personality, she became one of the key team members. She led the medical team, brought thousands of dollars' worth of donated supplies and encouraged the national medical workers who were our partners. Several friendships that emerged from that road trip continue to be important for Dena today.

Three of the last four summers, my family has joined a team on a mission trip (Honduras, Barbados, Mexico). My children were ages four and six during their first mission trip to Honduras. Each time they go, they are able to benefit more from their experience because of their age. But as a parent, I am grateful that they have been able to join us and participate in our efforts to get to know, love, serve and learn from people in other countries.

Road trips give people a rare picture of us as we really are. The summer we went to Malaysia, I made a big change. I had worn a beard for eight years—folks on the team going with us had never seen me without it. I decided that I'd shave off the beard for a variety of crosscultural and personal reasons. The night before we caught our plane, the team was gathered in our living room, and I emerged from my bedroom clean-shaven. The team saw me and immediately burst out laughing. I assured them that they were indeed looking at my actual face and that I didn't consider my face, as a face, all that funny. But I did laugh with them—the change was dramatic, for I really did have a baby face. And in a weird way, it was both vulnerable and bonding for us to experience that together. (Since then, rarely have people responded with hilarious laughter to seeing my face.)

Imagine what would happen to a church small group or couple's Bible study if they were able to go as a group for a week to work, pray, eat and live together. Relationships would leap forward; intimacy, dependence on one another and community might become real for the first time. This would be a powerful witness to the rest of the church body and to the community in which this small group focused its outreach. If parents tasted this kind of rich community, then the encounter for their kids might be more lasting and profound.

FROM ATTRACTIVE PICTURE TO COMPELLING REALITY

James and Eileen have long been frustrated by the lack of community among their church friends. The church is structured so that it is hard to get to know people as families. Several years ago they became convinced that a family camp for five to ten families with kids in grade or middle school would be a great start. They have mentioned this idea to the pastor to announce to the church, but this pastor is only really committed to all-church retreats and it never got a plug from the pulpit. For these last several years, they have mentioned their concern and idea to people who always express similar concerns and interest, but nothing ever comes of it.

James and Eileen have some vision for deeper relationships in their church. Why hasn't that vision been effective? While we could say that James and Eileen have had vision, it might also be possible to say that they've merely expressed a need. They haven't been willing to take any risky step other than to speak with their pastor, who hasn't told them no as much as he's indicated that he cannot be counted on to speak with vision toward this need. They have been unwilling to take risks and to articulate their hopes in the form of an invitation.

What needs to be their first step to see their hopes become reality? They need to find a small group of people to whom they say, in one way or another, "We're in; how about you?" By gathering two or three other families, and spelling out their hopes for deeper relationships, perhaps they will find these other families joining them in committing to the idea of a family camp. Then, as they talk to others, they could speak about something that was already going to happen, not simply something that could one day perhaps, just maybe, happen.

Each of the mission trips my wife and I have participated in involved some preparation months ahead. Pulling together the team, handling the raft of logistics, preparing the team with crosscultural training, and helping the team bring together the finances—these things take time and are daunting. Why even bother? In part because getting there, logistically and spiritually, is a crucial part of the trip and its value to those who go.

But once momentum for a trip has gathered, all the logistics required seem less daunting, because in fact the trip is becoming a reality. The biggest hurdle is the first. Speaking of a trip as if it really is going to happen, though so far no one is committed but you, is an act of faith in God and love for your friends. It is much like the love that is faith filled and vulnerable to say to someone else, "Will you marry me?" It has the same potential for disappointment, the same vulnerable display of unilateral commitment. The mere asking of the question deepens relationship, as does the reply of yes. Consider whom you can ask to travel with you, whether it is into an urban center for service or a retreat center for a spiritual renewal, whether it is for a weekend or for a week or a summer. And by all means, if friends take this kind of initiative with you, reward their vulnerability with a resounding "I was thinking about asking you to do the same!"

FOR REFLECTION

1. How can you take advantage of existing opportunities to leave behind your hectic life for a weekend or a day and be with fellow travelers in the pursuit of God?

2. What would it look like to take the risk of asking a group of friends to travel together? A mission project? A service project? A week at a family camp in the mountains?

3. What steps can you take to turn your fears and concerns of this risk over to God?

7

Friends Serve, Lead, See and Speak

The idea of The Servant as Leader *came out of reading Hermann Hesse's* Journey to the East. *In this story we see a band of men on a mythical journey, probably also Hesse's own journey. The central figure of the story is Leo who accompanies the party as the servant who does their menial chores, but who also sustains them with his spirit and his song. He is a person of extraordinary presence. All goes well until Leo disappears. Then the group falls into disarray and the journey is abandoned. They cannot make it without the servant Leo. The narrator, one of the party, after some years of wandering finds Leo and is taken into the Order that had sponsored the journey. There he discovers that Leo, whom he had known first as servant, was in fact the titular head of the order, its guiding spirit, a great and noble leader.*

ROBERT GREENLEAF, SERVANT LEADERSHIP

My friend Roger and I were members of the same leadership team, but I was new to the team and he had been on it for a while. As the new member to the team, I had a lot to learn. As a new member, I also had a lot of ideas. I didn't always understand why things went the way they did. These meetings always ended in a flurry of details and then abrupt leavings. But Roger often took time to call me and ask how I was doing after the meetings. He had a sense of where my feelings had been hurt or where my own communication choices were not wise. Roger gave me perspective and he identified ways forward, either relationally or tactically.

Roger was not my supervisor nor my leader in any formal sense; he was simply my colleague on the team. In the spirit of friendship, he offered me help, guidance and perspective, without coercion but with care. He served me in part through the things he observed and commented upon, and he spoke what was true.

◆　◆　◆

I have mentioned several times the seminal insights about friendship found in Aristotle's *Nicomachean Ethics*. Aristotle spoke of the three motives that bring friends together: (1) friends are useful to one another; (2) friends enjoy one another; and (3) friends share a common commitment to the good. Aristotle made the point that friendships that are motivated by only the first or second impulse are not likely to be long-lasting, because what we enjoy and what we need change over time, while friendships that share a common commitment to the good are more likely to endure. "Such friendships, then, are easily dissolved, if the parties do not remain like themselves; for if the one party is no longer pleasant or useful the other ceases to love him."[1]

In this chapter I'll focus on that third quality. Chapters three and four speak about ways that friends are useful to one another, while chapters five and six refer to how friends enjoy one another. This chapter and the rest of the book address the greater commitment friends share than merely the friendship itself. A common commitment to "the good" at least includes the pursuit of God.

Aristotle asserted that if a friendship is to endure, the friends need to share a common commitment to "the good." Many people today would be content with friendships that are characterized by usefulness and fun, leaving out any larger sense of purpose. The way this shows up among God pursuers is a slight to significant discomfort with leadership and intentionality.

- A household of singles living together assume they cannot properly have any leadership other than a strict democracy and that the goal of the household is to impinge on the individual desires of the members as little as possible. Mealtimes, food and music preferences—everything discretionary—are decided in a lowest-common-denominator way so that nobody is asked to do or commit to something they don't want.

- A church small group isn't comfortable with the idea that someone is a leader. The person who gathers the group together is willing to be called a facilitator, and everyone is more relaxed because the person refuses the mantle of "leader." "Perhaps we should rotate the role of discussion facilitator every week," someone suggests.

- A church or ministry has difficulty finding people who are willing to answer to the title or role of leader. "I could be an assistant or a sponsor," many say, "but I don't think I'd want to be viewed as a leader."

- Among several friends, everyone is worried for one friend, but no one will say anything out of fear of being viewed as judgmental or nosy. This won't keep people from talking to each other about their friend (out of "concern"), but they shrink from speaking to their friend except in the most elliptical and obscure terms.

Many recognize that deep and lasting friendship doesn't come easily, and yet they think it should be so. Friendship is supposed to be natural, effortless, spontaneous, transparent and intimate—almost a mystical experience into which we are supposed to fall (not unlike similar expectations for "love"), not a discipline we must follow or a pursuit for which we must train. Table 4 illustrates and unmasks some common false assumptions and half-truths about the nature of friendship. See if you recognize any of these assumptions.

Should friendships be influential? The obvious answer is yes. But what is the means for that influence? Leadership? Intentionality? As an example, someone might say, "Does that mean that, when you set up this lunch date, you actually had intentions to talk to me about things and even ask me to consider making some different choices? Have you been doing this all along?"

Yes, when someone is intentional with me, thinking ahead for a conversation or an evening together so that my life and choices might be influenced, it can get a little scary. Do friends actually do this?

Table 4. Assumptions and Half-Truths About the Nature of Friendship

Supposed "Friendship"	Supposed "Not True Friendship"	Real Friendship
Freed from the need for effort and intentionality	If it involves too much effort, it means we "just don't click."	Involves hard work, tough choices, costly risk.
Based on fundamental values of acceptance and tolerance	Seeking to influence means failure to accept people for who they are.	Means seeking the best for people and expecting mutual growth and change.
Triggered by spontaneity	Intentionality kills spontaneity.	Involves both spontaneity and intentionality.
Fueled by authenticity and transparency	Influence seems like manipulation; manipulation is deception; deception is the opposite of transparency.	Involves authentic influence that is not deceptive or manipulative.
Characterized by intimacy and equality	Leadership implies hierarchy, distorting and destroying friendship.	Involves mutual servanthood, submission, leadership and influence. These lead to intimacy and equality.

Of course, Jesus did this. He loved his friends by having vision for their lives, and he influenced them by modeling and by teaching. But that was Jesus. Surely he doesn't mean for us to be like him in this way? Can we be friends and receive intentional influence? Can we be friends and seek to influence the choices and values of others? Let's take another look at Jesus.

JESUS SERVES AND LEADS HIS FRIENDS (JOHN 13:1-17)

Peter was uncharacteristically silent, building up resistance until he exploded, "Lord, are you actually planning to wash my feet?" Peter had watched as Jesus had taken off his outer robe. He had scowled as Jesus had wrapped a towel around his waist and had taken up a bowl. He had squirmed when Jesus began to wash the other disciples' feet. Peter thought many things but remained silent until Jesus came around to him. It was clearly Jesus' plan to wash Peter's feet, but it was certainly not Peter's plan. "You will never wash my feet!" he exclaimed. It was the first of Peter's mistaken predictions about the future that evening.

Jesus was patient yet firm with Peter. "You do not know now what I am doing, but later you will understand." Jesus asked Peter simply to settle in, be at peace with his questions and wait for the answers that would certainly come. But at Peter's protest ("Never!"), Jesus said simply, "Unless I wash you, you have no share with me" (John 13:8).

Why was Peter so resistant? Because of a lack of devotion to the Lord? Probably not. Peter was resistant because he misunderstood the Lord to whom he was passionately devoted. "Lord, do *you* wash *my* feet? Shouldn't it be the other way around? Out of loyalty, I'll never let you *wash* my *feet*." Peter knew—just knew—that Jesus was the Messiah. But he just knew (mistakenly) that proper loyalty demanded that, if any feet were washed, he would wash Jesus' feet. Though it seems clear he loved Jesus, he loved his own idea of the Messiah more than he loved or even understood Jesus' purpose and destiny. This led to his downfall later that night.

Furthermore, Peter was stunned, not just at the actions of Jesus that night, but at the passivity of the other disciples. In a posture he would strike all evening long, Peter was certain of his exceptional loyalty to his leader. Even if the other disciples would permit Jesus to wash their feet, his loyalty would not allow it! Later Jesus said, "You will all fall away." Peter then said, in effect, "Not I, Lord. The others, well . . . I can totally see it. But not me. I'm prepared even to die for you." No, Peter (in his own mind at least) was the most loyal, the most devoted and hence the most stunned at this seeming reversal of everything right and proper. "Jesus wash *my* feet? Never!"

When Jesus said, "Unless I wash you, you have no share with me," he was saying, "Peter, get used to it. I am going to serve you—tonight by washing your feet and then again tomorrow. No, Peter, it is not you who will die for me but I who will die for you. Our relationship began with me serving you, and it continues with me serving you, and—get used to it, Peter—so it will remain. Unless I serve you, you receive nothing from me."

An eyewitness to these events, John, wrote, "Having loved his own who were in the world, he loved them to the end" (John 13:1). Of course, a dramatic way he loved them was by washing their feet—by giving them a sacramental picture, an indelible image, of the life he had lived with them. Yet his service to them didn't end when he put the towel away and returned to the table. He then said to them,

> Do you know what I have done to you? You call me Teacher and Lord—and you are right, for that is what I am. So if I, your Lord and Teacher, have washed your feet, you also ought to wash one another's feet. For I have set you an example, that you also should do as I have done to you. Very truly, I tell you, servants are not greater than their master, nor are messengers greater than the one who sent them. If you know these things, you are blessed if you do them. (John 13:12-17)

Jesus continued to serve the disciples to the end, in part by calling them to the life he had lived with them. Since, as Jesus said, blessing comes with service, Jesus was showing them the path to blessing through a life of service.

Why did he say this? Suppose Jesus had simply donned his robe, rejoined them at the table and stayed silent. What would they have concluded? "If he—our Lord and teacher—has washed our feet, we also ought to . . . wash his feet! Yeah! That must be it!" As unappealing as washing another human being's feet would be, that would be a logical conclusion. "He washes our feet; we also ought to wash his!"

Jesus knew that his model of servanthood was not enough; he also had to interpret his model, to explain to the disciples precisely the point they were to learn from his poignant sacramental drama. They were to serve one another—wash each other's feet—in the way Jesus had served them.

Jesus is a superior example of a servant leader. But he doesn't let us dismiss his example as unattainable. He calls any who would pursue God to be people who serve others in his name. Servanthood is not optional. Fortunately, it comes with a compelling promise: "You are blessed if you live like this."

FRIENDS SERVE BY TAKING INITIATIVE

I give you a new commandment, that you love one another. Just as I have loved you, you also should love one another.

JOHN 13:34

Jesus called his disciples to love one another just a few moments after he called them to serve one another. He used himself as a model and called them to love as he did.

We see that intentional influence belongs in the company of friends. Jesus loved, served and led his friends (John 15:12-15), and he calls us to serve and love one another similarly.

I would like to take another look at the groups of friends (pages 106-7) who find it awkward to embrace leadership in their midst. If one or more people were to step up and offer some wise and timely initiative, each member of these groups would be served better.

- *Household of singles.* One woman takes a bold stab at calling the rest of the household to make costly commitments to one another, such as a weekly schedule of house meals and free evenings. Another notices that little joint hospitality is happening and asks the group to invest time in getting to know and serve each other's friends. No formal leadership structure is established (though one might become useful). Yet to the extent individuals are allowed to ask each other to make commitments to work together, each member of the household gains deeper relationships.

- *Church small group.* After meeting for some time, Tom and Nancy notice barriers to depth in relationships, such as sarcasm, superficiality and an unwillingness to press individuals to say more than they are first willing to say about things that come up in the discussion. Tom and Nancy share with others the patterns they have noticed, humbly acknowledging their own role and participation as well. The result of their willingness to take this initiative is that these harmful patterns are addressed and the group's relationships with one another grow deeper.

- *Church without "leaders."* If people saw leadership as something that enhances and belongs in mutual friendships, they might be willing to step into that role in a church, knowing that they will grow to be better friends (among other things) as a result of their development as leaders.

- *Gossiping friends.* Several in the group become willing to speak to their friend in a way that is hearable and communicates their willingness to help that friend break out of destructive patterns or grow past relational barriers.

Initiative and intentionality are counterweights to the assumption that friendship is exclusively rooted in spontaneity. Both spontaneity and intentionality are crucial for friendships. In each of these cases, relationships wither without intentionality, yet imagine these groups with no sense of the sheer spontaneous enjoyment of relationships spoken of in chapter five. Each of these groups would soon grow oppressive and would bog down in overspiritualized fellowship.

FRIENDS INFLUENCE BY SERVING

Servanthood is both an end and a means to the pursuit of God. Jesus' servanthood operated as both a tool and a model in his influence strategy. It also advanced God's kingdom by meeting people's real needs.

It may be possible to conclude cynically, along with Lord Acton, that power corrupts. If that is true, then acts of servanthood—when someone uses his or her power or resources to help another—are always means to some extrinsic end. If I serve you today with the hope that you'll let me *use* you for a week, my servanthood doesn't have your best interests at heart. Cult leaders and con artists perfect this technique, and we recoil from their manipulation and deception.

If servanthood is not to be manipulative, then we must see it as a true and untainted benefit for the recipient. This it is, if we see it the way Jesus does.[2]

First, servanthood is a tool in our friendships. As we genuinely care for people through serving them, we build their trust. We must demonstrate the gospel in deeds if we expect people to believe what we say. Servanthood shows people that we care about them. It is not a technique allowing us to fool people into thinking we care for them. Rather, it is the way they begin to believe that our words or actions mean we actually do care for them. Service opens people to our friendship.

Second, servanthood is a model. It is not simply a means to some greater end, but it is also the goal of our influence. Jesus' servanthood not only built trust with the disciples; in addition, it showed them the way they could live as disciples. Servanthood is not simply a tool to get people to pursue God more intently; it embodies that pursuit.

Have you ever taught your friends how to do some activity so you'd have more people to share in the fun? I have taught poker and hearts to friends so that we could enjoy playing together, and a few times I have tried to teach bridge (difficult but rewarding to play). The point is not simply to enjoy the teaching but to enjoy one another more once we all know how to play.

Modeling servanthood and calling our friends into it is like teaching a game so you'll have table partners or like teaching a dance so you'll have someone to dance with. Life is more fun when our friends join us in the dance of servanthood, or as Jesus put it, "If you know these things, you are blessed if you do them" (John 13:17).

This is at the core of strategies to introduce people to God while inviting them to serve in some way. I know of groups of believing students who have invited their seeking friends to join them for a spring break Habitat for Humanity project. Building a home together for a needy family can be a great way to communicate the truth of Jesus' words that it is more blessed to give than to receive. This kind of activity is itself a parable depicting the spiritual reality that makes these transcendent words utterly practical.

FRIENDS SERVE BY SEEING: FORESIGHT

It is one thing to say that Jesus served and led even his friends; it is quite another to say that we can do it. Jesus always seemed to know what was going to happen. He did not take a poll or get sidetracked by his disciples' doubts or Satan's temptations. It was as if Jesus had a divine, internal gyroscope keeping him on course no matter the circumstances around him. Of course most of us do not experience life—let alone the pursuit of God—in the same way.

Yet we do have access to the same God, the same Holy Spirit and the same words of Jesus, which still have authority today. Furthermore, we can grow in our ability to rely upon God for wisdom, which he grants to those who ask him. While I maintain a list of friends with needs for whom I am praying, occasionally I will take longer times to pray for individuals. I take a few minutes to reflect on them one at a time. I ask, "God, do you want to show me anything for Lisa today?" or "How do you want me to pray for Mark?"

I want to emphasize two aspects of wisdom available to us: foresight and insight. Foresight is the ability of a person to see further into the future than others. Robert Greenleaf defines *foresight* as "a better than average guess about *what* is going to happen *when* in the future." It is the ability of a leader to step above day-to-day actions and to envision the future, with some (not necessarily total) confidence in the conclusions drawn. Greenleaf proceeds to say that "foresight is the *lead* a leader has."[3] It is part of what makes a leader a leader. Foresight contributes to the authority of a leader.

Foresight is not foreknowledge. It is not certainty but probability.

Foresight may be based on experience: "I know this road because I have been down it before." It may be based on intuition: "My sense is that this may be about to happen." It may be based on logic or reasoning. It may be based on divine guidance, through the promptings of the Holy Spirit. Regardless of the basis of foresight, it is an important resource with which we are able humbly to serve our friends.

Jesus demonstrated this kind of foresight as he led his disciples. Jesus told his disciples what would happen. He invited them to join a growing kingdom movement and told them what would happen to him, to them and to the movement itself. He painted a vision of the future in a way that was powerful and attractive. He also prepared them for the trials and sufferings they would face. In small events and long-range processes, Jesus described to his disciples the shape of things to come. Jesus used foresight as he led his disciples and others who came to him.[4]

Even the scene we have been looking at in John 13 includes several examples of Jesus exhibiting foresight as he prepared his disciples for his imminent departure. Jesus asked Peter to be patient, because Jesus knew that what Peter didn't understand then would be clear to him later. Later in this same scene, Jesus predicted his betrayal (13:21); he predicted his death (13:31-33) and resurrection (14:19; 16:16); he predicted Peter's denial (13:38); and he promised the arrival of the Holy Spirit (14:26; 16:12-15). In the midst of these short-term prophecies, Jesus told his disciples that he would return and take them to the place he would prepare for them (14:2-3). It was his clear ability to foresee the future in these examples that gave them the confidence that he would return, as he said. In fact, Jesus told his disciples why he was telling them all of this: "I have told you before it occurs, so that when it does occur, you may believe" (14:29).

Foresight is not certainty but probability. Perhaps for Jesus foresight and foreknowledge are the same, but for us it is an important distinction. Jesus used foresight, based on divine guidance, intuition or experience. We, too, can serve our friends by looking ahead.

Jesus used the narrow way as an image for the pursuit of God. In Matthew 7:13-14 he spoke of a road that we walk as disciples. He said the way is difficult. Friends in the pursuit of God have been helped to find their way to and down the road and are eager to help others make progress as well. People with foresight are able to see a little further down the road and help others travel it safely. We gain foresight through personal and group study of Scripture and through experience, thoughtful reflection, logic and intuition. Here are a few ways we can use foresight to serve our friends and deepen our friendships:

1. *Seeing opportunities to develop the friendship.* These opportunities could contribute to the friendship by helping friends enjoy one another more (through an outing, event or travel together), by helping friends be more useful to each other (by volunteering to paint an apartment or help one friend move into a new home), or by helping friends express and develop their common commitment to "the good" as they give time to the pursuit of God together through Bible study, retreats or conferences, service in church or other ministry efforts.

This has been a huge part of my role among my friends, and I have been the recipient of this type of initiative as well. I wrote in the first chapter of my friendship with Bill, which began when I was in college and has continued since. A few years ago, Bill began to reflect on the life he had chosen, watching others in ministry struggle and drop out for one reason or another. Bill decided to bring together a group of men who would be mutual mentors to one another and would help each other stay faithful to their wives, their families, their convictions and their callings. Bill contacted me, and together we laid a plan to gather a group of men we had both known for twenty years. Since then, four of us have been meeting annually for several days to listen to, encourage, exhort and pray for one another.

2. *Seeing opportunities for a friend's growth.* Foresight also may involve spotting growth opportunities and helping people take advantage of them. When we have experienced the benefit of personal prayer and

Scripture study, for example, we can help a friend begin to take such steps, encouraging our friend that after months of disciplined prayer and reading, he or she will see a difference in his or her life.

One of the main ways I have participated in this is by calling my friends to join with me in ministry. In part I am looking to see my friendships grow, but more importantly, I want to see my friends grow as disciples and lovers of God and people. I have invited friends to join me on mission trips (see chapter six), in small group leadership and in service projects in San Francisco, Santa Cruz, Boston and Washington, D.C.

Friends in our small group returned from a weekend retreat excited about what they had learned and experienced. They came to our small-group meeting with a hope that all of us would choose to take advantage of the opportunity when it came around again. I attend many retreats every year and even teach at a few. Yet as one who so often is encouraging growth opportunities for others, I found it genuinely refreshing to have someone speak of hope for my growth, encouraging me to participate in an opportunity to deepen my relationship with God.

3. *Seeing dangers in the road ahead*. Foresight may involve a perspective regarding the potential pitfalls in certain paths or in life in general. By reflecting on Scripture and experience, ours and others', we can spot turning points or critical junctures and help our friends avoid the worst possible outcomes. By speaking with humility, we can reduce the potential for a resistant or defensive reaction. The next chapter illustrates how we might have a gentle response to a friend we want to help.

The danger of speaking of foresight is, of course, the danger of speaking with too much confidence about our friends and their future. That is a temptation for some and can be destructive in friendships and harmful to our friends. However, my commensurate concern here is that we not withhold from our friends what we may have been given by God. So we need to learn to see and speak well, with humility and honor. Again, this is the central point of the next chapter.

FRIENDS SERVE BY SEEING: INSIGHT

If foresight is the ability to see further into the future, insight is the ability to see deeper into the present. Both insight and foresight are sources of knowledge or distillations of experience that give us an opportunity to speak into the life of a friend.

Jesus exercised insight. Jesus knew his disciples better than they knew themselves. Jesus knew what they were thinking, and he addressed their unasked questions. Jesus saw beyond the obvious physical needs of the multitudes who thronged to him. He knew the deeper needs—the emotional, social and spiritual needs—of those coming for physical healing. He saw the crowds not as annoyances and obstacles but as sheep without a shepherd. Jesus could understand people and circumstances that others around had no eye for. He relied on insight when dealing with the crowds or when talking with his disciples. He did so with the leper (Mark 1:40-44), with the bleeding woman (Mark 5:30-34), with the crowd (Mark 6:34) and repeatedly with Peter, James and John (Mark 8:32-33; 10:36-40; John 13:6-10).

While we don't have access to certainty about the unseen realm of people's hearts, we can take time to think deeply about the people around us in light of the Scriptures and our experiences. We then can use this insight to help people grow in their pursuit of God. Here are a few ways we can use insight to deepen our relationships and help our friends pursue God:

1. *Seeing potential in new relationships.* Lisa, my wife, was at a crossroads in her relationships. Most of her friends were involved in our campus ministry, yet she was in a new phase of life, with her primary focus the care of our young children. Used to taking most of the initiative in new relationships, both in our student ministry and in our young church, she delighted when another woman, a new attender at our church, began to take initiative with her. Lisa's friend, also named Lisa, saw potential for a friendship with my wife and took initiative. The two of them eventually hosted a regular study group for a handful of young

moms in our church. This initiative was contagious, and before long Lisa's husband and I became friends as well. Our wives encouraged us that this friendship was worth a try. Neither of these friendships would have happened without the initiative of our friend, who saw potential and invited response.

2. Seeing trends or patterns in the friendship. I have noticed that my friendships with single men change when they become romantically involved with a woman. That should come as no surprise, but in fact how the friendship changes is significant. If the romantic relationship is going well, including appropriate sexual boundaries, then my friend will be glad to answer the question "How are things going?" I can explicitly ask about purity and sexual temptation and my friend is not offended. Indeed he may be relieved. Yet if the relationship is struggling in this area, my friend will often not be very available for me even to ask. He fears being seen as a failure in this area. Over and over my friendships with single men go through a period where I must be available and sensitive but patient and not resentful. Eventually I am given a chance to enter in as a friend once again, sometimes only after the relationship has dissolved under the burden of its own dysfunction.

Insight involves sensing what lies behind the patterns we notice in our relationships. It is far beyond the scope of this chapter to go into depth on this topic, but I'll simply note that we gain wisdom when we pay attention to our relationships, in the form of seeing causes behind symptoms (for example, approval orientation, fear of conflict, need to be needed, spiritual hunger), seeing assumptions behind false beliefs (for example, about God, about others, about oneself, about parents, about values and priorities, about forgiveness and healing), and seeing deceptions behind feelings (for example, bitterness, anxiety, fear, depression). In each of these cases, insight makes connections between things that are observable and the causes, assumptions and deceptions that contribute to them. We need not have degrees in counseling or psychotherapy to be helpful to our friends. We simply need to pay attention and to speak about the things we see.

We also need not pluck out of thin observations whole theories about what really motivates people. We can speak with all the humility and compassion of a friend simply trying to be helpful. Prayer, on our own for our friends, and with our friends, for wisdom and guidance, makes this not an exercise in pettiness and self-justification but one of love.

3. *Seeing the need for reconciliation or understanding.* In chapter ten we will look at the process of seeking reconciliation as a crucial capability in friendship. I am referring to it here because one of the key ways we can demonstrate insight in our relationships with people is to know when reconciliation is needed.

My temperament is such that I enjoy contributing verbally in group settings. Often my mouth gets going and I say something for which I am later sorry. At some point I realize that I have just said something that has damaged trust with one or more members of the group. At that point the best thing I can do is stop the meeting and address those I have offended, asking for their forgiveness. While this is awkward and humbling, it is a way I can quickly attend to the damaged trust and broken friendship caused by my flippancy or aggression. I haven't always been quick to pursue this, but I have seen that it is best to pursue it at the point I become aware of it. (And Jesus' words in Matthew 5:21-26 back me up on this.) Others might not notice it or be as attuned to it, so insight on my part occasionally requires that I interrupt the conversational flow of the group in order to honor the relationships in it. Perhaps even more likely, some in the group have indeed noticed it and won't be able to continue well, either emotionally or cognitively, if I don't address it.

Insight and foresight both are sources of knowledge or distillations of experience that give us an opportunity to speak into the life of a friend. And this is precisely what makes this kind of initiative servanthood: if you have insight and foresight that you are willing to use to help me make better choices to pursue God, or to guide and improve our friendship, then you serve me by speaking in a gentle but persuasive way to influence my choices. By doing this you don't become my boss, my superior or my ruler; you simply live out friendship to me through serving by leading me in this way. And tomorrow, perhaps, I will get a chance to do the same for you.

Finally, friends serve simply by serving one another. Whether we plunk down a credit card to pay for the meal or pull up with a van to help someone move, when we use our resources, time and energy to help meet the need of a friend, we express our friendship in its most tangible form.

FRIENDS SERVE BY SPEAKING IN LOVE

Ultimately, a key way we deliver valuable insight and foresight to people is to speak to them. How we use words is crucial: we can cut people down or build them up; we can choose to honor them or we can use our words to diminish them.

The next chapter is about strategies for using words well, influencing people while leaving them intact, not attacked. At this point I simply want to summarize three ways we can serve people by speaking of the things we have seen in them.

1. *Calling for repentance.* Among his many responsible servants, King David had two very different men. Joab served as general of David's armies. When David had committed adultery with Bathsheba, Joab was given the job of making sure her husband, Uriah, was killed in battle. Joab did David's dirty work without complaint (2 Samuel 11:1, 14-15). On the other hand, Nathan, a prophet of the Lord, came to David to tell him a moving story. A poor man owned a beloved pet lamb, and a rich man, with a large flock of sheep, took and killed the poor man's only lamb to offer a meal to his friends. When David appropriately responded with rage at the rich man of Nathan's story, Nathan famously replied, "You are the man!" (2 Samuel 12:7). David responded in bro-

kenness, humility and sorrow for what he had done: "I have sinned against the LORD" (2 Samuel 12:13).

What enabled Nathan to serve David by speaking a prophetic call to repentance? First, Nathan saw more deeply into the situation than others. (God gave Nathan divine insight and emboldened him to use it to confront the king.) Second, Nathan spoke to David in a way that helped David to see his sin clearly. Third, Nathan spoke words of grace and forgiveness to David.

The story concluded in the final days of David's life: David welcomed Nathan to his bedside as a trusted friend, while David gave the order that Joab be killed for his continuing treachery (1 Kings 1:22-37; 2:5-6).

James and Amy were in trouble, and they came to Lisa and me for help. We had great affection for Amy and were delighted in her marriage to James, because they seemed so well suited for one another. Yet in the marriage Amy routinely felt taken for granted, not fully treasured by James. However, on this night James took the initiative to come because Amy, in a moment of anger, had slapped him.

Amy had every reason to trust us, which is why (I believe) she heard us say what we saw—that in fact James not only treasured her but also demonstrated it in many thoughtful ways. Amy had been blind to James's sensitive love for her, in part because of her previous relational and family history. Amy needed to cease questioning James's love and to take his words and deeds at face value. James in fact needed Amy to trust him, for his own damaged heart's sake.

Amy came to us looking for sympathy. Instead, she received what she needed even more: a loving dose of reality and a call to repent. She left that night grateful and restored to her husband in an enduring way.

2. *Calling for commitment.* The apostle Paul entered into deep relationships with the people of the church in Ephesus, spending three years preaching the gospel and giving of his extraordinary energy and commitment to the ministry there. He delivered his farewell sermon to

the leaders of the community in Acts 20:18-38, and it is clear from the text that they had more than a polite but distant admiration for him. They wept to think they'd never see him again.

In this context, Paul delivered to them something of what he had foreseen. The church in Ephesus would face dangers from without and within. Manipulators and deceivers would eventually dissemble and scheme to draw people away and fracture the group. So Paul called his young leaders, to whom he had entrusted the ministry in Ephesus, to take care and watch carefully over the flock. He called them to the same lifestyle he had lived among them and told them that his servanthood was a means for his own blessing, just as it would be for any who took up a similar lifestyle.

With today's sensibilities, we'd find it awkward to draw attention to ourselves as a model in the way that Paul did. I think we'd mostly hope that people wouldn't model their lives after us and that, if our life would be reckoned a model, it would be as a silent witness. The demands of humility would cause us to shy away from ever pointing out how perfectly and completely we actualize the gospel values we profess. Paul seemed willing, in the context of intimate friendship and deep appreciation for his leadership, to spell out the superlatives of his model.[5] His summary of his ministry with them is a great statement of his commitment to serve the church by speaking. He said, "I did not shrink from declaring to you the whole purpose of God" (verse 27). He did not say, "I told you everything you'll ever need to know." Rather, he said, "Everything I received from God I gave to you." In other words, when God gave him clarity about something, either regarding the faith's doctrine or its daily practice, Paul spoke up. He didn't see but not speak. He didn't see one thing but tell another. When God gave him clarity, he proclaimed it to whomever needed it. He could leave the ministry at Ephesus with a clear conscience, knowing that everything God gave him to say he had already said.

So in this final scene Paul served the Ephesian elders by speaking about what he saw ahead for the church, both the great opportunity and the real danger. He called the elders to commitment, to live out their callings as shepherds of God's flock, acting as nurturing caregivers to the tender sheep and as protective guardians against the wolves who endanger the flock. This they would do at great cost, as Paul made clear, but just as clearly he emphasized how the blessing is greater than the cost: "You know for yourselves that I worked with my own hands to support myself and my companions. In all this I have given you an example that by such work we must support the weak, remembering the words of the Lord Jesus, for he himself said, 'It is more blessed to give than to receive'" (Acts 20:34-35).

I have been fortunate enough to have been given dozens of chances to be a part of the process by which God has called people into vocational ministry. Part of my role has been to spell out the costs and also the benefits of this kind of life as I have seen and experienced it. In fact, it might be possible to leave people with the impression that I am an amazing sort of guy, a rare person who would be willing to sacrifice much for the sake of God's calling. Yet that isn't actually the notion I want to communicate: I'm not an amazing guy—but I do have an amazing God, and I have found a way to get the most out of life, as more blessing comes via giving than receiving, via serving more than being served. Whenever I am given the chance to invite people to count the cost and make a commitment, I must be as clear as Paul was in Acts 20 or as Jesus was in John 13:17: "If you know these things, you are blessed if you do them."

3. *Calling out gifts.* At one point in the story of the early church in Acts, the Jerusalem church was concerned about an emerging multiethnic church in Antioch. They sent Barnabas to Antioch to develop and shape its growth. When Barnabas arrived, he surveyed the scene and decided he needed additional help. So he left Antioch and made the 141-mile trip to Tarsus to look up Saul, also known as Paul. Paul was ideal for the role: educated outside of Judea, he was fully multicultural in language and training. Yet he was unproven as a leader. So Barnabas spoke up to persuade Paul to come. Barnabas's sponsorship of Paul was suc-

cessful, and a few months later that partnership brought about the first major missions movement of the early church.

One of the great ways we can serve people with insight is by speaking up about the gifts and talents we see at work in them. This can be self-serving if what we are doing is pumping people up with affirmation simply so that they'll do what we want them to do or serve the ministry we are involved in. In fact, it is as natural to see our own developed gifts in emerging leaders as it is for a musically inclined father to encourage any signs of musical talent in his child. Likewise, it is important for gifted teachers to affirm emerging teachers. However, it is also vital that we work to honor and encourage what God has placed in people and not simply shape people to resemble ourselves.

Table 5 summarizes the related topics in this chapter. Friends help one another by serving, leading, seeing and speaking. For this to happen, one friend must make a move toward the other in friendship. Serving involves a decision to extend oneself toward a friend. Leading involves risking rejection. Seeing with foresight and insight involves the work of reflecting, pondering the life and situation of another with compassion and clarity. Speaking the truth in love requires an articulation of what is seen in terms that are clear but humble and compassionate. Our inner dialogue can keep us from doing these things by tempting us to focus on our own needs, our own inadequacy, our own uncertainty, our own vulnerability. Only the call and resources of God can fundamentally help us to overcome these barriers and make the moves necessary to help these friendships not only survive but thrive.

Table 5. How Friends Help One Another

Friends Help One Another By	Crucial Move	Barrier: We Ask Ourselves
Serving—meeting real needs	Extending	"Who is looking out for me?"
Leading—taking initiative	Risking	"Who am I to lead?"
Seeing—with foresight and insight	Reflecting	"What if I'm wrong?"
Speaking—the truth in love	Articulating	"Will they still like me?"

Robert Greenleaf retells the story of Hermann Hesse's journey and its noble servant leader, Leo. Unfortunately, the experience of a group falling apart in the absence of servant leadership is not uncommon. Friendships, small groups, teams and even marriages can all fall into a lethargic existence or worse. Friends extend themselves and take risks on each other's behalf. They reflect enough to see deeply and love one another enough to say what they see. When this kind of servanthood is missing, relationships fall apart.

You may feel that any discussion of seeing and speaking should also cover the topic of listening, arguably a more important topic than either of the others. I quite agree, and I congratulate you for asking! The next chapter focuses on listening well and shows us how Jesus influenced his followers gently. We will consider how we can take a gentle approach, not being manipulative or controlling, yet still embrace our proper influencing role as fellow seekers after God.

FOR REFLECTION

1. How do you respond to the intentionality and effort others make in their friendships with you?

2. Have you seen Jesus serve you by calling you into service of others? Who has been instrumental in modeling this for you?

3. Which is easier for you: serving others or leading them? How can you develop into a better servant leader?

4. How have people offered you foresight and insight?

5. Think about a friend. What do you see in his or her life, or ahead for him or her, that you could help make clear?

6. How do you serve people by speaking? How have others received that?

Listening and Gentle Influence

But always to rigorous
judgment and censure
freely assenting,
man seeks, in his manhood,
not order, not laws and peremptory dogmas,
but counsel from one who is earnest in goodness
and faithful in friendship,
making man free.

Distant or near, in joy or in sorrow,
each in the other
sees his true helper
to brotherly freedom.

DIETRICH BONHOEFFER, "THE FRIEND"

It felt wonderful to have a listener as I rambled on and on. My friend Barney kept finding another question to ask whenever I stopped my run-away-train-of-thought gush. His questions showered me with affirmation as he took in the range of my tangents and made connections among them all. It seemed he had no agenda other than to listen to and sympathize with me in my perplexity.

I had just joined a small team. I was the youngest member and was prone to feeling misunderstood, and I was impatient for change. Barney listened, asked questions and affirmed me by the attention he paid me.

At the end of our long walk, at the end of the evening, at the end of a set of meetings that I had viewed as a waste of my time, he turned to me and asked, "How are you hoping to be a servant on this team, to your partners?" His question, phrased like that, placed no blame, incited no guilt. Instead it focused and clarified the challenge ahead. All my self-absorption was relativized in a moment by his penetrating question. "That question was worth the whole trip for me. Thanks for the perspective," I replied. I didn't leave that evening with the answer, but at least I was finally considering the right question.

Our lives are filled with decisions. Some flicker across our minds in an instant; some weigh us down for months and years. As Dietrich Bonhoeffer's poem on page 127 suggests, we expect that our warm, human friendships, rather than cold "laws" and "dogmas," will often inform us as we weigh these decisions. Our friends will give us information needed to make decisions among unclear alternatives. Our friends will give us insight into ourselves and others in ways that will help us choose the right path. Our friends will even shape our values and priorities.

Our friends will inform and influence our decisions both critical and trivial. Yet this fact alone doesn't imply that our friends have unhealthy influence in our lives. Of course we know "friends" that may exert pressure or manipulate us, inducing us to do what they want us to do, for their purposes and benefit, not ours. We also know that this activity is not true to friendship.

How can we find the kind of friends who will help us hear the voice of God, unwilling to sit blithely by while we charge off in the wrong direction but able to help us so that we are grateful, not resentful, to be helped? First of all, *having* such friends involves *being* such friends, and that is the focus of this chapter.

JESUS LED WITH QUESTIONS

Jesus' teaching methods were designed to elicit interest and response from people who were spiritually prepared to receive his teaching. His questions provoked people to think more deeply about the topics he taught. He was skilled at keeping people's attention and provoking them to think.

Jesus asked two questions that brought about the pivotal insight in the training of his young disciples (Mark 8:27-30). First, he asked, "Who do people say that I am?" (verse 27). The answers came quickly and easily. Every disciple had a popular answer; the whole country offered opinions about who Jesus was. Then the moment of truth came and Jesus asked, "But who do you say that I am?" (verse 29). The one word "but" told it all. "All of these answers are insufficient. Who do *you* know me to be?" The disciples sat still. Could it be true? Peter took the bait and—prompted by the Holy Spirit—declared, "You are the Messiah." By asking both questions, Jesus provoked the disciples to think and not be satisfied with rumor and supposition. The resulting declaration from Peter turned the course of events in a different direction: toward Jerusalem, toward conflict, toward Jesus' death and resurrection.

Why did Jesus teach this way? A look at Jesus' use of questions distills several advantages in Jesus' influence strategy.

- Questions kept people thinking during long discourses (Mark 4:13, 21; 7:18).

- Questions provided needed information regarding people Jesus was trying to help or heal (Matthew 9:28; Mark 8:23).

- Questions challenged people's assumptions about God, heaven, morality, Jesus' identity and so on (Mark 2:19; 3:4, 23, 33; 10:18; 11:30; 12:24, 35).

- Questions provoked pivotal insights (Mark 8:27-30; Luke 10:25-37).

An inductive emphasis suffused Jesus' teaching style, allowing people to come to their own conclusions about his identity and purpose. As people decided they wanted more of what he offered, he spoke with more authority into their lives. Do we allow Jesus' questions to penetrate our assumptions of what the kingdom is all about? Are we ready to use questions to do the same for others?

Friends need to develop an ability to ask good questions. This is crucial if we are to communicate with people in ways that will cause them to join or continue with us in our pursuit of God. Asking good questions and listening well to the answers will (1) help us get to know people more deeply and (2) provoke people to think for themselves about key issues of life and faith.

It may be obvious, but as people in pursuit of God with others, we must get to know those others. Asking good questions allows us to understand more about them—their background, their emotional makeup, their fears and hopes, their motives, their convictions. It also allows us to know how they understand God and their relationship with God.

Asking questions will allow people to think for themselves about what it means to be a disciple. Questions build ownership of conclusions through a process of discovery rather than simply being told what is right. Even if your friend's only real response to a question, after some reflection, is "I don't know; what do you think?" that can be a helpful way to begin the learning process. For example, this is what inductive Bible study is all about and why it is invaluable in building convictions in people. People are allowed to come to a biblical text and draw their conclusions based on the text itself, guided by a leader who keeps them on track with questions. The group's involvement in the inductive process forges group ownership of convictions. Group members may then enter into meaningful accountability with one another regarding convictions developed in this way.

TOOLS OF INFLUENCE

Most people do not know how to ask questions well. Many people prefer to talk rather than to listen, and skilled listeners are exceedingly rare. Yet Dietrich Bonhoeffer stresses the importance of good listeners:

> The first service that one owes to others in the fellowship consists in listening to them. Just as love to God begins with listening to His Word, so the beginning of love for the brethren is learning to listen to them.[1]

Furthermore, when people think about influence, often it takes the form of advice: "What I would do if I were you is . . ." Advice may be appropriate in some situations, but it undoubtedly is much overused. Unfortunately, for those who receive it, advice is also often undervalued.

Advice is overused often because some people feel that they have a responsibility as friends to tell others what to do. Their goal in these conversations is to dispense their own wisdom, hoping that it will have some positive effect on the one for whom their advice is directed.

Of course, another group of people avoid doling out advice or indeed making any overt attempt at influence with their friends. They believe that sincere friendship means pure acceptance of their friends, regardless of their choices and decisions.

Both of these strategies have merits, but both are deficient. People need wisdom, sometimes supplied by their friends. People also need acceptance, love and support, especially from friends. But as friends, we can aim for more than either a dispassionate dispensation of wisdom or an open and uncritical embrace of our friends.

My goal in the influence and support of my friends is not that they hear from me about what they should do but rather that they should hear from God. The distinction is not mere piety, nor is it a refusal to seek influence. I want to engage my friends in ways that will help them gain deep and godly conviction regarding their priorities and values, and then I want to help them more faithfully live by these priorities and values. My goal is *not* to get my friends to do what I want them to do.

Because getting my friends to do what I want them to do is not my goal, I don't pursue strategies aligned with this goal. Because I want them to hear from God, I employ strategies aimed at helping them do this. As we have seen, questions cause people to think; they provoke insight. Good questions imply that solutions are not obvious. As people ponder questions, they often gain insight.

We have many different verbal tools of influence available to us in our friendships, some of which can be helpful while others are detrimental. I think of them in a continuum flanked by two extremes: closed strategies, which make the questioner the expert, and open strategies, which make the responder the expert. (See figure 4.)

Influence strategies focused on the expertise of the influencer often focus on spelling out approved or correct behavior. This has the advantage of being clear: the actions desired may be quickly understood. At times this is appropriate, as when dealing with urgent situations that can be explained more fully later. (I use commands, not stories, when biking with my children, to keep them safely at the side of the road and out of the way of traffic.) Yet these tools—most obviously advice and commands—often leave friends without a deep understanding of the reasons why. In general, influence strategies in which the influencer is seen as the expert (bottom half of figure 4) leave a friend open to feeling manipulated (bad questions), controlled (advice, commands) or judged (judgments).

Influence strategies involving open conversation (good questions, stories, statements) focused on priorities and goals require a greater investment of time and listening effort, but they can be rewarding, as a friend comes to his or her own clarity about what choice would best fulfill his or her priorities and objectives. The friend is much less likely to feel manipulated or resentful, but rather grateful for the skill and attention of the listener.

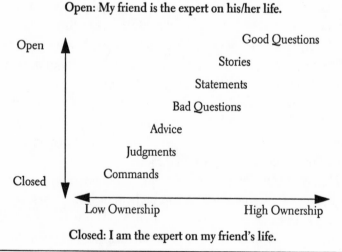

Figure 4. Verbal tools of influence

Often someone will try to ask questions, but the experience is not an altogether pleasant one, either for the listener or for the friend who is being questioned. That may be because the questioner thinks up questions the way a lawyer does when cross-examining an opposing witness. The questions come in the form of thinly veiled accusations or else efforts at making the responder see things the way the questioner does. "Why are you always so negative?"

It is no wonder that this kind of inquisition can be unpleasant. But that is not the kind of question asking I am suggesting is needed in our friendships. Robert Bolton speaks about the importance of open questions as opposed to closed questions:

> Questions are an integral part of verbal interaction in our society. As with many other kinds of responses, questions have their strengths and their limitations. Comparatively few people in our culture know how to question effectively. We often rely on questions excessively and use them poorly. . . .
>
> We distinguish between "closed" questions and "open" questions. Closed questions direct the speaker to give a specific, short response. Open questions, on the other hand, provide space for the speaker to explore his thoughts without being hemmed in too much by the listener's categories. . . . Closed questions are like true/false or multiple choice test questions, while open questions are like essay questions.[2]

Table 6 distinguishes between closed questions and open questions. Closed questions demand brief answers; open questions invite discussion. Closed questions seek specific details; open questions advance a process of discovery. Closed questions press the questioner's agenda; open questions serve only the responder's interests.

What about the "Why?" question? When I ask someone, "Why are you planning to do that?" it sounds like I think there are no good reasons. That may or may not be what I think, but that way of asking doesn't yield an open, nondefensive response. Rather, a better way to ask the question is simply to rephrase it: "What are the reasons you are planning to do that?" That rephrasing communicates something different. "Of the many possible reasons I can think of for planning to do that, which ones particularly motivate you?" People are much less likely to respond defensively to that question, and then real understanding can follow.

Table 6. Closed and Open Questions

Closed: I am the expert.	Open: My friend is the expert.
Yes/no questions: could, would, should, do, did, will, can	What, where, when, who, how
Content-oriented: directed toward specific information the questioner desires	Process-oriented: directed toward helping the responder move through a thorough process of thinking
Leading or manipulative	Stimulates thinking without hidden agendas
Threatening: out to prove a case	Nonthreatening: deeply curious with affection and honor
Why are you . . . ?	What are the reasons you are . . . ?

Table 6 can summed up simply: people are the experts of their own lives. Even when I seek the guidance of others in my life, I want them to acknowledge that I at least have a few clues. When we seek to help others, we must do it with humility. Focusing on using open questions is futile or even deceptive if we believe we really are the experts in our conversations with friends regarding their lives. If I ultimately believe my job is to get my friend to see her situation the way I see it, then I will ask leading or manipulative questions to draw her into the web of perspective I have spun. However, if I sincerely believe that she is the expert on her own life, then I will ask her the kinds of open questions that make it possible to hear from her regarding motives, desires, objectives and goals. (I won't have to remember to ask such questions; I will simply, naturally ask them because these will be the questions I actually have.) My friend won't feel manipulated or trapped but rather served by the good questions that help her understand her own thinking, her own desires and how God speaks to her in the midst of those things.

Table 7. Planning a Helpful Conversation, Example 1

Presenting issue	Thinking about looking for a new job
What does the person seek?	Your advice about how much longer he should stay in his current frustrating and stress-producing job.
What concerns do you have?	You know the job is frustrating but are aware of character growth opportunities in it. You aren't convinced that he should leave his job right now.
Advice you'd just love to give:	Don't quit your job quite yet. You haven't learned all you can through it, and your perseverance will be rewarded.
Closed (bad) questions you'd be tempted to ask:	• In the past, have you quit jobs quickly when they became the least bit frustrating? • What does it say about you that you don't want to stay in this job?
Open questions that would help him to better understand his own motives and priorities:	• What are some of the things God is teaching you in your current job? • How do your current stresses help you depend on God? How do they hinder your dependence on God? • What kinds of near-term goals can you work toward that will help you to learn and benefit from your current job? • When would be a realistic time frame to consider leaving?
Goal for your helpful conversation:	That the person identify some of the ways God is working in his current job and how facing and not running away could provoke more growth. To help him identify signs that it is actually time to move on.

Imagine a friend has come to you to talk about his stressful job, perhaps to ask for your advice. You find that within just a few minutes you have a sense of what you think your friend should do, and you are sorely tempted to give him some advice. I'm going to take us through a little exercise in which we acknowledge that we'd like to knock some sense into him. We won't actually give advice, and we'll refrain from asking manipulative questions. In the end, I'm suggesting that this strategy of asking open questions (in which our friend is the expert and he knows we know it) will best help him discover a good solution or approach. Table 7 spells out our strategy.

Next, imagine that a friend has come to you telling you that she is planning to drop the commitment she has made to a team on which you serve or perhaps you lead. She is seeking your approval for this, though it hasn't occurred to her that you'd have any problems with her decision. Let's do the same exercise (table 8). Again, we are going to acknowledge that we'd love to give advice or to ask questions that will leave our friend completely clear about our lack of enthusiasm for her decision. Even as

Table 8. Planning a Helpful Conversation, Example 2

Presenting issue	Thinking about dropping a ministry commitment
What does the person seek?	Your approval for her decision to drop the commitment she has made to your team.
What concerns do you have?	You fear that her decision to drop her ministry commitment is based in self-protection, risk avoidance or conflict avoidance rather than in wisdom.
Advice you'd just love to give:	Don't drop your team commitment! Stop working so much on weekends!
Closed (bad) questions you'd be tempted to ask:	• How do you think the people your ministry serves will feel? How will your partners feel? • What could be a higher priority than serving in this way?
Open questions that would help her to better understand her own motives and priorities:	• What are the commitments in your week you most enjoy? • What is satisfying about them? • What priorities make dropping this commitment look attractive? • What priorities would be sacrificed by making this choice? • How could these tradeoffs be avoided?
Goal for your helpful conversation:	That the person consider priorities and make a good decision in light of those priorities. This could include dropping the ministry commitment, but for the right reasons.

we acknowledge this, however, we are going to try to avoid giving advice or asking manipulative questions.

Let me give one final example. A believing friend in her mid-thirties is considering whether to break up with or to marry her long-time boyfriend, Stan, who is sweet to her and cares for her but is not passionate about life and ministry in the way she is. Stan has proposed and she has not given her answer, though she gets the feeling that Stan would be content to wait if she asked him to do so. She feels life with Stan would be secure, if a little boring. Your friend comes to you asking your advice regarding the wisdom of saying yes to a man she is not sure she passionately loves, after months of trying. Table 9 outlines a plan.

Table 9. Planning a Helpful Conversation, Example 3

Presenting issue	Considering a marriage proposal
What does the person seek?	Your advice regarding whether to say yes or not, given her ambivalence toward her suitor.
What concerns do you have?	You fear she is tempted to settle, undervaluing herself and her hopes and dreams for her life, trading passion for security.
Advice you'd offer:	Though you quail at the thought of giving your friend advice in matters of the heart, you'd say, "I just think you aren't ready to say yes to him."
Closed (bad) questions you'd be tempted to ask:	• Do you really think you could be happy with a man with whom you share so little? • Could you really marry someone so shallow?
Open questions that would help her to better understand her own hopes and to hear from God:	• What are your hopes for the future? • What have you hoped for in a marriage partner? • How does Stan satisfy those hopes? In what ways does he not? • How important is that to you? • What can you do to allow God to give you clarity in this decision?
Goal for your helpful conversation:	That your friend consider the big picture and make a decision out of faith, not fear. As this decision has great consequences for her, you want her to fully own it and not simply do what you would do if you were in her place.

All of these scenarios, but especially the third, illustrate the dangers of advice. If my goal in a conversation with a friend is simply to give advice, I run several risks. First, it is a risk if my friend takes my advice—it could turn out wrong. Second, it is a risk if my friend doesn't take my advice—it could strain our relationship in the future. (Even if I wouldn't see it that way, my friend might.)

On the other hand, if my goal is to have a helpful conversation, my friend owns the result—she hasn't been manipulated by advice or entrapping questions. If it turns out badly (and of course it still might), I am still in her life as a friend to listen, to pray, to speak about it and help discern God's voice.

Wouldn't it be great to have friends who knew how to listen without judgment and yet who wouldn't withhold from us God-given insight into our lives? Wouldn't it be great to be such a friend?

JESUS ENGAGED PEOPLE WITH STORIES

Since Jesus relied on group settings to communicate the gospel message, he needed skill to communicate to many people in ways appropriate for each. He did this most often through stories. Obviously, Jesus was a great storyteller. Many of his "greatest hits" parables, like the good Samaritan or the prodigal son, were told in response to a question asked by someone else. These stories were Jesus' way of communicating essential gospel truth in a hidden or obscure form so that those who were ready to understand would receive the benefit of the parable but those who were not ready would not understand it.

In order to understand why and how Jesus used stories, we must look at his statements regarding this in Mark 4:

> When he was alone, those who were around him along with the twelve asked him about the parables. And he said to them, "To you has been given the secret of the kingdom of God, but for those outside, everything comes in parables; in order that
> 'they may indeed look, but not perceive,

and may indeed listen, but not understand;
so that they may not turn again and be forgiven.'" . . .
"For there is nothing hidden, except to be disclosed; nor is anything secret, except to come to light." (Mark 4:10-12, 22)

In his explanation, Jesus gave us a clue as to why he spoke in parables. Verse 22 makes it clear that he didn't speak in parables in order to permanently obscure the truth, but that the truth might eventually be fully grasped. Jesus taught in parables so that people would begin to see and perceive, hear and understand. But they would do so only as they had been given the secret of the kingdom of God. These people stood before Jesus after the telling of the parables, asking him for understanding. They had listened to him, when he began telling them to "Listen!" They had understood, not the parable, but that the parable itself was important.

In fact, Jesus indicated that they did not understand the parable at all (Mark 4:13)! But they did understand that the message was worth pursuing further. This one fact differentiated the Twelve and others who stayed later from all the rest who returned home after hearing the story. They alone had been given the secret of the kingdom. The secret had something to do with the importance of Jesus' words. The kingdom had everything to do with Jesus.

So Jesus told parables in order that the meaning might be communicated, but only to those who were ready to receive the meaning. "For those outside," Jesus' words remained obscure. For them, as he said, "everything comes in parables . . . so that they may not turn again and be forgiven" (Mark 4:11-12). Jesus did not want anyone remaining on the outside—those separated from Jesus and unwilling to enter into relationship with him—to be forgiven. Rather, he wanted something even better for people on the outside. He wanted them to become insiders, entering into relationship with the only One who, on earth, has the authority to forgive sins (Mark 2:10).

One group who were clearly on the outside in the Gospel of Mark were the Pharisees. Jesus had to be careful in his communication with them, because from the beginning they demonstrated an unwillingness to consider the possibility that he was from God (Mark 2:7, for example). It is not that Jesus did not care about the Pharisees or that he made no attempt to communicate with them, but he demanded that they respond to him. He warned them of the danger of their conclusions (Mark 3:28-29). For those who had ears to hear, as some eventually did, Jesus' gospel invitation offered salvation through faith in him.

Imagine the setting in which the first apostles taught their young disciples about the gospel. This would have been before anything in the New Testament was written. As they gathered for meals and for prayers, one of those revered people who actually walked with Jesus would sit back and in hushed tones would begin to describe the extraordinary events of the Gospels that we now view as commonplace. "There was that one time when we fed five thousand people with a few loaves of bread and a couple of fish!" Whether it was the telling of a miracle, a powerful parable, the events of the Passion week or the glorious resurrection stories, the gospel would be told primarily in narrative form. People would be taught Jesus' ethical code in the form of parables they would learn by heart or sayings of Jesus in the context of some event in the lives of the disciples. Narrative was the primary way the truth about the gospel was communicated. Certainly the same can be said about the Old Testament. The facts about God, his nature and his character, are not revealed systematically or propositionally but through narrative—the unfolding of a story about a people and their God.

YOU ARE MY WITNESSES

The Urbana 96 Student Mission Convention had as its theme "You Are My Witnesses," a phrase taken from Isaiah 43:10-12. The publicity poster for the event featured a blowup of an eye, and the caption read, "What have you seen God do lately? A life transformed by Christ is a compelling witness." I especially appreciate that little adverb *lately*.

We must be able to tell our own story. The classic form of this is our own testimony.[3] Every follower of Jesus Christ is commonly expected to have a form of his or her testimony to share with anyone who may ask. This is a good beginning, but our repertoire of tales to tell should be ever expanding. We will have tales of God's *recent* work in our lives, of our tough struggles of faith or obedience, of our developing relationships and the values we developed through them, of prayer and God's recent answers to our prayers. In other words, if we don't have current stories of God's goodness to us, of struggles we have faced or of answers to prayer, it may be that our relationship with God was more alive in the past than it is in the present.

Our own story, in this sense, is more than just a history; rather, it is a "gospel"—it recounts God's work in history. We tell our stories the way Jesus told his stories, for those who have "ears to hear." When we speak of our experiences, valuable friendships or relationships, or insights, we invite people to join us, to learn with us as we have learned.

For example, here is how I as a campus minister have used a story from my own life. I had some concerns regarding John and Liz's romantic relationship, and I wanted to talk to John about them, though I didn't know how open John would be to my concerns. I could have had an intense one-to-one discussion with him. But instead I waited until it arose in normal conversation between John, his good (Christian) friend Kirk and me as we sat over dinner in the dining hall. At that point I asked John more about his relationship with Liz and shared about my own relationship with my wife, Lisa, as it developed before our engagement. I also talked about other relationships I'd been in. Both John and Kirk were challenged as I talked about some of the mistakes I made. I was able to share how those early mistakes and the encouragement of friends deepened my own convictions about health and purity in romance. Then I followed up with a question to Kirk about his romantic history and then another question to John. When we were through, we all knew each other better and both of them had something to ponder in this area.

This was the perfect setting in which to tell my own story. It was here that I could acknowledge my own weakness and sin in a way that was vulnerable and yet implicitly raised questions for John about his relationship with Liz. As John heard from me, he could demonstrate either openness or defensiveness and unwillingness to listen. I could gauge his level of receptivity through the questions he asked or even through body language. I was able to gauge John's openness to a more direct challenge from me regarding the specific issues of his relationship with Liz.

As in this case, the first conversation is not usually the last, and through telling my own story I may be able to discern openness and pursue the topic in the future. Often the third person (Kirk in the example above) will be more open to the story and its message than the one for whom it is originally told, and this was indeed the case. Perhaps a later conversation between the others who heard the story will be the setting in which conviction is formed.

I have friends who routinely ask their family members to "spot God," that is, to identify places in their day or week when they saw evidence of God's work or his communication with them. Each member of the family, children and parents alike, partakes in witness to the work of God by telling brief stories. What have you seen God do lately?

FOR REFLECTION

1. Think about your own experience of being asked good, open questions by a friend whose chief interest was to listen to you and help without giving advice. What did that feel like for you? Who do you know who is good at it?

2. Are you able to choose open rather than closed strategies in your conversations with others? How would you like to grow?

3. Find someone with whom you can share the model of conversation in this chapter. Try to pick an actual decision you are currently facing. Let one of you ask the other open questions, without advice, without judgment, focusing first on priorities and goals and only later getting to actions and decisions. How did that feel? Now reverse the roles and repeat the process.

4. How have you seen God work lately? Identify a story you can tell about things you've learned

   - about God's love for you

   - about reconciliation with a friend

   - about the benefits of crossing cultural boundaries in friendship

   - about integrity at work

9

Competition and Comparison Among Friends

If you are in love with precedence and the highest honor, pursue the things in last place, pursue being the least valued of all, pursue being the lowliest of all, pursue being the smallest of all, pursue placing yourself behind others.

CHRYSOSTOM, *THE GOSPEL OF ST. MATTHEW*, HOMILY 58

I think we have a lot we can learn from each other," I said brightly.

"I can see that you have a lot to learn from me. I just don't see that I have anything to learn from you," she said quenchingly.

I had taken a step to be vulnerable in order to build trust. I was speaking to a peer and teammate after it was clear I was likely to be appointed as leader for the team after its current leader's imminent departure. I thought she might even be a little intimidated by me (it has been reported I have that effect on some people), and so I was trying to emphasize that I saw Stacey as a partner. I knew our relationship would be essential in the team as each of our roles evolved.

I just wasn't prepared for her response. Frankly, I wasn't used to being told I had nothing to offer. After clarifying that I had indeed heard her correctly, I stammered that, while I thought there were areas in which Stacey's ministry instincts were strong, I had to (if I did say so myself) acknowledge that I had complementary strengths. I thought this was self-evident, and I thought she would give way at this point. But she didn't back down. She merely asserted that she was as strong or stronger in those areas that I thought were my strengths, in addition to accepting my estimation of her relative strengths. This conversation completely flummoxed me.

Six months later, having grown in ease with one another and understanding better how we were able to benefit from working in partnership together, Stacey and I were able to laugh about the entire conversation. In fact she had been somewhat insecure with me, and it was this insecurity that manifested itself as bravado in our original conversation. Over time this insecurity lessened, and eventually we each learned from the other's strengths in ministry. We came to enjoy mutual respect and partnership that made it fun. But it had been a rocky beginning.

What makes relationships competitive, filled with comparison and lacking grace and sympathy? My children, who as I write are eight and ten years old, are each other's best friends, yet they don't always share well. When I was their age, I was like them. Actually, I still am. Of course, at age twenty, I knew not to grab someone's toy, but competition showed up in more subtle ways. I still had difficulty sharing the limelight—I wanted my ideas to be accepted and to carry the day on the ministry team on which I served. If a Bible study were a pickup basketball game, I was the equivalent of a "ball hog."

Now, twenty years later, I know how to share the air time in a group discussion, but I still am tempted to size up a man on the basis of the size of his house or the accomplishments of his children.[1] I wish it weren't true, and it isn't always, but competition and comparison never quite seem to go away.

JOHN AND PETER'S FRIENDSHIP (JOHN 20—21)

Early on the first day of the week, while it was still dark, Mary Magdalene came to the tomb and saw that the stone had been removed from the tomb. So she ran and went to Simon Peter and the other disciple, the one whom Jesus loved, and said to them, "They have taken the Lord out of the tomb, and we do not know where they have laid him." Then Peter and the other disciple set out and went toward the tomb. The two were running together, but the other disciple outran Peter and reached the tomb first. He bent down to look in and saw the linen wrappings lying there, but he did not go in. Then Simon Peter came, following him, and went into the tomb. He saw the linen wrappings lying there, and the cloth that had been on Jesus' head, not lying with the linen wrappings but rolled up in a place by itself. Then the other disciple, who reached the tomb first, also went in, and he saw and believed.

JOHN 20:1-8

It didn't begin as a race. It began as a bewildered and urgent response to a confusing bit of news: someone has taken the body of the Lord. Peter and John began to run from their hideout to the garden tomb. But as they ran, each began to exert more effort, until it finally became a sprint for gold. As it so often was between these two, it came down to loyalty: which one loved him more? Usually, Peter had the upper hand. It had been Peter who walked on water to Jesus. It had been Peter about whom Jesus said, "On this rock I will build my church" (Matthew 16:18). Yet lately Peter had distinguished himself in ignominy, not glory. Peter had, as Jesus predicted, denied three times that he even knew Jesus. John, on the other hand, had been at the foot of the cross ready to receive Jesus' mother into his care at Jesus' solemn request.

What began as urgency ended up as one more attempt at proving their love for Jesus. John, the Gospel writer, told us the outcome of this all-important race: the beloved disciple won. Peter was an older brother and head disciple; John was a younger brother and probably a significantly younger man and in better physical shape. Yet Peter, arriving second, tried to claim the loyalty position by being the first to go into the empty tomb. Then John (as he narrated) retook the lead by saying that when he went in, *he saw and believed.*

This scene frames the background for John and Peter's experience in John 21. It was a confusing time once again for the disciples. Jesus had risen from the dead, but it wasn't clear exactly what that meant for them. Peter's vision of what life was supposed to look like had been shattered, and yet nothing had put the pieces back together. So Peter decided to do something he knew. "I'm going fishing," he announced, and several of the others joined him.

Jesus met the crew as they were tired from being out on the lake all night with nothing to show for it. Unrecognized, he spoke to them with sympathy, "You have no fish?" (John 21:4). He told them to try once more, and indeed they netted a huge catch of fish. John recognized this as déjà vu, and he nudged Peter and said in hushed tones, "It is the Lord" (verse 7). Peter, once again in a display of over-the-top loyalty, swam to shore to be first to reach Jesus. Yet when Peter arrived, he found he had nothing to say to the Master.

Eventually Jesus asked, "Simon son of John, do you love me more than these?" (verse 15). I read this as "Do you love me more than these others love me?" Peter had indicated, a few nights previously, that even though he could easily see the others falling away, he would certainly not do it. Peter had said, in many different ways, that he was the most devoted of Jesus' disciples. I think Jesus was actually asking him if he wanted again to claim that he was uniquely committed and devoted to Jesus. "Peter, do you still want to claim that you love me more than anyone else does?"

If Jesus was indeed pointing to the other disciples, asking Peter once again to make his heroic claims to unique loyalty and devotion, then this explains why there is no comparative in Peter's response. Peter didn't say, "Sure, Lord, I love you more than they do." Rather, all the swagger and boasts were gone. Peter was indeed humbled, and yet he asserted that he loved his Lord. Not more than others, not the best. "But yes, Lord, you know—you know all things—you know I love you."

Jesus didn't contradict Peter. This was a hopeful sign, one that is very encouraging to me. Jesus took Peter's responses at face value. He gave Peter a chance to undo those denials one by one, the three increasingly agitated affirmations of Peter's love for Jesus negating the three increasingly vociferous denials of the recent past. After telling him to take care of his sheep and his lambs, Jesus said, "Follow me," and then he told him, "Yes, Peter, you will get your chance to die for me."

And then we see John back once more as a character in his own narration. Peter asked, "What about him?" (John 21:21). Peter wanted to know, "Is this everyone's destiny or just mine because I denied you? You *do* love him more, don't you?" The competitive relationship they'd had since the beginning showed up at the end. "Lord, will he face what I must face?" To this Jesus simply replied, "Your story only is yours to know; follow me."

Before we look at the end of the story with Peter and John, let's back up and examine an earlier scene where their dynamics emerged. We, too, need to hear Jesus' caution and invitation to the disciples.

THE SPIRITUAL DANGER OF COMPETITION (MARK 10:35-45)

It was the kind of thing that could have splintered the group. Yes, James and John had done a foolish thing: they had asked to be appointed Jesus' next in command. But the anger of the ten left no room for quick apologies. Fighting words were used—the band that had preached of God's love and had ministered God's power was breaking apart in a petty power struggle of its own.

Jesus called the group together and put out the fires of discord. He said, "Gentiles think that way. But it is not so among you." He didn't say, "It should not be so among you." He spoke of fact, not advice. "This is the way it works, folks. You want to be great? Be a servant!"

Jesus' teaching here was not simply a rebuke of James and John. The anger of the ten revealed that they were thinking just like the Thunder Twins. Jesus didn't try simply to smooth things out with everyone. He brought the fractious group together and in no uncertain terms told them that they had it all wrong.

Competition can easily impede friendships focused on a pursuit of God. Rather than desire to have the most toys or the biggest muscles, we can want to have the deepest friendships or the most honor as a leader. The problem here is that for every winner of this game there are many losers.

Jesus turned this competition on its head. You want to be first? "Pursue the things in last place," as Chrysostom said. You want honor? Show honor to others. Or as the apostle Paul said in Romans 12:10, "Love one another with mutual affection; outdo one another in showing honor." This kind of competition makes everyone a winner and displays the abundance of the kingdom. It doesn't endanger the company of friends; it fuels it.

While in college, I spent one summer in Boulder, Colorado, working on a painting crew, scraping and prepping and painting houses in the heat of the day. I received no paycheck that summer. I was in Boulder with about twenty other students who lived in two crowded houses, men in one, women in the other. We all looked for work, and what income we received went into a single bank account, out of which our expenses for the summer were paid. We were in Boulder to learn about God and about how to talk to people about our faith in a way that was attractive and real. We were there to show hospitality to people, to begin relationships with people and encourage them to join us in pursuit of God.

That summer was a turning point for me. Up until then, almost all of my male friendships were somewhat competitive by nature. Who was smartest, wittiest, best? These questions were always beneath the surface. But it was different in Boulder, and I've seen this make a difference since. Working side by side—while painting or while giving of ourselves to relational ministry—drove competition from our relationships. We had better things to do with our time than wonder who was wittiest.

Peter and John, shown still competitive at the end of John's Gospel, were side by side in Acts 3—4 when Peter healed the lame beggar, and they were both dragged before the council and warned. Peter and John did not arrive at their breakthrough by finally settling the argument "Who loves Jesus more?" They settled when they were both drawn into mission. When thousands entered the community and people needed leadership, Peter and John needed each other and stood together in partnership. They faced success together; they remained together when they faced opposition, even the threat of death.

What made the difference for Peter and John from the story at the end of Jesus' life to the scene a month later when they were together at the temple steps, healing the lame man? Peter saw the man and said to him, "I have no silver or gold, but what I have I give you; in the name of Jesus Christ of Nazareth, stand up and walk" (Acts 3:5). With Peter tapped in to the limitless power of the Holy Spirit, he could give what he had and be no poorer. John and Peter were no longer in competition for Jesus' attention, for with the advent of the Holy Spirit each had within him a deep well of God's presence and power. So they did not need to compete at that point.

Consider what at least for me is a familiar experience: eating a plate of french fries while at a table full of people. If I have a small plate, sitting right in front of me, I experience no competition for those fries—they are mine and I'll probably eat every last one. If I have a big plate sitting in front of me, I'll still experience no competition—the fries are still mine, but I will probably feel like sharing, so a few others will get a few fries. When that plate is finished, I'll be happy, though others may still be hungry. Now imagine a small basket sitting in the middle of the table. This is where competition comes in, as the fries are not mine. Everyone eats some of the fries, but I notice that I eat them more quickly than normal. How many fries I get will be proportional to how rapidly I munch. We all experience sharing, but we are all still competitive in regard to the fries (assuming I'm sitting with people who are as calculating about their fries as I am). Finally, imagine sitting down at a table with a huge basket of fries. I look at that basket and think, *Even if everyone eats as many as I would want to eat, we'll still have leftovers.* Now there is no competition for the fries, and we can go back to eating the fries at our own individual ideal consumption rate. Everyone shares; everyone gets full; no one goes hungry. If we're able to see it this way, life in the kingdom is like life at that table with a huge basket of fries.

Jesus told his disciples on the night before he was betrayed, "I have said these things to you so that my joy may be in you, and that your joy may be complete. This is my commandment, that you love one another as I have loved you. . . . You did not choose me but I chose you. And I appointed you to go and bear fruit, fruit that will last" (John 15:11-12, 16).

Fullness, joy, lasting fruit—these are the results of a life oriented toward loving others, as Jesus commanded. The basket is full to overflowing; everyone is full, no one goes hungry and no one is sitting around wondering who got the most.

Imagine a group of singles where everyone is trying to find deep friendship, especially in a relationship that could lead toward marriage. Finding yourself in such a group, you could make a choice, perhaps with another like-minded individual, to host events where your focus, rather than to find such relationships for yourself, is to help others build friendships in a natural way. Your comments and actions during these events aren't motivated by a desire to meet your own needs but rather by a desire to serve and honor the others you've invited. Would it be possible, in this way, to alter the dynamics of this singles group? I believe so. Would others begin to catch on? Quite possibly. Would you be the loser for choosing this strategy? I think Jesus' promises in Mark 10 back me up when I say, "Not likely!"

COMPETITION AND RESENTMENT

Now as they went on their way, he entered a certain village, where a woman named Martha welcomed him into her home. She had a sister named Mary, who sat at the Lord's feet and listened to what he was saying. But Martha was distracted by her many tasks; so she came to him and asked, "Lord, do you not care that my sister has left me to do all the work by myself? Tell her then to help me." But the Lord answered her, "Martha, Martha, you are worried and distracted by many things; there is need of only one thing. Mary has chosen the better part, which will not be taken away from her."

LUKE 10:38-42

Again we come to take a look at Martha and her sister, Mary, perhaps the most developed characters in the Gospels beyond Jesus, his mother and a few of the Twelve. Martha was the older of the two, responsible for her home and eager to welcome Jesus into it. Mary was the younger sister, an impractical, dreamy, poetic type. For her to choose to sit at

Jesus' feet and listen to teaching, she had to be strong-willed or else oblivious to the social requirements of the day. Perhaps she was some of both.

Martha's outburst—"Lord, do you not care?"—likely came after many futile attempts to capture Mary's attention. Martha saw her efforts on Jesus' behalf as being evidence of her devotion to her Lord. Yet Mary was the one who got to sit at Jesus' feet and drink deeply of Jesus' teaching and manner. Martha resented Mary's choice, but temperamentally it would have been a difficult choice for her to make, just as it would have pained Mary to have to leave the circle and draw water for the soup.

It is possible for people with a Martha temperament to resent Mary types, and even vice versa. As one who relates more to Martha than Mary, let me first acknowledge that Martha types get a lot of affirmation and positive feedback by being as productive as they are. When the preparation is going well and the meal is served, all you hear is "Martha, you sure can cook!" and "This is great, Martha!" The Mary types, at this point, are less productive, less practical—and often less honored. But when all is not going well, or our hearts aren't in the right place, we Martha types can be jealous of the people who don't carry their weight in the kitchen and yet get what we want, namely affirmation from God. We know that kind of affirmation matters most.

At times in my life, prayer has been easy and consistent for me, but mostly it is a discipline I practice with mixed results. I wish it weren't true, but for me as an activist, prayer seems too passive, like it's doing nothing. Reading a book on prayer—now that's something! (I've done that a lot.) So when I see people for whom intimacy with God seems to be second nature, it can be irksome to me, and I can break out like Martha, "Lord, don't you care about me? I'm busy working for you." Of course, Jesus never actually asked me to work for him. In fact, the more I relate to Martha's attitude of "I'm busy working for Jesus," the more distant I feel I am from God.

One friend of mine who experiences a deep and familiar intimacy with God got to that point, in part, by going to a coffee shop once or twice a week, where she would enjoy her time in reading and prayer in a comfortable environment with a refreshing drink (usually tea) in her hand. She imagined herself on an extended coffee break with God. When I heard about this, my heart and head reacted oppositely. I thought, *That seems unnecessary, extravagant, easily distracting.* But I also reacted, *That sounds wonderful.* Rather than striking my usual posture of self-justification and critique, I tried it for myself. And so I've done this too, not weekly but monthly for a few hours. Usually I start my morning in an open church sanctuary, where I can pray and sing, and then retire to a French bakery café to enjoy a chocolate croissant and a glass of fresh orange juice. There I continue to pray, hear from God and write in my journal, uninterrupted by phone or e-mail.

The hope for us Martha types lies not in complaining about Mary but in joining her at Jesus' feet.

COMPARISON, TEMPERAMENT AND CULTURE

My friend Jody is naturally enthusiastic about everything she does. While she has been exposed to cynicism and sarcasm from her college classmates and other friends, she remains positive and upbeat about life. One of the ways her delightful personality (to know her really is to love her) exhibits itself is in her habit of speaking about her preferences—for music, food, entertainment, worship style and so on—as if they are statements of fact. You don't hear Jody say, "I didn't like that movie" or "That's my favorite flavor" but rather "That's the best flavor!" or "That was a terrible movie!" Jody is a natural evangelist because in part she is not content merely to express her opinions; she wants to win people to her position. "Try my flavor, just a taste, and you'll agree it *is* best!"

At some point in my friendship with Jody we talked about how she communicated her preferences, and it became a matter of gentle kidding with her, a shared insight activated by a brief, affectionate comment reminding her of her tendency to state preference as conviction. What we understood is that even in areas where her preferences were deeply and tenderly felt, as in her preference for liturgical forms of worship, other well-meaning people could hold equally strong but opposite preferences.

Consider and compare the following examples of hospitality:

- I recently enjoyed a meal and stayed overnight at some friends' house. The meal, preceded by sparkling cider and delightful hors d'oeuvres, was beautifully presented, if not elaborately so. My hosts presented me with a gift box of chocolates—a certain hit with me. After a warm evening of laughter and conversation that ranged from favorite movies and television shows to family plans for the upcoming holidays, I was shown to my guest room, including a TV/VCR combination that faced the bed. My hosts, knowing of my interest in a particular TV show, and knowing I had traveled on that evening and hadn't been able to see it, had the tape of the show ready for me to watch when I retired for the evening. When I finally fell asleep, I had been lavished in an extravagant hospitality of welcome and abundance.

- My wife and I have often invited people from church into our home for Sunday brunch of whatever we can throw together, often with no certainty of what we'll be able to provide at the time we make the offer. Upon our arrival at home after church, we'll bring our guests right into our kitchen and converse with them as we prepare the meal. The importance of our meal together is that we *are* together, which would not have happened at all without a willingness to have people in our home when we aren't necessarily at our best or most prepared. We could achieve our top priority—time with our friends—with spontaneity and flexibility.

Both of these versions of hospitality have their strengths. In the first, people are deeply honored and thoughtfully treated. In the second, people are casually welcomed but intimately invited in, valuing spontaneity and togetherness. In fact, many binary choices about how to pursue friendship or how to pursue God have their competing strengths and corresponding tradeoffs. It might have been possible for Martha to recognize that her choice—to cook the meal—made the evening possible while Mary's choice made it intimate. Martha could have experienced satisfaction in her choice without resentment of Mary's. Jesus was patient with Martha, repeating her name in a show of affection. He didn't condemn her choice, but he did say that Mary would be protected from Martha's jealousy.

As I get older the number of things I assign to the realm of preference grows and the number of things that I know that I know as truth seems to shrink. This, of course, is one of the benefits to moving out in a crosscultural friendship or ministry context. We learn that some things we always took as givens (language, food, expression, view of time, view of privacy and so on) turn out not to be so. Where we once might have thought of ourselves as flexible and open-minded, through crosscultural friendship we realize that the spectrum of open-mindedness is much broader than we had initially thought.[2]

My first ministry teammate, Jennie, and I experienced a common tension: I wanted to develop and stick to the plan, and she was never comfortable with the plan and always wanted to rethink it, based on her latest concerns and feelings. Growth in understanding our differences helped us to work together more effectively, without feeling constant, inexplicable tension with one another.[3]

Later, when I married Lisa and she and I worked closely in ministry, I began to experience the opposite tension. Lisa is even more planning-focused than I am, and her preference for putting things on the calendar made me seem to prefer spontaneity by comparison. Our partnership makes our family life work better than either preference without the balance of the other. She is able to nail things down and get them on the calendar, and I am able to help us remain flexible as circumstances change or plans don't work.

Table 10 contains a brief list of pairs of values that stand in tension with one another. Neither side of the paired values is more biblical or unequivocally preferred over the other. Both sides have their advantages and disadvantages. Yet they can produce tension in friendships, small groups, churches, organizations or workplace environments. Consider the list for your own preferences in comparison with those of a friend or spouse.

Table 10. Value and Preference Pairs

Breadth in relationships	Depth in relationships
Tradition and history	Creativity and innovation
Appreciation for authority and structure	Ability to think unconventionally and take risks
Planning	Spontaneity
Leadership	Responsiveness
Hospitality as elegant thoughtfulness	Hospitality as warm inclusiveness
Tasks and goals	Relationships and people
Being on time and following the schedule	Being present in the moment and being flexible
People honored for what they have done	People honored for who they are
People seen as unique individuals	People seen as members of their groups
Involvement in society	Prophetic stance toward society
Directness in communication	Attentive listening to posture and tone

The tendency to make preferences into absolutes is often a major contributor to any type of relational or organizational conflict. Making moral distinctions between such competing values can result in divorce, unreconciliation in families or between friends, church splits (even denominational splits) or severed business partnerships. We need an ability to navigate these value and preference distinctions in our relationships. With humility and tentativeness, we must remain open to the culture and values of another.

Listen to two friends, Ming and Jody, describe the development of their unlikely, crosscultural relationship:

Jody: When I first met Ming, I immediately assumed we had nothing in common. I certainly would never have predicted we would become close friends. Coming to college, in my mind, meant an opportunity to remake myself from a studious high school student into an outgoing, fun-loving party girl. Ming, on the other hand, seemed to be everything I wanted to distance myself from: quiet, studious, introverted.

Ming: When I first met Jody, she seemed in a different world. She was loud, exuberant and flirtatious—fitting my stereotype of a blonde, white girl from Texas. I remember going on an off-campus trip and Jody shouting, "I get shotgun!" before reaching the car. Jody's willingness to assert her desire to sit in the most comfortable seat was jarring to my Chinese American upbringing, where you never put your own wishes forward so obviously. I remember thinking, *Who does she think she is?*

Jody: Our junior year, at Ming's gracious initiative, we became friends. It was an intentional decision. She came to me and asked me if I would choose to invest in a friendship with her. No one had ever done that with me before, and though it felt a little awkward, I also felt honored to be chosen so deliberately.

   Ming and I both had to make a deliberate choice to be friends, because we are so different from each other. She is Asian American; I am white. She is introverted and fairly quiet; I am extroverted and (especially at that point in my life) somewhat loud. She is spontaneous and casual; I live by my schedule. She loses her keys once a week; I input my finances into Quicken religiously. But we both love Jesus, and we both recognized a need in our lives for the kind of friend that would walk with us on the journey of following him.

Ming: Our friendship grew and blossomed. We began to get together to pray and to share on a regular basis. Beyond the extrovert-introvert differences, as well as some different expectations from our white and Asian American upbringings, we found similar desires and struggles in our relationship with Jesus and our desire to follow him faithfully and well. I loved how passionately Jody wanted to know Jesus, and I respected choices that she was making to put him first. I liked how Jody had easy access to her emotions, and I found that it made it easier for me to be vulnerable in friendship as well. Underneath Jody's emotional openness, I saw real depth. Her strength made it easier for me to explore my own emotional needs.

One of the turning points in our growing friendship came when she started to date Curtis, who like me is second-generation Chinese American. As they wrestled with what it meant to date cross-ethnically, Jody grew more and more interested in entering with humility into Chinese American culture and experiences. This really helped our friendship to grow, as few white friends have expressed this much interest in wrestling with issues of race and ethnicity. Jody's willingness to try built trust and bridges that deepened our friendship.

Jody: Since that day our junior year, Ming and I have worked in ministry together, shared a room and been in each other's weddings. I have learned the value of knowing and loving someone very different from me. I have learned about honesty, reconciliation and crossing cultural barriers. We are friends for life. I am so thankful that Ming took the risk eleven years ago.

Ming: I continue to thank God for Jody as a friend who has been willing to challenge me, to stay faithful in friendship and to extend her commitment to me, to keep following Jesus in risky ways and to open her life to me in a vulnerable way. She has helped me in huge ways to know myself more, love Jesus more and value friendship more.

Competition and comparison can be the grating rub that dooms relationships and prevents intimacy. Or it can be part of the grit in the tumbler of our discipleship, wearing away at our pride and polishing our manners in friendship. It is a matter of perspective and commitment. Take some time to inventory your relationships and the places you experience conflict or tension. Thank God for the people in your life who are different from you and from whom you can learn.

FOR REFLECTION

As you read this chapter, it is likely that specific people and relationships came to mind. Take a minute to thank God for these people, even before considering the questions.

1. How have you seen competition in your friendships? What form does it usually take?

2. What specific gifts from God do your greatest "competitors" exhibit, for which you can begin to thank God and them?

3. How has a common commitment to ministry improved your friendships?

4. How have differences in values, temperaments and cultural background produced tension in your friendships? How have they produced growth and understanding?

10

Reconciliation and Forgiveness Among Friends

"It seems the deuce of a town," I volunteered, "and that's what I can't understand. The parts of it that I saw were so empty. Was there once a much larger population?"

"Not at all," said my neighbor. "The trouble is that they're so quarrelsome. As soon as anyone arrives he settles in some street. Before he's been there twenty-four hours he quarrels with his neighbor. Before the week is over he's quarreled so badly that he decides to move. Very likely he finds the next street empty because all the people there have quarreled with their neighbors—and moved. So he settles in. If by any chance the street is full, he goes further. But even if he stays, it makes no odds. He's sure to have another quarrel pretty soon and then he'll move on again. Finally he'll move right out to the edge of the town and build a new house. You see, it's easy here. You've only got to think a house and there it is. That's how the town keeps on growing."

C. S. LEWIS, THE GREAT DIVORCE

A familiar phone call went something like this: "Hey, Brian, I hope you get this message in time. I'm sorry, but I seem to have double scheduled. I won't be there at 12:30. I'll try to reach you later. What's next week look like?" I became adept at unraveling the double-schedule knot, because I found myself caught in it every few weeks. More than a few times I had actually *triple scheduled.*

I hold two competing values: I fill my life with activity, yet I prize being available for requests from friends. So sometimes I would agree to an opportunity before I knew whether I had the time. Fortunately, I had patient and understanding friends. (Perhaps they would be called "enablers" today.) But I came to see that my choices and conflicts had consequences for my friends and my friendships. I saw that I viewed my time as more important than my friends' time. I didn't simply need to apologize for the inconvenience of having to reschedule; I had to ask forgiveness that my yes was not yes. I had to acknowledge that I had sinned in my cavalier devaluing of my friends and their time.

◆ ◆ ◆

When I worked in Santa Cruz with the campus Christian fellowship there, we often played Ultimate Frisbee as a group on Saturday afternoons. The U.C. Santa Cruz campus was an especially beautiful setting for this. It had a wide expanse of green lawn laid down like a soft blanket between the redwoods of the campus above and Monterey Bay down below. One afternoon the play was especially competitive, and the women who were playing were excluded and ignored by some of the men. A few others noticed this and began to throw the Frisbee only to women, in an indignant attempt to even out the play. Eventually tempers flared. People quit playing.

Instead of sheepishly avoiding the issue or simply being embarrassed by what happened, we seized the teachable moment as a community. This situation became an opportunity for us as a fellowship to talk and decide how to respond to the situation. The women in the group could have simply decided not to participate in competitive games with the men. But they didn't. Rather, we all decided as a group to play by different rules and inclusive conventions. Two men who had lost their temper reconciled with one another. Instead of postponing group Ultimate Frisbee for a while, we announced another game the following Saturday. The play was more relaxed and more people were included. In one small way, people learned to value people more, and discipleship entered a new practical area of life.

◆ ◆ ◆

C. S. Lewis, in his novel *The Great Divorce*, conceives of a picture of hell very different from the medieval nightmare of flames and pitchfork-carrying devils. The essence of this place is the inability of anyone to get along with anyone else. Quarrels break out. Fights even with pistols are common, though no one is killed (this being hell). But people keep moving away from others, unable to abide human company for more than the briefest interval without angry incident. Lewis begins his fable with the disclaimer "This is a fantasy. . . . [It] is not even a guess or a speculation at what may actually await us."[1] Yet Lewis has, as usual, made a powerful conjecture. In a world devoid of God and his general grace to all people, no reconciliation or forgiveness is possible, and apart from reconciliation, relationships are impossible.

According to Jesus' teaching, healthy relationships require reconciliation. Jesus set the expectation for disciples when Peter asked him, "Lord, if another member of the church sins against me, how often should I forgive? As many as seven times?" (Matthew 18:21). Peter considered himself to be excessive here. The popular rabbinic teachings of the day usually required people to forgive only three times. Jesus set the standard much, much higher: "Not seven times, but, I tell you, seventy-seven times" (verse 22). In other words, "Don't even bother counting, Peter. Forgiveness is total. Forgiveness is absolute. Forgiveness is not optional." People in pursuit of God must be consummate forgivers.

Jesus told his disciples that they should not take lightly losing their tempers and calling their friends names in anger (Matthew 5:21-26). Jesus said calling someone "You fool" could make one "liable to the hell of fire" (verse 22). At this point, the entire assembly of disciples probably sat before him condemned. So Jesus then stressed the importance of reconciliation. It is more important to reconcile with a brother or sister whom you have sinned against than to continue on uninterrupted in your worship of God. The image of leaving the gift at the altar was a startling one: in the middle of a solemn ceremony, imagine disrupting the proceedings to leave and return hours or days later! Yet Jesus' teachings indicate a radical reordering of priorities.

A FOOL, A FIREBRAND AND A RECONCILER

Abigail, a responsible and resourceful woman of means during the time of David, provides a great model of the reconciliation teaching in Matthew 5, 7 and 18. The story of Abigail is told in 1 Samuel 25. The setting is the nation of Israel at a time when King Saul was on the throne but David had been anointed and was in hiding from Saul, who sought his life in a jealous rage. David had already spared Saul's life once, but it had benefited David little in generating goodwill with Saul.

David served Nabal, a wealthy sheep owner, by providing timely protection for his shepherds, for his shearers and for his huge flock. In return, David asked Nabal for some spare food for him and his men. Nabal, easily in a position to fulfill David's humble and reasonable request, not only declined but went out of his way to insult David. When David heard of this, he said, "Every man strap on his sword." We'll kill 'em all!

So when Abigail entered the story, she had an urgent situation on her hands. As a decisive and responsible representative of Nabal's household, she took responsibility for the unraveling mess and stepped in quickly. She prepared an ample gift and set it on donkeys to go ahead of her. This had to begin to soften David's flinty heart.

When Abigail saw David, she hurried and alighted from the donkey, and fell before David on her face, bowing to the ground. She fell at his feet and said, "Upon me alone, my lord, be the guilt; please let your servant speak in your ears, and hear the words of your servant. My lord, do not take seriously this ill-natured fellow, Nabal; for as his name is, so is he; Nabal is his name, and folly is with him; but I, your servant, did not see the young men of my lord, whom you sent.

"Now then, my lord, as the LORD lives, and as you yourself live, since the LORD has restrained you from bloodguilt and from taking vengeance with your own hand, now let your enemies and those who seek to do evil to my lord be like Nabal. And now let this present that your servant has brought to my lord be given to the young men who follow my lord. Please forgive the trespass of your servant; for the LORD will certainly make my lord a sure house, because my lord is fighting the battles of the LORD; and evil shall not be found in you so long as you live. If anyone should rise up to pursue you and to seek your life, the life of my lord shall be bound in the bundle of the living under the care of the LORD your God; but the lives of your enemies he shall sling out as from the hollow of a sling. When the LORD has done to my lord according to all the good that he has spoken concerning you, and has appointed you prince over Israel, my lord shall have no cause of grief, or pangs of conscience, for having shed blood without cause or for having saved himself. And when the LORD has dealt well with my lord, then remember your servant." (1 Samuel 25:23-31)

Abigail's appearance before David seems (to Western eyes anyway) like duplicity, even if honorable in motive. How could she claim she had any guilt here? "Upon me alone, my lord, be the guilt. . . . I, your servant, did not see the young men of my lord, whom you sent" (verses 24-25). How was she guilty?

Abigail claimed guilt because of her culture's way of looking at and valuing hospitality. As lady of the house, she should have seen David's men when they came, but attending to other duties interfered. If she had done as she ought, this conflict would never have arisen.

She took an ingenious approach. Was she *most* at fault for the bloodbath David had premeditated? Hardly. In fact, she brought a reproach to David: his intention was beneath him as anointed king and as one whom the Lord God had vindicated and protected. But her first word to him was of her guilt. She was willing to take the speck out of her own eye (Matthew 7:1-5), leaving David impressed enough to begin to see clearly to remove the battering ram from his. David praised her and her good sense, because she kept David's hands clean of killing innocent blood.

So how is Abigail a model for us? Table 11 outlines it in summary.

Table 11. Abigail as a Model for Us in Conflict

What did Abigail know? What did she do?	Application
Verse 17: Even before the conflict happened, she was understood to be a person of action who would not freeze up but would do the right thing. Her servant said, "Now therefore know this and consider what you should do."	Be ready for conflict. Think ahead and make commitments that you won't flee—for the sake of your friendships and for the sake of your (current or possible future) marriage. Otherwise, while you waffle you will gossip, complain, and become fearful and resentful.
Verse 18: She was willing to intercede on behalf of her husband. She was willing to enter in and make peace. She spared no expense of time or money. She understood the urgency.	Don't be casual about relational tension. Relational conflict is not always a matter of physical life and death, but Jesus made it clear that spiritual life and death hang in the balance (Matthew 5:21-26). Forgiveness and reconciliation are that important.
Verse 19: She sent someone on ahead of her as an advocate to make peace.	Find someone who knows both parties involved and who has a stake in a positive outcome (Matthew 18:16).
Verse 24: She put herself in the one-down, or subordinate, position. She didn't indulge in self-pity, saying, "It's not my fault this happened!" though in this case she was more in the right, while David was more culpable.	Choose not to make a sinful response even when you are wronged. Often the justification for a sinful response is the original sin in the first place. "He [or she] started it!"
Verse 27: She addressed the original complaint. She made amends.	Start not with your own complaint but with every way in which you were or could possibly have been in the wrong. Don't begin even with trying to be understood, which implies, "You were wrong to think that I was in the wrong." Agree first. Understand, and you may come to be understood.
Verse 31: She reminded David of the promises associated with his life and future—she called him to live up to what God was doing in him. She spoke of the future as if it were guaranteed: "When the LORD has dealt well with my lord, then remember your servant."	See the results of your actions clearly. Small choices now can make huge differences later— for you, for others, for your small group, fellowship or church, for nonbelievers.
She stopped speaking and trusted in God to calm David's anger, to save her life. She didn't flee the conflict but rode right into it.	Have faith that God will come through for you. Ultimately, it is not up to your words, gestures or schemes. Others' hearts are in God's hands. Pray to God, who softens hearts and restores friendships.

What were the results of Abigail's faithful choice? First, David was extraordinarily willing to learn from someone less powerful. David received a challenge from Abigail as a gift from God. Second, David's reputation and conscience was kept clear of guilt. This figured prominently in Abigail's speech to David. Third, God responded to bring justice to the situation beyond what was in David's power, through the death of Nabal. The result was the same—Nabal's death—but in this way it was an act of God's righteous judgment, not of David's vengeful anger. Fourth, through God's judgment of Nabal, David received the confirmation of God's work in his life and his advocacy for him. With the death of Samuel at the beginning of 1 Samuel 25, David might well have been feeling that he was without a sponsor-protector in Israel and still hotly pursued by Saul. This reassured David that God was still at work on his behalf.

The final result of Abigail's faithful choice to confront David was that David was so impressed with Abigail that, after Nabal's death, he proposed marriage to her. She ended up with a more reasonable husband, though admittedly it was David who received the better deal.

Let us learn from Abigail. She did all she could do and then trusted God for the rest. When it comes to reconciliation, all we can do is all we can do. Others' hearts are in God's hands, not ours.

THE POWER TO FORGIVE

The parable of the unforgiving servant (Matthew 18:21-35) provides insight regarding the relationship between forgiveness from God and our forgiveness of others. Jesus told a story of a servant who came before his master owing an enormous debt—in today's dollars, roughly equal to $1.5 bazillion.[2] The servant did not ask for mercy but simply for time, promising that he would pay it all back. The master had pity on him and forgave the entire amount. But the servant went out and immediately found a fellow servant who owed him the equivalent of four months' wages—a significant sum, but paltry by comparison. The servant demanded payment, and his fellow servant begged for a little time. The forgiven servant could not forgive, nor could he even spare time—he demanded immediate payment and threw his fellow servant in prison.

The climax to this parable comes in the following scene, when the master heard what had happened. He called the "forgiven" servant back to him and confronted him with the ingratitude and inequity of his behavior, and then he *unforgave* his debt! He threw the man into prison, waiting to repay his formerly forgiven debt. Jesus then summarized with a warning: "So my heavenly Father will also do to every one of you, if you do not forgive your brother or sister from your heart" (Matthew 18:35).

The idea of God unforgiving people's sin is, understandably, an uncomfortable one for us. Through the death of Christ, we who believe in him are forgiven, permanently, once and for all. How is it Jesus could tell a story involving a king who would unforgive his servant? When the servant entered the room to face his master the first time, he had racked up a huge debt, completely unpayable within the economic realities of the time. Yet he did not ask for forgiveness but simply for a little time to pay off his debt. He was completely out of touch with the magnitude of his trespass against his master. His request for extra time is pitiable in its absurdity.

Yet the master forgave him his debt. He should have walked out of that room dizzy and babbling like a baby! He should have discovered for the first time what life is like without a huge burden of debt weighing him down. Yet he left his master's presence in much the same frame of mind as he had entered it: he was thinking of ways he could scrape together enough money to pay back his debt. The man walked away and noticed his fellow servant. If he had experienced true forgiveness, his heart would have overflowed with compassion for his fellow servant. He would have said something like "Don't even mention that hundred-denarii debt to me again! I forgive you. I have been forgiven so much more by my master; what a great master we have!" Instead he demanded payment. He did not understand that his master had forgiven him.

So when the master recalled his unforgiving servant, he recognized that his offer of forgiveness had never been received by the ingrate, and so the offer was withdrawn. The man was thrown in prison, to waste away under the burden of his debt. Jesus said that this is how it is with God. God offers his children forgiveness, by the blood of Jesus, accessed through faith in him. In order to receive forgiveness, we must acknowledge the immensity of our sin. We must recognize our complete inability, apart from God's forgiveness, to erase the debt. The servant never acknowledged the scope of his sin nor humbled himself to ask for forgiveness, so he never lived as though he was forgiven. But if we receive God's forgiveness, we will necessarily become the kind of people who are forgiving. Unlike the servant, we become lighthearted and overjoyed with the freedom that comes from our own receiving of God's mercy. We will be like $10 million lottery winners, who will gladly give away $100 bills to our friends in celebration.

Essential to the act of forgiveness is the ability to have compassion for the one who has sinned against us. The unforgiving servant did not have such compassion on the other servant (though it would have been ridiculously easy, given recent events). When we see ourselves clearly as the bazillion-dollar sinners that we are, we will be better able to have compassion on people who, though their sin may deeply wound us, are themselves wounded victims as well. This compassion, the heart insight to match the head insight of the magnitude of our sin against God, enables us to see people who need our forgiveness as broken people and not simply as vicious victimizers.

HOW TO RECONCILE

Jesus also gave practical help regarding how to deal with conflict and how to pursue reconciliation. We have seen how Jesus modeled high standards in the relationships among his disciples. He also taught his disciples how to live with one another in their forgiveness.

Jesus gave instructions for any situation needing reconciliation in Matthew 5:23-26 and 18:15-20. In the first case, the offender approaches the offended; in the second, the offended is to approach the offender. In other words, whether you sinned or your friend sinned, if you realize that you are not reconciled, don't wait! Approach your brother or sister. In the second case, the offended makes the first overture alone. Hopefully, this takes care of it. The offender acknowledges sin, asks for forgiveness and receives it and fellowship between the two is restored. Only if the offender is not willing to repent are others to be involved, first two or three, then the entire church. At each point, hopefully, repentance and forgiveness is the result, not defensiveness and further distance between people.

Jesus also gave some guidance as to the tone and nature of the help we should offer others, especially as forgiveness and reconciliation are concerned. Jesus called his followers not to be judges or hypocrites but humble brothers and sisters to one another:

> Do not judge, so that you may not be judged. For with the judgment you make you will be judged, and the measure you give will be the measure you get. Why do you see the speck in your neighbor's eye, but do not notice the log in your own eye? Or how can you say to your neighbor, "Let me take the speck out of your eye," while the log is in your own eye? You hypocrite, first take the log out of your own eye, and then you will see clearly to take the speck out of your neighbor's eye. (Matthew 7:1-5)

This can help us as we think about people who have sinned against us. We so often want to place ourselves in the role of judge, proclaiming what is right and who is wrong! Even Jesus refused to be put in that position (Luke 12:14). If we live harsh, critical, judging lives toward others, those same judgments will come back around and others will judge and condemn us. We also are not to be hypocrites, willing to offer advice to others when our own lives display the same sin. We must first take the log out of our own eyes. We first scrutinize our own motivations, actions and words.

This may mean that we don't always tell a brother or sister when that one has sinned. Our first call might simply be to forgive, as Jesus said in Mark 11:25. As we grow in our understanding of our own sinfulness, then we will be in a position to help brothers and sisters in humility without hypocrisy.

Recently a friend asked me, "Are there any guidelines as to when to confront and when just to forgive?" It is not an easy question. Consider the complexity of situations: power dynamics, strength of prior relationship, type of sin, awareness of the one who sinned. In general, I'm an advocate of direct communication rather than avoidance, but it seems one rule needs to be taken seriously: Do what you do to strengthen the relationship and bring it closer to health. Silent grace may foster health. Often frank and honest conversation, from the person ready to forgive, will help. But this is a messy business, and clearly no single strategy or simple equation will work in every case. A truth-at-any-costs strategy can easily backfire, heightening rather than relieving tension.

Clare and Tim, college-educated European Americans, had chosen to live and work in a poor border community in Mexico. One time they were thrown out of a party for some close friends of theirs. A visiting relative of their friends had lived and worked in Los Angeles for many years and had been mistreated and put down by many white people. She was drunk that night, and Clare and Tim received the brunt of everything that had happened to her. They left feeling terrible—not personally responsible but realizing that a cultural situation they were part of was responsible for her pain.

When they saw this woman at church again, she didn't remember or was too embarrassed to acknowledge what had happened. They spoke kindly to each other, and Tim and Clare decided simply to forgive her and move on. Was this a missed opportunity for deeper intimacy and understanding? Or did their decision most reflect the need for grace and humility in the face of intractable crosscultural conflict? It is difficult to second-guess the choice of this young couple trying tangibly to demonstrate the gospel.

Just as it is difficult to navigate reconciliation from the offended person's perspective, being a softhearted offender is perhaps even more difficult. One of the most common responses in a Matthew 18 situation, when people approach us regarding sin, is defensiveness. We so want to be righteous that our first instincts are to deny that we did anything wrong or to place blame elsewhere.

When I was in the Yucatán peninsula in Mexico for a summer, I discovered an interesting linguistic artifact. Whenever I or anyone else broke, spilled or dropped something, I would hear someone explaining with the words *se cayo* or *se rompio*. I was new at the Spanish language and missed most of the nuances of communication. But I soon figured out that what people were saying could be directly translated, "It fell" or "The milk spilled itself" or "It broke itself." In fact, the culturally correct way to talk about little tragedies like this was to place the blame on the object that fell, broke or spilled rather than to place blame on the human agent involved. (What a happy invention, a linguistic graciousness and propensity to pardon!) Though the English language does not have such a helpful linguistic feature, a tendency to scan the scene for worthy objects of blame is innate to us all.

In fact, the tendency to place blame externally to ourselves is as old as humanity. Consider, for example, Adam and Eve when confronted by God for their sin in the garden. Adam blamed Eve for his disobedience and indirectly blamed God for making Eve. In her turn, Eve blamed the snake for tricking her (Genesis 3:12-13).

Even the Pharisees had an elaborate system set up such that their sin could never be traced back to themselves. "Defilement" (their word for sin) was usually traced to "unclean" cups, "unclean" hands, "unclean" food, "unclean" marketplaces or "sinners" (unclean people). Defilement always had as its source something external to themselves.

Jesus confronted this attitude directly in Mark 7:1-23. The Pharisees asked Jesus, "Why do your disciples not live according to the tradition of the elders, but eat with defiled hands?" (verse 5). Jesus harangued on the "traditions of the elders" for a while, but then he addressed the question. He said, "There is nothing outside a person that by going in can defile, but the things that come out are what defile" (verse 15). He elaborated further with his disciples,

"Do you not see that whatever goes into a person from outside cannot defile, since it enters, not the heart but the stomach, and goes out into the sewer?" (Thus he declared all foods clean.) And he said, "It is what comes out of a person that defiles. For it is from within, from the human heart, that evil intentions come: fornication, theft, murder, adultery, avarice, wickedness, deceit, licentiousness, envy, slander, pride, folly. All these things come from within, and they defile a person." (Mark 7:18-23)

Fundamental to our ability to reconcile is our ability to acknowledge our own sin. The Pharisees' system hermetically sealed their lives from sin, or so they thought. By making it impossible for them even to acknowledge their own sin, let alone repent, their system isolated them from any chance they would have to be forgiven. Today we don't have cups and food to blame, but we can blame all sorts of things for our unkindness or thoughtlessness or unfaithfulness. We blame the traffic or the weather or a lack of sleep. We accuse neighbors, spouses and bosses. Defensiveness was not a problem just for the Pharisees; it is intrinsic to the human condition. But Jesus pointed the way to a solution. Sin comes out of our own hearts, so when we sin, we must look there first.

I have had a number of close friends, especially (but not limited to) my wife, who have been willing to approach me about issues of sin in my life. Often it has involved something I have said, a defensive posture I have taken or a verbal attack I have made. My standard approach to such conversations used to be to defend, defend, defend . . . and then, perhaps, finally, to give in. The result was that I was able to see and acknowledge my sin, and in fact I was usually grateful for my friends and their "tough love." Yet the grueling process, the resistance and my defensiveness, cost my friends dearly. Oh, how I made them pay! All for the privilege of being a good friend to me.

My own breakthrough came when I recognized this pattern and noticed that I was risking my friendships for the sake of my pride. In more sober moments, I understood that these kinds of friendships were far more valuable than the few minutes of pride I had at risk.

If I am to welcome someone who values relationship with me enough to seek reconciliation, I must have as my fundamental posture the recognition that I am a sinner, that out of my heart come all sorts of evil. If this is my self-understanding, then when confronted in love, I can easily respond, "Yes, I did that. In fact, this is just the tip of the iceberg. I have done much worse. Please forgive me." This takes the sting out of the confrontation and allows us to embrace the process of reconciliation, not simply chafe under it.

KEEPING SHORT ACCOUNTS

Recently I spoke on the topic of reconciliation and forgiveness, and I asked the group a few questions. I asked, "How many of you have asked someone's forgiveness in the past month?" Just a few hands went up in the medium-sized crowd. Then I asked, "How many of you have sinned against someone in the past month?" Of course, as people began to understand my point, they all raised their hands. I asked them what I ask now, why was there such a contrast? We know we are sinners. If someone asked me, "Are you a sinner?" my theological convictions and my practical experience would converge: "Yes, of course." But when confronted with my sin, I fear the *particular* acknowledgment it requires. I want to claim my innocence.

And frankly, often others don't want me to acknowledge my guilt any more than they want to acknowledge their own guilt. People would rather say, "It was nothing," than to say, "You are right—you did hurt me. But I gladly forgive you." If they don't have to acknowledge my sin, then they aren't confronted with their own. So our standards for relationships drop to a mutual minimum level. We sin and are sinned against and say nothing.

This is not a picture of a wholehearted pursuit of God. This is capitulation to the low relational standards of our society. Jesus presented to Peter a relationship in which forgiveness is asked for and received seventy-seven times! He described a quality of relationship unknown to most of us today.

One phrase that fills out the image of a seventy-seven-sin relationship is the advice to "keep short accounts." If we have deep, consistent relationships (not five-minutes-over-coffee-and-doughnuts-after-the-worship-service relationships), then we will be sinning against each other often. That's OK; that's expected. In contrast, rather than letting those sins pile up, keeping track of them like little IOUs, we instead deal with sin as soon as we are cognizant of it. Hence we keep short accounts, not letting the debts build up but wiping the slate clean through repeated mini-reconciliations. Since we hardly expect to go through the day without sinning (though we strive for that), why not grow in our expectation that we will need to ask for forgiveness on a daily basis? Especially this will be true for people we live with: spouses and family members, roommates, coworkers.

We will spend the most time with people closest to us, and therefore we will sin against them more. In chapter six I spoke of the value of road trips. This is one of the chief benefits of a mission trip or vacation together: we are given chances to rub against each other to the point where reconciliation and forgiveness can become a normal part of our relationships.

I began this chapter acknowledging that I had a problem with double scheduling and repeatedly had to ask to reschedule with people, often at the last minute. Recently an old college friend read that opening story. When she read it, she told me how familiar it was. She spoke of a time when she had expected to meet me and did, only to realize that I had triple scheduled, with others waiting also. Her disappointment intensified when she realized she was third priority. Hearing her recount her version was much more painful than my own confessional telling, though she told it with affection and grace, evidence of a long-ago forgiveness.

The only way I was able to get out of this habit was to stop seeing it simply as a mistake, an understandable oversight in need of correction or perhaps even a quirk of my personality, a tic that made me lovable to my friends. I needed to see it as sin, another painful example of my willingness to view my time as more important than that of my friends, my not treating people as I would wish to be treated. Once I began asking for forgiveness for double scheduling, rather than simply apologizing, I began taking it seriously and I noticed a change. I double scheduled less frequently, because I was more careful with my schedule and more thoughtful with my friends. Dealing with my sin as sin helped me to become a more faithful friend.

For those of us who serve as leaders in some setting, Christian or secular, we must embrace opportunities to seek reconciliation between us as leaders and the members of groups we lead. As we examine and confess our own sin in the presence of the group, we can model humility and nondefensiveness. The results of doing so are often unexpected. Leaders are tempted to dig in through defensiveness, perhaps fearing a loss of face or a weakening of their authority. Yet when leaders refuse to acknowledge obvious sin and error, they *do* lose trust and their authority *is* weakened, especially when they are patently in the wrong. On the other hand, they will be honored in the long run if they are willing to humble themselves by acknowledging sin and failure. The biblical injunction should guide us: "Humble yourselves therefore under the mighty hand of God, so that he may exalt you in due time" (1 Peter 5:6).

We recognize our need for God and for forgiveness, not just from God but also from those who have been sinned against. This experience will take us a long way with people who have come to trust us through our servanthood and have allowed us to lead them into a greater discipleship. This will remain in their minds a powerful model of humility and repentance. It is also one of the most difficult things for a leader to do.

It is crucial to recognize that we do not avoid or work through these times of conflict as quickly as possible so as to return to a "normal" state of relating. Conflict, tension and the resolution of true reconciliation can be embraced as some of the central activities of the group as a group.

Recently I caught myself mid-sentence. I had begun to say, "I think the most logical way to do it would be—" and then I stopped. We were talking in a group of twelve about how to organize a set of values we'd put up on the board. This was not a case of right versus wrong, merely shades of preference. I continued, "Let me rephrase that. One possible way to do it would be . . ." My catching myself was greeted with affectionate and knowing chuckles as we all were familiar with my overbearing rhetoric and its consequences on group process.

In fact, I often sin against people in group discussions because of my impatience or rhetorical bite. This is an area of struggle in my life—God is sanctifying me, but he is not done yet, obviously! This has taken a toll in the groups I have led, but never more so than when I remain obdurate and unrepentant. God's primary work in me has been to shorten the amount of time it takes for me to see and acknowledge my sin in the midst of others. As a result, some of my most powerful and trust-building experiences with groups have been when I as the leader have had to ask the group's forgiveness. Often I am able to see only through my tears of repentance the love and trust of my friends as they extend forgiveness and mercy to me.

FOR REFLECTION

1. How attuned are you to a need to reconcile in your relationships? In what healthy ways and what unhealthy ways have you tended to respond to sin in your friendships?

2. Plan a conflict resolution process with someone you are in conflict with now or typically experience conflict with:

   - Name a current or typical conflict and the familiar circumstances.

   - What will be the result if things are not addressed? In the short term? In the long term?

   - Is there anyone who can act as advocate or intermediary, someone you both trust?

   - What would it take on your part to address the original cause of tension?

- How can you put yourself in the one-down, or subordinate, position? To what can you confess without requiring prior initiative on the part of the other?

- What would it cost you to take the initiative in this relationship?

- What do you need to receive from God if this is to end well? For what will you need to pray?

- What good will come if this conflict is dealt with speedily, in humility?

3. Practice saying words that actually ask for forgiveness, not simply acknowledging that something is wrong. "I am sorry I _____. I need your forgiveness. Please forgive me."

11

Jesus' Vision for the Company of Friends

Dispel my illusions then by telling the truth; for truths of this sort are very rarely told.

I wish that we five, who now love each other in Christ, could make some such arrangement. Just as others have, in recent times, been meeting together in secret to plot wickedness and heresies against His Majesty, so we might arrange to come together now and then in order to dispel one another's illusions, and to advise one another of ways in which we could improve ourselves and be more pleasing to God. For no one knows himself so well as those who observe him, provided they do so lovingly and with the wish to do him good.

ST. TERESA OF ÁVILA

In retrospect, I realize I should have noticed the clues. My wife encouraged me to get some time with my friend Peter on a Saturday afternoon, usually prime family time with Lisa and my kids, Mark and Becca. My friend Peter had asked if we could meet his friend at the local YWCA. He had told me 1:00 p.m., but we were running late and he didn't seem to care. As we walked up the walkway to the YWCA, I saw signs for an event that was happening, with balloons. I did not read the signs.

So when we arrived at the Y, I expected to meet a friend of Peter's, a woman I didn't know. Instead I met fifty friends of mine, gathered to celebrate my fortieth birthday. (The party was a few days early, so I wasn't expecting it.)

Several friends had come from California; others from all around

New England. My wife, with lots of help from others, had pulled off a great surprise and honor. Several friends staged a game show with the questions focusing on facts from my screwy life and odd personality. Several people spoke a few kind words, and then we continued to talk together and enjoy one another around festive food.

◆　◆　◆

Once again I'd like to consider Aristotle's insights regarding motivations for friendship. Ideally, friends (1) enjoy one another, (2) are useful to one another and (3) share a common commitment to "the good." We could extend Aristotle's insights to address healthy marriages, which above all need to be characterized as robust friendships thus described.[1]

Aristotle's insights extend beyond individual friendships, however. They also describe fundamental prerequisites for a healthy community, a company of friends in pursuit of God. Aristotle's three points show up as the fundamental prerequisites of community: fellowship, accountability and partnership.

In this chapter we examine the nature of the company of friends as Jesus depicted it in the Gospels. Jesus used several images of inclusion to describe the nature and goal of the community he began. These images emphasize different ways the community relates to the world, to God and to itself as well as the ways members of the community relate to one another.

Community speaks of commitments a group of people hold in common. *Fellowship* entails common life, a sheer enjoyment of time spent together. Jesus illustrated this aspect of community with the image of a party, a feast or banquet. *Accountability* requires common commitments to integrity, reconciliation and mutual concern and indicates that these commitments mean something, for the good of each and all. Jesus illustrated this aspect of community with the image of family. *Partnership* involves common mission, an outward focus that is not in competition with community but is instead an essential outgrowth of it. Jesus illustrated this aspect of community with the twin images of salt and light.

THE PARTY

Jesus was (as we have seen) comfortable at parties. And even more remarkable to our contemporary minds, partyers were comfortable with Jesus. His first miracle, at the wedding feast in Cana, was the production of 150 gallons or so of wine, no small endorsement of the revelry involved. Jesus was accused of being a drunk and a glutton. This was a charge to which he did not admit, but it had basis in his willingness to enjoy the parties he attended. Jesus taught the Pharisees how to throw a proper party. He did not teach them not to have parties, merely that they were going about partying in the wrong way (Luke 14:7-14). In fact, if the Pharisees threw parties as Jesus directed, they would have been in for some wild times!

Jesus also taught people the importance of the party known as the kingdom of God. In Luke 14:15-24 Jesus described a party that the invited guests did not value. They gave all sorts of excuses rather than come when called. The host of the party was determined to have a full house, so he invited random people in the streets and highways and even told his servants to compel people, so determined was he that none of his original guests were to be able to come late to his feast.

The most powerful picture of the party is given in Luke 15. The setting for the telling was, in fact, a party. Jesus was quite obviously celebrating with the tax collectors and "sinners," and the Pharisees were all standing around grumbling. The setting was probably a semi-public courtyard setting where the Pharisees (certainly not invited guests) were able to hang around and view the proceedings, at least enough to draw their own conclusions.

So Jesus turned from the party scene and told the Pharisees several parables, all relating to the question in the minds of these critics: "Why does this man receive sinners and eat with them?" Jesus' first two parables, of the lost sheep and the lost coin, focus on the one who goes out and finds the lost item of value. Both the shepherd and the woman find their missing treasure, and both respond in joy and celebration. Jesus summarized, "There is joy in the presence of the angels of God over one sinner who repents" (Luke 15:10).

Jesus was able to see a reality that the Pharisees could not. The Pharisees looked at the partyers and saw sinners. Jesus looked at them and saw a cause for rejoicing. He saw them in the process of turning back to God. The context for this repentance was not a dirgelike procession of penance but an exultant expression of joy. Jesus partied with his sinner friends because to do anything else was to miss the reality of the situation.

Jesus finished his two stories, but the Pharisees still were not moved. So he told them another story. He told them the story of the extravagant father with two rebellious sons.

The rebellion of the younger son is well known. He told his father, "Dad, you are as good as dead to me. Give me my share of the inheritance now." His father, amazingly, complied. The son left home and his money soon left him. He wound up in poverty and hunger, feeding pigs but not eating as well as they were. Then he realized, "My dad's servants are better fed than I am now. I could go ask my dad for a job. No mercy—from here on out I'll work for what I get." So he returned home.

He did not expect what he found. From the day the son left, his father had habitually looked out the picture window and down the road, always wondering when his son might return. This day, the father squinted and stared out the window at a filthy person approaching the house, until he could see through the grime and scruff that it was indeed his son. He wasted no time. He ran out to meet his son and embraced him. The son tried to choke out his prepared speech, offering a fair work-for-hire proposition, but his father cut him off. His father then cranked up the makings for a huge party. The fatted calf (the choicest animal) was to be killed, and everything else in proportion was to be made ready. The party began as the younger son, bewildered, was led into the house like visiting royalty.

The rebellion of the older son was more subtle, but more perverse. This son never left home, never cashed in his inheritance, never disobeyed his father. Yet this son, too, was in rebellion. When he heard about his brother's arrival, he protested and refused to join the festivities. His father begged him to come and celebrate. The older son said, "Look,

I have served you for so long, and never disobeyed you once, and what have I received? Not even a goat to have a barbecue for me and my friends! But this son of yours comes back, who wasted your hard-earned money on prostitutes, and you want me to party with you? No way!"

The older son's speech reveals his own form of rebellion against his father. Both sons had the same problem. They both viewed their father as a harsh taskmaster. The younger son left home, living out his wishes to throw off his slave status and find freedom. The irony, of course, is that he only then realized what true slavery was like. He came back, offering to enter the household as a servant, but his father treated him like a beloved son. But the older son never thought of his father as anything other than a taskmaster. Even when his father had come out to beg him to join the party, the older son would not let go of his image of his father. He simply added "unjust" to his prior understanding of his father as demanding and unappreciative.

It is interesting that Jesus never finished his story. The last line is the father's invitation to the older son to come and join the party. This invitation is the invitation Jesus offered the Pharisees: "Come, join the party of the kingdom of God!" Jesus invited the Pharisees to join in the celebration of the reconciliation of people to God. The question that remains at the end of the story is, will any of these uptight Pharisees loosen up and come on in and join the party?

Though the story seems to put the younger son in a bad light, the older son was worse off. The younger son, by virtue of his participation in the party, came to see his father as something other than a slave driver. He came to understand firsthand the generosity of his father. He experienced grace, and this transformed his relationship with his father. It allowed him to enjoy partying with his dad.

But the older son never experienced grace. He wanted a goat but thought he had to work for it! His dad just said, in effect, "My dear son, all that I have is yours. You could simply have asked for a goat!" But the son didn't want to be given a goat; he wanted to earn it. The older son, like the younger son in his original plan to return, wanted to work for what he received from his father. But his father's grace was not available by working for it. The father gave out of his love and generosity and joy.

This, then, is the picture of the gathering of God's people: a giant party, thrown in celebration of all of us sinner types who have turned around and have embraced the generous grace of our Father God. There are many people who prefer to work for God than to receive freely from him. These people will resent the notion of the party because they resent the notion of grace. Grace robs them of the chance to work and be compensated for their labors. Grace robs them of their pride. And yet to these Jesus still holds out an invitation. "Come, join the party. Lay down your shovel. Stop working for me. Lay aside your pride and independence. Come, eat, drink, enjoy my abundance."

This is the flavor of the community of God's people. The pursuit of God in the company of friends is not a grim obedience but a joyful celebration. God administers grace to his people through the ability of a community to enjoy and play with, honor and celebrate one another.

You may have noticed in a church small group that people are motivated to attend for a variety of reasons. Some come because they want to learn more about the Bible or to grow in their relationship with God. Some come because they like the intimate setting in which to worship and pray with a few friends. And some come simply because they want to get to know, or continue to be with, some close friends.

I have had a tendency to be impatient with people who seem to value most highly the social dimension of a group, and this extends back to my time in youth group when I was a teen. When Scripture study gave way to game or movie nights, it always seemed less valuable than what we were there to accomplish, which (by my reckoning) was to learn things about God and the Bible.

I no longer think this way, or at least, when I do find myself thinking this way, I resist or repent. I recognize that the fellowship component of church or a small group or any company of friends is just as crucial as the learning and worshiping components. I don't want to focus on learning about good relationships as an alternative to actually experiencing them. A small group without fellowship in its diet would be as inviting as that elder son, standing aloof from the party, continuing to till the soil long after the band music had begun to play. "We *had* to celebrate," the father said. Take him at his word; we still have to.

THE FAMILY

Jesus used the image of the family of God to illustrate the nature of the community he was establishing. The parent of this family is God, who as a perfect Father knows how to give good gifts to his children. God is not prone to outbursts of random rage, like an alcoholic parent. God is consistent and trustworthy, better by far than "evil" human fathers (Luke 11:11-13). But we enter into the family of God not simply with a relationship to our Father God but also with relationships to other brothers and sisters. Jesus spoke of this in Mark 3:31-35:

> [Jesus'] mother and his brothers came; and standing outside, they sent to him and called him. A crowd was sitting around him; and they said to him, "Your mother and your brothers and sisters are outside, asking for you." And he replied, "Who are my mother and my brothers?" And looking at those who sat around him, he said, "Here are my mother and my brothers! Whoever does the will of God is my brother and sister and mother."

Jesus defined a new type of family. Birth into this family differs from natural birth. Membership comes by the will, that is, by the choice to do the will of God. Yet for those who make this choice, they enter into a new set of relationships, with Jesus and with one another, as brothers and sisters.

Jesus made a similar promise to those who heard him speak about the difficulty that people with wealth will have in entering the kingdom of God. He said afterward, in response to Peter's question: "Truly I tell you, there is no one who has left house or brothers or sisters or mother or father or children or fields, for my sake and for the sake of the good news, who will not receive a hundredfold now in this age—houses, brothers and sisters, mothers and children, and fields, with persecutions—and in the age to come eternal life. But many who are first will be last, and the last will be first." (Mark 10:29-31).

He promised a multiplicity of brothers and sisters and mothers and children to those who left behind allegiance to their earthly families and staked their claim with the family of God. This astonishing promise became reality for these first disciples. Jesus' promise remains intact for us today, describing a reality in which we participate.

The challenge and the countercultural nature of this way of thinking about the people of God is lost on us who are used to hearing Christians refer to one another as "brother" or "sister." That, combined with a decreasing set of expectations regarding the importance and the role of the family, dilutes the power of Jesus' image of the family. Therefore, we must recover the biblical strength of God's family as an experience of community. The original role of the family is to teach humans how to relate with other individuals and in society. Likewise, the family of God teaches young followers of Jesus how to relate to their brothers and sisters. Theoretical, deductive and detached teaching cannot communicate this. It requires practical, actual involvement in the tangible family where God is Father and Jesus is our older brother.

People in a healthy family make and keep commitments to one another. They are helpful to each other, seeing the success of one as the success of all. Small failures to keep the integrity of the family are noted, repented of and forgiven, not swept aside, ignored or accumulated until the breaking point is reached.

When Jesus taught his disciples about forgiveness and reconciliation, he spoke of how to treat "brothers."[2] Jesus encouraged his disciples to reconcile quickly with their brothers. He challenged his disciples not to be hypocritical judges of one another, studying each other to find the minute specks. Rather, he challenged them to self-criticism and then encouraged them to be loving brothers with one another, helpful but not critical. He told them how to reconcile with their brothers as well as how often. Obviously, Jesus considered sibling love to be critical in the new family. There is no room for gossip, resentment and festering un-forgiveness in the family of God.

The family, as Jesus described it, is a compelling, if perhaps unfamil-iar, safe haven. It is not a place where the truth is not spoken; rather, it is a place where people can be trusted with the truth. We speak about things that we see, and we receive the words spoken to us as truth spo-ken in love.

> Take care, brothers and sisters, that none of you may have an evil, unbelieving heart that turns away from the living God. But exhort one another every day, as long as it is called "today," so that none of you may be hardened by the deceitfulness of sin. For we have become partners of Christ, if only we hold our first confidence firm to the end. (Hebrews 3:12-14)

The writer of Hebrews, using the same family image, was speaking about a set of relationships where people are speaking to one another about the dangers of sin, calling each other to repentance and clarity for the sake of their hearts. The chief strategy seems to be one of debunking the "deceitfulness of sin." This involves helping people to combat sin, not by simply telling them, "Don't do that," but by helping them see the ways that sin has deceived them and tricked them into nursing attitudes that, given time, could cause them to turn away from the living God. This is not a holier-than-thou attitude, but neither is it a it-is-none-of-my-business attitude. The writer of Hebrews, knowing the stakes, was asking people to be involved in their family members' lives in this man-ner in a daily ("as long as it is called today") way.

This level of participation in one another's lives is rare. The writer of Hebrews described this as a daily thing, but in many churches it isn't even practiced annually. Imagine the announcement coming at church, "To-day we are celebrating Exhortation Sunday, the point in our church year when we get to tell each other what we really think! During the greeting time this morning, make sure you tell each person you speak with at least one negative thing you've thought about them but never said."

If not that, what would it look like? Daily truth speaking begins with an understanding that we are all susceptible to the deceitfulness of sin.[3] Sin gets into our hearts and makes promises that it cannot deliver. Each of us has a heart that is susceptible to some deceptions and relatively immune to others. This is why we need each other to help us debunk the lies and reject the false promises of sin.

Our role as family members is to help each other see through the lies. A family member who isn't susceptible to a particular sin can often help others spot its deception and in return receive the help he or she needs from others. It is a little like the game of debunking the promises television commercials make to sell their products; spelling out the lie is most of the work of debunking it.

My wife and I serve one another in this way quite often. I am particularly susceptible to impatience, and she is prone to anxiety. She helps me to see that my impatience is founded on the deception that what I want to do is always urgent and important, trumping other concerns and other people. I am able occasionally to help my wife to see that her anxiety springs from a false belief that worry is like prayer—"God responds if I am truly worried enough." We can help one another by seeing each other clearly with compassion and reminding each other of the truth.

Imagine helping our friends see the lies they have been lulled into believing, without being or sounding superior, because we know we are susceptible to believing in similar lies. Loving frankness, speaking the truth in love and exerting gentle influence is what we are striving for.

Yet loving frankness is the exact opposite of how the classic dysfunctional family is described today:

> Families learn to tolerate the hurtful. They come to expect it. They learn to discount their own perceptions and their reality. They succumb to the dysfunctional family rules, Don't Talk, Don't Feel, Don't Trust, Don't Think, Don't Question. All in an attempt to cope.[4]

I believe the ultimate solution for the dysfunctions of families today is a functional family with God as Father, with Jesus as older brother and with all members empowered by the Holy Spirit to live according to the relationship between Jesus and the Father (John 17:20-23). Yet that is like saying the solution to our problems is to get rid of them. How do we get from where we live to the life Jesus offers?

As I began to hear and read more about the problems of families, I encountered a new word: *reparenting*. This describes a self-conscious process that a counselor or therapist might enter into with a patient. The patient might be struggling with self-esteem, inability to trust others or a deep-seated need to be needed. These needs, or others, can be traced back to a deficiency in the parenting the patient received as a child. The dysfunctional background is addressed, and hopefully healed, through the counselor entering into a parental role, reparenting through consistency and unconditional positive regard.

As a friend, I do not see my role as that of a therapist. Rather, if any word would be appropriate to describe the process of a group of people becoming family for one another, it is not *reparenting* but *refamilying*. I personally am cautious and skeptical about entering into a parental role, but I expect God pursuers will experience the fellowship of a small group as something of a family. Ideally it is in this family where functional means of communication and commitment are relearned and the dysfunctional patterns are unlearned or corrected.

The perspective of healing and growth in the company of friends takes the pressure off any single relationship. The healing process happens not simply in a single relationship between mature Christian and new Christian but more broadly in the web of relationships of the community. A leader brings his or her skills into a group, not as the new father or mother, but simply as one of the many brothers or sisters of the new family. The Christian community has the potential to be a surrogate family in which people build a healthy foundation of identity and security in the love of God and are called toward love of God and of others.

As I use the image of refamilying, this is not meant to indicate an emphasis on pulling people out of their biological families. Often cults with high demands of obedience and loyalty force their new members to cut all ties with family members and other close friends outside the community. This is not what I'm describing here. In fact, through this refamilying process people will often become more loyal and loving members of their biological families.

Entering into the family of God will mean that people will grow in their ability to love people in healthy ways. As members of the family of God begin to learn more healthy and functional patterns of communication and relationship, they will deeply desire open communication with their biological families. Of course, these disciples hope that their family members will eventually enter the family of disciples and that they, too, will experience the freedom and healing found in Jesus. Yet, to some unhealthy families, an injection of truth, honesty, open feelings and efforts at real reconciliation may be threatening and appear disloyal. However, the opposite is true. For these people, their love for their families motivates their risks at confrontation with family members. Their unwillingness to relate in the same unhealthy patterns is an act of redemptive love.

I've been in several small groups where it seemed that the unwritten rules included "Don't rock anyone's boat." When people shared about their lives, they got polite nods, questions focused on background information and promises to pray, or they heard encouragements. They didn't get what they needed.

◆ ◆ ◆

The small-group members were stunned. They had just heard Ron say, "I have decided I need to go out and buy a Porsche 911 Targa." Ron had earlier spoken of his recent layoff from work. At that point his fellow small-group members were prepared to speak encouragement and pray for him. Now they simply didn't know what to say. He had a fine automobile, probably a $30,000 vehicle in good working order. But his self-diagnosis was that his personal crisis wasn't anything that the purchase of an $80,000 automobile wouldn't solve. The small-group members were shocked and silent.

The evening ended with Ron's words hanging over the group. Ron didn't get prayed for, but neither did people talk to him about their concerns. Ron and Julie were committed members of the small group and the church. If the group members had spoken up, they might have asked, "Ron, how are you feeling about the loss of your job?" "Help us understand the connection between your loss and the desire to purchase a Porsche." "How have you and Julie both talked about what is next for you as a couple and family?" "How does the purchase of a new car fit in at this time?" But none of these questions were asked, nor any of a dozen more.

Perhaps this was all for the best. Asking questions like this gets personal very fast. Ron might have felt hurt, having his choices and priorities subtly (if not explicitly) challenged. Others in the group who drove expensive cars (though no one drove a Porsche!) might have felt the heat of unwanted scrutiny. So they left, unwilling to speak to Ron about it. In each of the cars driving home that night, except for Ron's, the group members were talking about Ron's nutty idea, that disappointment and uncertainty can be medicated by an outlandish car purchase. However, they never mentioned it to Ron.

This group did learn one lesson that night. They learned that, despite the theory of their being a small group for one another, they couldn't really rely on one another to speak the truth. Or even to ask about the truth. Or perhaps even to care. They learned that they could expect gossip, not truth spoken in love. They could expect niceness but not wisdom. This incident taught, or more likely reinforced, the unwritten rules of communication in the small group, at great cost to the group and to everyone in it.

◆   ◆   ◆

Consider a few common attitudes and try to identify some of the many strategies sin uses to dupe us into adopting these destructive states of the heart. Table 12 illustrates how we might think through both the lies of sin and a few Scripture references to help point a way through to faith. Both the lists of the deceptions of sin and the responses of faith are meant to be illustrative, not exhaustive. As you read the list, you may consider which of these attitudes of the heart are typical for you and which deceptions carry the most attraction.

Table 12. Debunking the Lies of Sin

Attitude of the Heart	Sin's Deception: What Is Promised?	Faith Provides Power over the Deception
Bitterness or resentment: harboring a grudge or an unforgiving spirit.	To forgive will cost you some of the power you have over the person. You have the right to complain, to be the victim, to pity yourself. You should protect yourself—the person might do it again. You will be spared the effort of reconciliation.	Understand how we've been forgiven by God (Matthew 6:12; 18:21-35). Love your enemies (Matthew 5:43-48). The punishment for others' sin is in God's hands (Romans 12:19-21).
Regret: a belief that a mistake we made in the past virtually rules out a happy future. A re-evaluation of our life and choices in the face of suffering.	You have made a choice that will be irrevocable: you will never be able to be in God's will again. Joy, happiness, hope and love are placed permanently out of the realm of possibility for you. Others may experience these things, but you never will.	God works through all things (Genesis 50:20; Romans 8:28). We are "more than conquerors." Things that we thought were stumbling blocks prove to be stepping stones with faith (Romans 8:37-39). Peter failed and was reinstated (John 21:15-17).
Sloth, laziness: avoiding hard work and suffering; devaluing the significance of what we are called to be doing. Escapism.	Rest is more important than work. Leisure will restore you. Indulgence in your own rest is required to be able to accomplish anything. You will always have tomorrow to do what you don't do today.	God was a worker (six days of creation, one day of rest). Make the most of the time, for the days are evil (Ephesians 5:16). See Proverbs 6:6-11; 13:4; 26:13-16; Galatians 6:7-10.

Consider the case studies outlined in tables 13 and 14. Each of these people has issues that you are able to see because of your proximity to them, and they are affecting you. You want the best for these friends, but you know that well wishing on its own will not help them. You need to speak to them and to listen to them, with humility and gentleness.

Of course, conversations that begin with questions may go in very different directions, and no simple case study can serve as a rigid template for these kinds of conversations. But these case studies illustrate how we might be better *family* to our friends through a willingness to help them spot the lies they have chosen to believe.

Diane, always a flamboyant storyteller, had just confessed her defeat: she ended a one-day fast three hours early by eating three Eskimo Pies. Her plea to our small group: "Pray for me; I feel so weak and guilty."

Table 13. Debunking the Lies of Sin, Case Study 1

Jay, a coworker at your office, is a young Christian who has responded well to your friendly initiative. You have seen one another in social situations outside work. You have observed Jay in the office and on the road—he is a fast-moving, ambitious guy who drives aggressively and uses his horn a lot. Last week Jay received word that he didn't get an important assignment he was hoping for. Upset, Jay has begun to find fault with anyone and everyone, including you.

What might be a good way to proceed with Jay?	"How are you doing? I've noticed these things . . . Are they connected?" You need to build a relationship with Jay without being judgmental.
What questions do you have?	Is Jay aware of how he's treating people? Is he eager to grow? "Jay, how do you see this decision? Where is God in it? How could this be viewed as an opportunity?"
What would you hope Jay could come to see?	Jay's anger, impatience, entitlement and/or jealousy. I would want him to see the way sin has deceived him to believe that it is possible for God's good intentions for him to be thwarted by someone else's decision regarding his career. I would hope Jay could see that God is giving him an opportunity to trust him.
How might you reflect what you've seen to Jay in a hearable way?	You likely have your own story of an initially disappointing event that was later revealed to be a work of God's grace and love for you, though you didn't recognize it at the time. "Jay, I am praying for you, that you'll be able to see how God is at work for your good in this job. I think you'll enjoy it more, and that enjoyment will produce better results for you than your current evident frustration."

The small-group members each responded by giving Diane what they thought she needed: encouragement ("At least you skipped lunch") and understanding ("I find it's impossible for me to fast") and relief ("Don't feel guilty"). Unfortunately, no one engaged her or asked a question.

Finally someone thought to ask, "Diane, what was your intention in fasting?" Diane had hoped to spend the day in prayer for some friends facing deep struggle. Instead she was so distracted by her hunger that

Table 14. Debunking the Lies of Sin, Case Study 2

Your ministry partner, Anne, always seems nervous about your ministry's upcoming outreach events, to which many people contribute by playing music, hosting, taking care of logistics and inviting their friends. It seems her demeanor is affecting the faith and expectations of the rest of the team. You decide to talk with her.

What would you like to ask Anne?	"How are you feeling about the events? How have they gone for you?" "What do you feel good about? Not good about?"
What might be possible heart issues to address?	Anxiety, fear, lack of trust in God, inability to trust others with their role in the program, feelings of carrying the whole thing on her shoulders. Anne seems to fear that "God won't show up." Perhaps she thinks, *My worry is the only thing holding this outreach event together.* These thoughts are deceptions. Anxiety robs Anne of the enjoyment and satisfaction of the event, as Jesus is taken out of the picture. It also affects the team's faith and vision.
How could you discuss these issues with Anne in a way that enables her to be receptive?	"I normally think of you as a fairly joyful person—that's why I was excited to work with you on these events. But I've been noticing that you seem very tense. It seems like anxiety has been robbing you of your enjoyment of our outreach. I'd really love to see you enjoy it—for your own sake and because I think, if you have fun, it will be contagious for the rest of the team. As it stands, it is more your anxiety that the team is catching from you. What could we do to help you receive a little more freedom from Jesus, for your sake and for the team's?"
What are your hopes for Anne and for the team?	If Anne has a valid critique of the outreach events, I want to hear her express it productively, not as worry. I want her to grow in faith. I also want the team to respond well to her, not just writing her off because of her needless worry.

she couldn't pray well. Another question: "What did you believe about God at 8:00 a.m. that you forgot or didn't really believe by 3:00 p.m.?" As her fast day began, Diane firmly believed that God was available to her through prayer, and she viewed her fast as a privilege to be able to focus her day and her heart on prayer for her friends. But by 3:00 p.m. all she could think was that if she were to eat a single morsel of food, she would have failed God and his requirements of her. (Hence, when she failed by eating one Eskimo Pie, eating two more hardly seemed to matter.) After she spoke, one member of the group summarized, "It seems that your fast day changed from something you were asking God to do into something you were doing for God. I can relate to you: I take a gift from God and I turn it around and I present it to him on a platter. Or I feel guilty when I cannot. Diane, God didn't ask you to do something heroic for him." At this point, everyone indeed could relate to Diane, and a broader discussion ensued.

Gently speaking the truth in love, and not fearing the truth, is the biblical picture of how a family is supposed to relate. In the context of secure love between them, brothers and sisters are asked to help one another out by mutually debunking the lies of sin in an attitude of humility and compassion. St. Teresa of Ávila expressed, in the chapter-opening quote, her wish that this kind of loving frankness could be achieved in her little group of spiritual friends and confessors. She went on to say, "Even preachers have the habit of so framing their sermons as to displease nobody."[5] For something written over four hundred years ago, her words reflect a remarkably contemporary understanding!

SALT AND LIGHT

A third set of images of community and corporate life involves salt and light. Jesus used these in the Sermon on the Mount as he described the gathering of disciples sitting and listening to him:

You are the salt of the earth; but if salt has lost its taste, how can its saltiness be restored? It is no longer good for anything, but is thrown out and trampled under foot.

You are the light of the world. A city built on a hill cannot be hid. No one after lighting a lamp puts it under the bushel basket, but on the lampstand, and it gives light to all in the house. In the same way, let your light shine before others, so that they may see your good works and give glory to your Father in heaven. (Matthew 5:13-16)

These images—salt and light—are corporate images. Jesus described how Christians are to relate to the world as a community. When Jesus spoke of salt and light, he was not speaking of individual grains of salt, nor of individual photons of light. He spoke of the entire community as a pile of salt or a beam of light.

In fact, his images are powerful only to the extent they are corporate. A pile of salt can be used to flavor meat. But a grain of salt, alone, is essentially worthless. That grain must combine with hundreds of other grains of salt so that together they may have some effect. Likewise, the power of light is in its intensity. A single particle of light by itself will accomplish little. The power of light is directly proportional to its quantity. Salt and light have an effect on the world only as they represent gatherings of individual units into a corporate entity: a pile of salt, a beam of light.

The third image, that of a city, describes what the community will become. The community of the kingdom, living under an alternate political structure, with a new culture and values, will be like a city set on a hill. It will be visible in the world yet distinguishable from the world. It will be available to the world yet not controlled by its politics. People from all over the world will come to this city, but for each of them it will require a lifetime of cultural adjustment. The citizens of this city will be said to be in the world but not of it.

A book on evangelism developed Jesus' image with its title *Out of the Saltshaker*.[6] Author Becky Pippert's vital point was that salt left in the saltshaker does no good at flavoring the society it is supposed to be flavoring. Yet a mistaken implication could be made that individual Christians, freed from the burdensome demands of the community, should focus exclusively on evangelistic relationships with non-Christians. These Christians are supposed to salt their conversations with allusions to their Lord and serve people in ways that illuminate the gospel and attract people to Jesus.

Yet Jesus' image itself does not challenge the community to spend little time as a community. Rather, the images of salt, light and the city on a hill imply that the community, *as a community*, will be the flavoring, illuminating and attractive force drawing all people into the society of the kingdom. Yes, we need the salt to leave the saltshaker! But if salt leaves its shaker grain by isolated grain, then it does nothing to flavor anything. It simply dissolves into its surroundings, unnoticed and ineffective.[7]

In my ministry to college students I am always trying to draw students, believing and nonbelieving, into the company of friends, the campus Christian fellowship. However, I cannot do that alone. On my own I can lead people into a pretty good discussion of a Bible passage. I can even get them praying. But one thing—one crucial thing—I cannot do alone: I cannot model community. I cannot demonstrate for people the nature and texture of kingdom relationships. I need partners committed to joining me to do that.

This isn't just my problem, and in this way at least I'm not at all unique. No one can model kingdom community, relationships focused around a pursuit of God, alone. Not even Jesus did this. Repeatedly he pointed to the close relationship he had with his Father as a model.[8] Jesus and the Father were in consistent, constant community, and as Jesus sent the disciples out, he sent them out as partners. Perhaps even more striking (judging from his confidence and temperament), not even Paul ministered alone: he carried his community around with him even as he pursued mission with unmatched zeal.

It is possible to identify two ways to miss this aspect of Jesus' teaching on the company of friends, incarnating the community as salt and light. First, we can remain at all times in the saltshaker and assume that our goal as a company of friends is to become as close as possible. People who have tasted of true and deep community often have tried to replicate it with ever-increasing intensity of commitment, but without an outward ministry focus, the community life becomes ingrown and eventually implodes. Second, we can decide that mission is the goal, and that getting those salt grains out of the saltshaker (or light photons out of the flashlight) is the top priority, but give no thought to partnership. So the community is scattered, expending little packets of energy and flavoring all over the map, without illuminating or seasoning anything.

When my wife and I were first married, we lived in a house with seven others, all members of the InterVarsity fellowship at U.C. Santa Cruz as senior students or staff. It was a rich, attractive community and students in the fellowship loved being in our home, sharing meals and life with us.

When my wife and I moved to Boston to work at Harvard, we mourned the loss of this rich fellowship and community. We tried many things to build community with students and surprised them repeatedly by our availability for relationships. However, the turning point came when two single men decided to live with us and volunteer with the ministry. Soon the ministry-oriented community became a very attractive place for students to be. They began to see a household of relationships focused around a joint pursuit of God. We began to hear from students how attractive our community was and how much they wanted life like that after college.

The church is the gathered community of God's people who operate as salt and light in society. As a community, we let our light shine before all people (Matthew 5:16), so that they will see this light and glorify God. People will be curious; they will be incredulous; they will inquire. The source of this light, they will find, is not just one or two remarkable human beings but dozens of normal human beings reflecting like mirrors the awesome brilliance of their Father, God. This is the light that will shine and bring glory to our God in heaven.

FOR REFLECTION

Take some time to reflect on the components of community before reading the next chapter to see them put together into a single, three-dimensional image.

1. How open are you to the celebration necessary to build healthy community? How do you see it as a priority in your small group or friendships?

2. In the tension between fellowship (looking inward) and partnership in mission (looking outward), where does your company of friends tend usually to give greater priority? How can you seek a balance?

3. Debunk the lies of sin. In a group of two or three, read the following list and pick a few that are attitudes you are susceptible to, with each person perhaps contributing one to the list. Then spend some time identifying both the deceptions that make this attitude attractive or powerful (at some level) and Scripture or other ways of embracing faith that serve as antidotes. The three that were included in the text, given as examples, are included here for the sake of a complete listing.[9]

   - *Anxiety:* a lack of peace that springs from dwelling on some dark scenario that we think will occur in the future. (See 2 Chronicles 20:20; Isaiah 7:9; 51:12; Matthew 6:25-34; Philippians 4; 1 Peter 5:7.)

   - *Bitterness, resentment:* harboring a grudge or an unforgiving spirit. (See Matthew 6:12; 18:21-35; Romans 12:19-21.)

   - *Covetousness:* discontent with what we possess or with our station or situation in life, negative comparisons with others, lack of generosity, hospitality, gluttony, hoarding, consumerism. (See Philippians 4:11-13; 1 Timothy 6:6-12; Hebrews 13:5-6.)

   - *Critical spirit:* exalting oneself by harshly evaluating others, leading to cruelty, unreasonable demands and gossip. (See Matthew 5:7; 7:1-5; 1 Corinthians 4:1-5.)

- *Deceit:* lying, knowingly falsifying the truth, unwillingness to confess sin. (See Exodus 20:16; Psalm 32; 51.)

- *Despondency, despair:* believing that we are at a dead-end with no way out, a no-win situation. Leads to burnout, lack of interest in prayer, Scripture and ministry (See Psalm 16:11; 23; Matthew 11:28-30; Hebrews 10:35-39.)

- *Divisiveness:* causing disunity in a group by exalting the distinctives of oneself or a subgroup to which one belongs. (See 1 Corinthians 1:10-13; 12:12-13, 24-26; Galatians 5:19-21; 6:7-10.)

- *Impatience:* the feeling that we should be getting on with something more quickly than we are. Leads to a lack of peace, bouts of anger, lack of love for others and trying to receive a blessing "our way." (See Proverbs 21:5; Isaiah 40:28-31; 50:10-11; 64:4; Matthew 5:5; John 15:6; James 1:3-6.)

- *Jealousy, envy:* becoming angry or upset when we see a person get something we wish we had. (See Psalm 37; 73; Galatians 5:19-21; 1 Thessalonians 5:18.)

- *Lust, immorality:* lack of self-control in the sexual area. Lustful thoughts. Inappropriate sexual activity. Use of pornography, visual stimulation. Creating inappropriate sexual tension. Habitual masturbation. (See Mark 7:20-23; 1 Corinthians 7:8-9; Galatians 5:14-21; 6:7-10.)

- *Pride, self-adulation:* savoring something one has done or said (or some distinctive) as particularly good, clever, wise, creative. Positive comparisons to others. Competitiveness, provoking others and making others look bad. (See Deuteronomy 8:14-18; Jeremiah 9:24; Ezekiel 18:29-32; Matthew 23:12; 1 Corinthians 1:28-31; 4:7; James 4:6-8; 1 Peter 5:5.)

- *Regret:* a belief that a mistake we made in the past virtually rules out a happy future. A reevaluation of our life and choices in the face of suffering. (See Genesis 50:20; 1 Samuel 12:20; Romans 8:27-39.)

- *Self-protection:* covering up, withdrawing or pulling away from community and ministry in order to avoid the pain of self-revelation or intentional suffering. (See Mark 8:34-37; Luke 10:25-37; 1 Corinthians 12:12-27; Philippians 2:1-11; 2 Timothy 2:1-13.)

- *Sloth, laziness:* avoiding hard work and suffering; devaluing the significance of what we are called to be doing. Escapism. (See Proverbs 6:6-11; 13:4; 26:13-16; Galatians 6:7-10; Ephesians 5:16.)

12

Three-Dimensional Community

Innumerable times a whole Christian community has broken down because it had sprung from a wish dream. The serious Christian, set down for the first time in a Christian community, is likely to bring with him a very definite idea of what Christian life together should be and to try to realize it. But God's grace speedily shatters such dreams. . . . He who loves his dream of a community more than the Christian community itself becomes a destroyer of the latter, even though his personal intentions may be ever so honest and earnest and sacrificial.

DIETRICH BONHOEFFER, *LIFE TOGETHER*

Community is not a paint-by-numbers affair. Community is not made simply by moving into a house together. Broken relationships are not mended by enforcing arbitrary commitments. Flailing teams are not automatically reinvigorated by vision retreats. Dietrich Bonhoeffer warned against trying to apply rigidly any schema or system to a real expression of community.

For anyone who has tried to live intentionally in committed Christian community, Bonhoeffer seems a prophet. Too often we can hear complaints about particular expressions of community with little or no diagnosis as to how to actually deepen the experience and impact of community.

Different expressions of community will have different characteristic strengths and weaknesses. It can be tempting merely to compare our current expression with the one we loved in the halcyon days of yore. But this is a losing strategy, certain to bring only dissatisfaction and not liable to be a help to our current small group of friends. In fact, Bonhoeffer warned that it is likely to destroy what little experience of community we do enjoy.

Instead, I'd like to bring the three images from the previous chapter together until a more complete picture emerges. This is not a checklist but a three-dimensional vision with depth and texture and infinite variation. Community, like any successful friendship, involves fellowship, accountability and partnership. Fellowship expresses the community's common life; accountability, its common commitments; partnership, its common vision. Table 15 summarizes these three dimensions and their distinctives.

Table 15. The Three Dimensions of Community

Community Involves	Key Image	Common	Fundamental Quality	Without It a Group Is Characterized By
Fellowship (enjoy one another)	The party	Life	Love	Joylessness
Accountability (serve one another)	The family	Commitments	Truth	Sin and hypocrisy
Partnership (commit to the good)	Salt and light	Vision	Mission	Factions or drift

Using the terms discussed above, how healthy are these communities? As an exercise, before reading the discussion that follows the descriptions, rank them by how closely the requirements of community are met.

- **Ego Associates:** an interactive communications agency. "We create and develop award-winning brands in today's marketplace. Founded in 1998, Ego Associates is a hybrid between a traditional branding company and an interactive agency. Our purpose is to explore new modes of brand communication through the use of emerging information technologies. Since its inception, Ego Associates has evolved into an industry-recognized creative force fueled by a dynamic team-centric culture that fosters solutions-oriented thinking. Our mission is to trigger imaginative thinking to build and strengthen relationships between brands and users. 'Leave your ego to us.'"

- *Four couples in a small group:* These four couples have been meeting in a small group for over nine years, and they have seen it all! They continue to meet every week for Bible study and fellowship and once every month for dinner and an evening of fun. Five years ago one couple moved away, but the group has remained unchanged other than that. They rotate leadership among the members, sometimes studying Scripture and sometimes reading books together. They take summers off but are pretty consistent during the year. They see each other at their three-thousand-member church occasionally. They used to live in the same community, but three of the couples have moved to neighboring towns (for the schools) and so they aren't geographically as close as they used to be.

- *Special Forces Operational Detachment Alpha.* The "A-Team" consists of twelve Special Forces soldiers—two officers and ten sergeants. All team members are SF-qualified and cross-trained in different skills. They are also multilingual. The A-Team is almost unlimited in its capabilities to operate in hostile or denied areas. A-Teams can infiltrate and exfiltrate their area of operations by air, land or sea. An A-Team can operate for an indefinite period of time in remote locations with little or no outside support. They are truly independent, self-sustaining detachments.

- *Vegetarians united.* A group of five women move into a house together after they graduate from college. They share a commitment to vegetarianism and (in part, necessity-based) simple living. The house they move into has four bedrooms, and rent is split according to room size. They have pretty crazy schedules but try to eat at least one meal per week with one another. Over the next three years, they each figure prominently at the four weddings and a funeral (one woman's dad dies of cancer) that follow the maturing of these five women.

Once you begin to look for them, you will notice that small groups abound in society: teams, clubs, households, e-mail lists, user groups, parents' groups, advocacy groups and a whole host of groups that use the term *community* to describe themselves. We hear of online communities, academic communities, ethnic communities, the medical community, the intelligence community, community college communities and product communities, such as "the AOL community" and "the Saturn community." Whether or not these groups and self-proclaimed communities satisfy what we understand as community is at least arguable. Some groups gathered around arcane and nonspiritual activity may satisfy the requirements of community far better than spiritually minded groups that call themselves community but fail in one or more ways.

Now, if you haven't taken a few moments to consider the relative strengths and weaknesses of the preceding list of supposed community, take a minute to do so before reading further.

- *Ego Associates.* This group has a highly developed sense of mission and "a dynamic team-centric culture." These people are aggressive marketing professionals who seem to enjoy their work and are proud of what they do. Of the three components, certainly it was mission that brought them together, and their usefulness to one another keeps them working together. They say they value relationships on the team. Yet company volleyball games don't generate revenues or satisfy clients. In a pinch, they knuckle down and work at a brutal pace. My guess: in five years, one or more of the principals will be gone. Ego will get in the way.

- *Four couples.* A need for fellowship and their mutual desire to grow in their pursuit of God brought them together, and after nine years, they've certainly been successful at something. A great deal of love and some measure of truth permeates these relationships, but it is sad to say, they have little sense of mission. Could those fun evenings be opened to seeker friends? Could they decide to run their group, for a couple of months, as an evangelistic small group, inviting friends to consider common questions of faith? Could they decide to do a week-long ministry trip together? Any chance to partner in ministry would create an urgency in their relationships and small group that seems not to exist currently. They take summers off, perhaps simply as a capitulation to the exigencies of busy summer schedules, but perhaps it is symptomatic of a lack of a sense of deep need for this small group. If they were in mission together, I believe they'd have a deeper sense of their mutual need for one another, even during the summer.

- *Special Forces Alpha Team.* The description here is of a group of twelve people that functions like a machine—every part well oiled and highly trained and tested. They are completely mission driven and must work together to accomplish the purpose. It is possible to imagine that, when they are not working hard, they are playing hard, but that isn't explicitly mentioned. Do these people love each other? They will be asked to risk their lives for one another; one hopes they do.

- *Vegetarians united.* They seem to love each other and share a few commitments, namely eating no meat, sharing rent and being involved in one another's lives. Yet it seems they are not able to make any other commitments to one another to grow as people or to take on some outward focus or cause. They are strong on fellowship, weaker on accountability and weakest on partnership in mission. After the spate of weddings, these women, with little to keep them together, will likely drift apart. Vegetarianism conveniently brought them together but won't be enough to keep them together.

Jesus painted his vision for community with imagery, three-dimensional pictures of an attractive company of friends gathered for the purpose of a joint pursuit of God. His imagery can be fleshed out in dozens of helpful ways, but it also clarifies when key components are missing. Jesus did have a vision for the company of friends. Are we captivated by his vision?

FROM HERE TO COMMUNITY

An early initial experience of Christian community can imprint upon us a particular form of communal expression. This can be great if it helps us persevere when we find ourselves someplace else, but it can also be devastating if we never learn to readjust our expectations.

- A freshman in college pines for his youth group at home, failing to take advantage of the campus Christian group, in large part because he doesn't like the songs.

- A college graduate visits eight churches two or three times each but never settles because she doesn't feel at home anywhere other than her college fellowship, which she still visits once a month or so.

- A couple often comment to each other that their small group seems shallow compared to the small-group experience at their previous church, but they never take any initiative to deepen relationships with other group members.

Joining a community is a step of faith. You cannot know what it is like or how well it will satisfy until you commit. Visiting a small group may give you some idea, but it will be a different experience after you've been going for six months. Unfortunately, there is no shortcut or quick fix. It means making a choice and taking a risk.

When we commit to a group of people, we simplify our lives. We no longer need to make a decision every week about whether to attend small group. We make one decision: "If I'm in town, I'm at small group." Some nights will be great, but frankly some meetings will be duds. (I've led my share of dud small-group meetings.) But a week-in, week-out commitment will, in its accumulated effect, pay off. Eventually this kind of commitment means that even "dud" small-group meetings contribute to our sense of intimacy and friendship with those in our group. (We can all look back on such meetings and moan in chorus, "Yeah, that really was a dud!")

But of course, just being in the same room for two hours per week does not ensure that satisfying friendships will form and deepen. We may, in fact, all be sitting in the room looking at each other and wondering why no one else seems to notice how shallow our relationships are. So beyond a commitment to attend, we need a commitment to give priority to developing relationships.

My wife and I regularly sit down to schedule our lives—her nights at class, my travel days, our date nights and so on. During those times, we also talk about whom we'd like to have over for a meal, whom we'd like to speak with some evening on a longer phone call and whom we'd like to spend the weekend days with as a family. And we talk about the hopes we have for some of these friendships. For example, we are each separately friends with members of a couple we'd like to enjoy more as a couple, and recently we talked about how to do so.

The complexity of our lives makes this kind of initiative in friendships difficult to sustain. It is difficult enough to get food on the table for the family, let alone try to schedule meals with friends, constrained by kids' activities and bedtimes and work deadlines. We desire to have deep friendships, but when faced with the complexity of our lives, we can easily settle for the comfort and quiet of the home with the kids in bed and the parents soon to follow.

Commitment gets us in the same room with a group of people or a few friends. The resource we spend is time. Intentionality means we spend energy thinking about how to make the time we have with them satisfying at a variety of levels.

I have sought male friends who have kids similar in their ages with mine to meet with on a regular basis and speak about the tensions of time and balance of family life, professional life and spiritual life. But every time I invite a man in my church into that kind of a consistent relationship, it feels risky and vulnerable. Most recently it was Bob. Bob's initial response to my invitation was "Yeah, that sounds great." But I felt exposed until Bob, after a couple of breakfast meetings, reminded *me* that we needed to get together soon, reciprocating my effort as affirmation of his heartfelt interest in the friendship.

But now that I am meeting with Bob every few weeks, I actually have to have something to say and questions to ask. Early on in any friendship, I often feel some need to help people see me in the best light. It is not that I am dishonest but that I will present a certain limited perspective. It is inevitable, really, in that people cannot find out everything about me all at once. But over time, I recognize that this is not satisfying, and so I need to make a third choice. Beyond commitment, beyond intentionality, I need to make a choice for authenticity, to reveal myself not as I wish I were or want people to believe I am but as I really am. And I know that getting to know my friend in the same way will take a choice on his part as well.

So I find I cannot simply go to breakfast with Bob every few weeks without thinking about Bob in the intervening time. If our relationship is to grow, I need to both have something self-reflective to share as we come together and have questions to ask of Bob. If he mentions concerns, I need to pray for them and then remember to ask him about them. If I am going to have an authentic friendship, I need to lead in self-disclosure. And at least for me, to lead in self-disclosure I must exert some effort at self-understanding so I will have something to disclose.

These three moves—commitment, intentionality, authenticity—will make a huge difference in our ability to join in and benefit from, even to create or to improve, community in the settings in which we pursue it. Table 16 summarizes these steps toward deeper community. Each is a move of increasing depth, and making these moves brings community closer.

Table 16. From Here to Community

Choice	Movement	Risk in Faith
Commitment	From consumer to member	Time
Intentionality	From passive to active	Energy
Authenticity	From concealment to openness	Vulnerability

FOR REFLECTION

1. Identify a few groups of which you are a member in your church, school, workplace or other part of life and ask yourself the question, do these qualify as well-balanced communities? What would be needed to make them better?

2. Which of the three choices summarized in table 16 could you make in your relationships to deepen your experience of community? What, if anything, holds you back?

The Mission of God in the Company of Friends

We few, we happy few, we band of brothers;
For he to-day that sheds his blood with me
Shall be my brother; be he ne'er so vile,
This day shall gentle his condition;
And gentlemen in England now-a-bed
Shall think themselves accurs'd they were not here,
And hold their manhoods cheap whiles any speaks
That fought with us upon Saint Crispin's day.

SHAKESPEARE, *HENRY V*

Our fledgling church plant's outreach team had a vision: "Invite tens of thousands, welcome thousands, incorporate hundreds." For an infant church of maybe eighty regulars, that was quite a vision. Our first attempt was arguably misguided yet well intentioned. We bought local address labels and sent out a mailing of ten thousand with a friendly letter and a flyer introducing our church. We later learned of mailing companies that have an automated and relatively inexpensive process to send out bulk mail to lists. However, this first time we inserted letters and cards into envelopes, affixed labels and stamps, sealed and mailed all ten thousand envelopes by hand. It took thirty people four or five hours to do it.

If we had experienced even a 3 percent return, it would have been impossible to seat the three hundred people in the room we were renting at the time. Sadly, we didn't have that problem. We received nearly two thousand returned envelopes because the addressee had moved. We figured later that perhaps twenty people ever showed up because of our mailing. Still, because of other publicity and personal invitations to friends, our body more than doubled that fall and did the same again a year later, by which point the outreach team could claim success for its original vision.

If some observers were tempted to chalk up the mailing as a big waste of resources and a failure, none of us who experienced it would have. We were in on an enterprise much bigger than any of us would have planned on our own. We had a sense that we were on a mission from God, being sped along by his backing and serving as witnesses of his unfolding dramatic plan. The mailing was an almost sacramental experience, an outward and visible sign of an inward and spiritual reality, that God was moving in our church and had confirmed his intention to bless our efforts and multiply our ministry. That fall we welcomed into our worship dozens of people who were visiting church for the first time or returning to a church after years of alienation from God. Our church's advertising tag line spoke of the reality we were experiencing: "Practical. Spiritual. Fun."[1] It wasn't just a marketing gimmick: church (both the weekly event and the deeper relational reality) was practical. And spiritual. And very, very fun.

◆　◆　◆

Warfare of any kind produces deep bonds and forges intimate friendships, a "band of brothers." The mission of God, heartily engaged in, offers such martial opportunity. Deep friendships are enriched by the mission and thrown into tension by it, as the momentum of the work of God alternately brings us together and sends us out.

GATHERING AND BEING SENT OUT

Jesus' call to his disciples to spend time with him and with one another was not absolute. Jesus also sent out his disciples two by two to preach, to heal and to cast out demons.

> He called the twelve and began to send them out two by two, and
> gave them authority over the unclean spirits. He ordered them to

take nothing for their journey except a staff; no bread, no bag, no money in their belts; but to wear sandals and not to put on two tunics. He said to them, "Wherever you enter a house, stay there until you leave the place. If any place will not welcome you and they refuse to hear you, as you leave, shake off the dust that is on your feet as a testimony against them." So they went out and proclaimed that all should repent. They cast out many demons, and anointed with oil many who were sick and cured them. (Mark 6:7-13)

Jesus prepared his disciples to go out on their first preaching mission. In order to prepare them, he had to equip them with all the resources they would need for their journey. What they needed most of all, however, was not food, money and extra clothing but dependence on God and on Jesus' words. So, in preparation, he stripped them of any extra supplies on which they may have been tempted to rely. Jesus knew what would happen to them if they trusted their Father and him in this way. Furthermore, he also prepared them to know what to do if they entered an inhospitable town. The disciples were not to blame themselves nor to doubt the message they had been given. Jesus told the disciples merely to warn the town and move on. Jesus' foresight in this case probably prevented some of the disciples from becoming discouraged and quitting upon finding a particularly unresponsive town. They were able to press on to places that were receptive, and they were able to rejoice as they saw the fruit of their ministry among open people. When they met with receptivity, they were to put down roots and stay awhile.

Jesus' instructions to his disciples indicate his priorities in mission:

- *Partnership, not heroism.* Jesus valued risk taking and dependence on God, but not more than partnership. He wanted the disciples to be given a chance to depend on him for their sustenance and power, but he still gave them a partner to lean on for the trip.

- *Partnership over coverage.* Jesus' plan valued getting the word out, but not more than partnership. He sent the disciples out because he wanted people in the towns and villages to hear the message, but he made a choice to send them in teams rather than as individuals. If community is part of the message (and not just a convenient medium), then it would have been impossible for the gospel fully to be portrayed without teamwork.

- *Depth over breadth.* Jesus wanted whole towns to be affected, but he wanted individual households to be impacted deeply: "stay there until you leave the place" (Mark 6:10). He said not to hop from welcoming house to welcoming house. When they arrived in town, one household would welcome them and they would stay there and give more attention and time to them. In this way they would leave witnesses to the kingdom in the town when they left.

This illustrates the redemptive tension between the gathering work of Jesus and the sending out of his disciples.

Community involves gathering a company of friends. But the purpose for that community always involves a scattering, a move outward from the center. This side of heaven, there is no proper gathering without a sending out and no proper sending out without a gathering. We cannot find equilibrium, a place of rest where tension no longer exists. We do well enough simply to find a balance, where our lives are lived in a respiratory rhythm of our being gathered into a community and our being impelled outward by God's love for those who are not in it.

We may experience this tension in a variety of ways:

- A household of friends struggle with their individual plans and time demands pitted against their common hope that they would be able to spend time together as a community.

- A ministry team working with a youth group considers taking time away to be together as a team, but some on the team feel that they should instead spend the time away with the entire youth group, not just the leaders.

- A small group reads a book together about evangelism but are not willing to open their small-group evenings up for the possibility that seeking friends of theirs would come.

- A newlywed couple decides to take a year off from participating in a church small group so that they can focus on their new relationship.

We can see the gathering and sending-out impulses back to back at many places in the Gospels. Table 17 gives a few paired examples.

Table 17. Gathering and Sending Out: The Ministry and Call of Jesus

Gathering Impulse	Sending-Out Impulse
Love: "I give you a new commandment, that you love one another. Just as I have loved you, you also should love one another" (John 13:34).	*Witness:* "By this everyone will know that you are my disciples, if you have love for one another" (John 13:35).
Joy: "I have said these things to you so that my joy may be in you, and that your joy may be complete. This is my commandment, that you love one another as I have loved you" (John 15:11-12).	*Purpose:* "You did not choose me but I chose you. And I appointed you to go and bear fruit, fruit that will last. . . . I am giving you these commands so that you may love one another" (John 15:16-17).
Relationship: "Let us go across to the other side" (Mark 4:35). Jesus spent time with his disciples in the boat.	*Mission:* "Go home to your friends, and tell them how much the Lord has done for you, and what mercy he has shown you" (Mark 5:19). Jesus sent out the former demoniac, commissioning his first apostle to the Gentiles.
Exclusivity: "Jesus went on with his disciples to the villages of Caesarea Philippi" (Mark 8:27). Jesus spent extra time alone with his disciples, teaching them of his identity and mission.	*Inclusiveness:* "He called the crowd with his disciples, and said to them, 'If any want to become my followers . . .'" (Mark 8:34). Jesus gathered the crowds and issued a universal invitation to follow him.
Sabbath and rest: "Come away to a deserted place all by yourselves and rest a while" (Mark 6:31).	*Ministry:* "You give them something to eat" (Mark 6:37).

Unhealthy versions of Christian expression often are characterized by one or the other of these extremes. The gathering and sending-out contrast could be seen also as relationship versus task, as reflection versus action, or as introversion versus extroversion. Temperamentally, one side of this tension may predominate for us as individuals. To recognize a temperamental preference is reasonable; to generalize that to a ministry strategy absolute yields an imbalance. To pursue healthy Christian community we need others for whom the opposite side of the contrasting impulses predominates.

It is probably difficult to overstate the danger of failing to balance an emphasis on gathering with an emphasis on sending out. From ingrown small groups and cliquish campus fellowships to cozy churches and even megagatherings, an overemphasis on the community relationships at the expense of the apostolic vision produces instability or complacency as a group.

COMMUNITY AND MISSION IN TENSION (MARK 6:30-44)

After Jesus sent the disciples out to preach, they eventually gathered around him with enthusiasm and the flush of success. The disciples had healed people, cast out demons and preached the good news about the kingdom of God, and they returned with the enthusiasm of schoolchildren, saying, "And then we healed a blind man!" "And then *we* healed two lepers!" "And then *we* cast out six demons!" Mark, in this passage, referred to the disciples as "apostles," meaning "sent-out ones." He didn't use this word lightly—they literally had been sent out. But this is the only time the evangelist used that word to describe them. Jesus understood that having been sent out, they needed a time of gathering and refreshment. So he said to them, "Come away to a deserted place all by yourselves and rest a while" (Mark 6:31). Just the promise of that invitation restored their energy enough for them to hurry into a boat and try to remove themselves from the crowds.

The problem with that little plan was that any place with Jesus, his disciples and the crowds that pursued them was no longer a deserted place. Mark told us that the people recognized "them"—not just Jesus but the disciples as well, because they had been out among the people preaching to them (verse 33). The disciples had become celebrities—healers and preachers—and along with Jesus were popular with the crowds.

Perhaps it was insensitive of Jesus not to remember his words to them, "Come away to a deserted place." Perhaps the disciples can be forgiven for their willingness to become sarcastic with Jesus and resentful of a crowd who had come to be with Jesus and with them. It seems like a human reaction to the disappointment of not finding rest that had been promised.

Imagine the disciples' emotions. Jesus promised them peace and quiet, and instead they met with crowds and requests for healing and silent claims for compassion. Jesus did in fact have compassion on the crowds, but as he preached to the crowds words of life, the disciples were sitting there, impassive, or glaring at the crowds, resenting the interpenetration of their lives with their ministry. So when Jesus said to them, "You give them something to eat," they lost composure (verse 37). They became sarcastic; they literally made fun of Jesus for making what sounded to them like a foolish suggestion. "Oh yeah, right, we'll just go out and buy five thousand Happy Meals for these good people! Swell idea, chief!"

What did Jesus have in mind when he said, "You feed them"? These were the very people the disciples had been sent out among to preach and heal. Many of these people had welcomed them into their homes. A few of these people had put meals on the table for them. The disciples had recently experienced being fed and cared for in the very act of ministry; now they were viewing ministry as a threat to their survival and care. Jesus wanted the disciples again to receive blessing while serving others, knowing that this was not simply a two-week mission trip but was to become a lifestyle for them.

Imagine a very different day: When they arrive, the disciples stare in wonder and delight at the size of the crowds. People they know, their friends, gather around. The disciples welcome them and introduce them to Jesus with enthusiasm. "He's the one I told you about!" Then Jesus begins to teach and the disciples are again entranced by hearing the stories and images that first captivated their imaginations. Later, Jesus says, "I have compassion on the crowd; let's feed them."[2] The disciples say, "But how?" And Jesus invites them to host a miracle. Wow! What a day! If I were able to experience that, no matter what my week was like, that would be a highlight.

Jesus didn't forget his words to them or his promise of rest. But Jesus did want to teach his disciples about their calling as shepherds of the flock of God. Often, for the sake of our obsessive focus on something we feel we need, we can fail to see the opportunity to receive something even better. The disciples' experience of community was never as rich as the moments after they had returned from their ministry trips excited about what God had empowered them to do. Nevertheless, their experience of community was never as impoverished as when they began to resent the impinging crowds and lost sight of the miraculous sufficiency of their Lord in their midst.

The fundamental dynamic is the paradox of the feeding of the five thousand: when we make ourselves and our resources available to give, we find that we experience more abundance in the community of God's people. Community and friendship are deep wells, and the more we draw from them, the more we find they contain. If we come to see that community is enriched and not impoverished by mission, and vice versa, then we would not be tempted to make choices to protect the one against encroachment by the other.

Let us return to the groups of people we considered earlier in the chapter and see how their lives could be different by making different choices in the face of the tension between mission and community:

- This household of friends decide to lay down their tendency individually to protect their schedules and priorities for the sake of making time to be a real community. They find ways to invite people into their home at times when they can welcome them as a group. It means that each of them must cut out some involvements, but they take on other involvements as partners and friends and find these rewarding and reinforcing of their household community and its purpose.

• The youth group ministry team decides that they will go away alone for the weekend, without the youth, but their focus during the weekend is listening to God, in Scripture study and prayer, and to one another about the work God is doing in the youth. The team returns from this time away renewed, energized and resourced to care for and lead the youth ministry.

• The small group gaining a vision for evangelism decides to open up its meeting format so that they would be comfortable inviting their friends. As small-group members get to know one another's seeker friends, their sense of partnership with one another grows. Soon they decide to gather each week in trios for prayer and preparation for the seeker-oriented events sponsored by the small group. As their group grows, their sense of enjoyment and ownership grows as well.

• The newlywed couple receives wise counsel that even during their first year of marriage they need good friends who know them, love them and can help them to navigate the challenges of their new life together. The time they spend investing in other friendships pays huge dividends in the wise and timely help they receive for their marriage, and it sets a pattern that their marriage will deepen in the context of community, not isolation.

LOVE FOR ONE ANOTHER AND THE MISSION OF GOD

We have already seen much of Jesus' teaching that touches on love. I want to look specifically at Jesus' commands to his disciples to love one another. These are found in the Gospels exclusively in John in the upper-room discourse (John 13—17). I want to look at four brief passages within the scope of the entire discourse. The section in John is well worth studying in context, perhaps especially by a group of people who are committing together to grow in their life with God. We have already examined the opening passage, regarding Jesus' servanthood of his disciples and his call for them to serve one another. This introduced the themes that he returned to again and again as he spent the final night before his death with his disciples.

> I give you a new commandment, that you love one another. Just as I have loved you, you also should love one another. By this everyone will know that you are my disciples, if you have love for one another. (John 13:34-35)

> If you love me, you will keep my commandments. . . . They who have my commandments and keep them are those who love me; and those who love me will be loved by my Father, and I will love them and reveal myself to them. . . . Those who love me will keep my word, and my Father will love them, and we will come to them and make our home with them. Whoever does not love me does not keep my words. (John 14:15, 21, 23-24)

> As the Father has loved me, so I have loved you; abide in my love. If you keep my commandments, you will abide in my love, just as I have kept my Father's commandments and abide in his love. I have said these things to you so that my joy may be in you, and that your joy may be complete.

> This is my commandment, that you love one another as I have loved you. No one has greater love than this, to lay down one's life for one's friends. You are my friends if you do what I command you. (John 15:9-14)

> I ask not only on behalf of these, but also on behalf of those who will believe in me through their word, that they may all be one. As you, Father, are in me and I am in you, may they also be in us, so that the world may believe that you have sent me. The glory that

you have given me I have given them, so that they may be one, as we are one, I in them and you in me, that they may become completely one, so that the world may know that you have sent me and have loved them even as you have loved me. (John 17:20-23)

In each of these passages, Jesus' love is both the basis for his call to love one another and a model. Just as the Father's love for Jesus is the basis of Jesus' obedience to his Father (John 15:10), so Jesus' love for his disciples is the basis of their obedience. Furthermore, Jesus' love is the standard of the love he wants his disciples to have for one another.

In regard to pursuing God in the company of friends, we can draw at least four conclusions from these passages.

First, if we love Jesus, we ought to love our fellow Christians. We know this is so because Jesus' command is to love one another (John 13:34; 15:12), and love for Jesus means we'll keep his commands (John 14:15).

The command to love our fellow Christians is not a weak, intangible, mushy command; rather, the love we are to have for our brothers and sisters is real, and it issues in costly service. It is the love Jesus had for his disciples (John 13:34: "just as I have loved you"). The love of the broader company of friends is not optional for anyone in pursuit of God.

Second, to not love one another means to step out of Jesus' love and friendship (John 14:15; 15:13-14). Joy—full joy, Jesus' joy—is at stake. Our relationship with Jesus does not move forward if we are not actively working at loving our brothers and sisters.

A disturbing question comes out of this conclusion. Is Jesus' love conditional? It almost seems so from the way Jesus described his love and the disciples' abiding in it. Yet this can be challenging to those who claim that the essential quality of Jesus' love is its unconditionality (see Romans 8:37-39).

I want to use an image to illustrate how, even though Jesus' love is unconditional, our experience of it depends on our response. Let us think of Jesus' love like a warm fire in the dark of night. His love illumines our way in the dark and warms us in the cold. Jesus' words have pointed us in the direction of the beam: we know which way to walk as we study Jesus' words. If we continue to walk toward the fire of his love, then we will continue to enjoy the warmth and light it affords. Jesus' joy will be in us, and our joy will be full. We will be his friends, enjoying his companionship and deepening our relationship with him.

However, like sheep prone to wander from our intended path, we often stroll away from the burning flame of his love. As we move away, we no longer feel the warmth against the cold. We find ourselves in greater and greater darkness as we step further from his revealed light. Has his love stopped burning? No. His love continues and in that sense is unconditional. But our enjoyment of his love has diminished. We have failed to "abide," or remain, in Jesus' love.

Is all lost? No! What can we do? Repent! As we turn around and head back toward the flame, we once again enjoy his warmth and illumination. We once again are able to bask in his goodness and be filled with his joy. In fact, we experience the grace of his love in this: when we wander away from his love, we *do* feel the cold and see the dimming light. Some may grow angry at this, but in fact these sensations are how God alerts us to the danger of our wayward course. Of course, this was the experience of the younger, prodigal son in the parable of the waiting father. He woke up to the cold chill on his face as he stared longingly at the pods he was feeding the pigs, and he met the warm embrace of his Father's burning unconditional love for him upon his return.

This, in fact, describes a common experience for a follower of Jesus Christ. While it was possible for Jesus perfectly to abide in his Father's love by sinless obedience, that is not the case for us. Jesus loves us even when we sin, but part of his love for us involves calling us back to his standards of righteousness *for our own sake*. Jesus is not so petty that he, like a jealous lover, turns away from us the second we let our eyes wander from him. Rather, Jesus' constant and unchanging love for his disciples consists in directing our paths. Even when we turn from him, he directs us with the beam of his love, revealed through his words, toward goodness, toward himself. Again, he does this for our sake. Jesus said, "I have said these things to you so that my joy may be in you, and that your joy may be complete" (John 15:11). He loves us by giving us his commandments.

The surprising conclusion of this examination of Jesus' very individual and unconditional love for each of us is that he loves us by telling us to love one another. If we fail to love one another, we distance ourselves from the love of Jesus!

Third, love for the company of friends is instrumental to our evangelism and witness in the world (John 13:35; 17:23). The effectiveness of Jesus' entire mission was dependent on the disciples' love for and unity with one another.

Often nonbelievers see the body of Christians as a fighting, bickering mess. Even within individual denominations and churches, political power dynamics and not love for one another often dominate decision making. So long as this is the prevalent impression Christians make on the world, our efforts to preach Jesus will be thwarted. We must love one another for the sake of those still seeking God.

Furthermore, we cannot trade off loving believers with evangelistic activity. All of our efforts at evangelism will fail if we have no active and practical love for brothers and sisters. In fact, much of it does fail because Christians are not seen as having this kind of love for one another, both globally throughout history and locally today.

Fourth, the mission of God is advanced in two ways through our love for the company of friends in the pursuit of God. On the one hand, God's purposes for us impel us to grow in love. This is the mission of God *in* each of us. On the other hand, God's purposes in others and in the world are carried out as our hearts grow in love and as others respond to the love of God in us. This is the mission of God *through* us. If people around us know that we love each other, this will have an impact on their lives.

A powerful experience of community is magnetic. Karl, a sophomore and a young leader in the InterVarsity fellowship, met Joe, an agnostic, through studying for their common major, physics. Karl invited Joe to a fellowship meeting, and Joe was welcomed into the life of the group.

Joe was invited into a small study group of physics majors in the fellowship. These men were good friends and often spent all-nighters studying, laughing and praying together. One beautiful (and rare, for Cambridge) spring day, a month or so after Joe began to hang around Karl and the others, the group were eating lunch together. Someone casually remarked that nature itself argues for the existence of God. Joe, not yet a Christian, said, "Well, I think the best argument for the existence of God is you guys. I've been watching how you care for each other, and I can't explain it apart from God." It was clear that Joe was not far from the kingdom of God. By the end of the next week, Joe had committed himself to follow Jesus.

A powerful experience of community is indeed magnetic. The early church experienced this kind of community, and people were drawn into it daily (Acts 2:43-47). This is still true today, when loneliness and superficiality are widespread. As disciples love one another in ways that even the world can see, others will be attracted to that and will desire to join the company of friends in the pursuit of God.

FOR REFLECTION

1. In your own rhythm of being gathered and being sent out, where are you most likely to become stuck? What steps can you take to embrace a healthy rhythm of doing both?

2. How have you experienced the tension between community and mission? How have you seen community be enriched by mission?

3. How have you seen your own ministry outreach enriched by community? How would you like to grow in this?

The Eternal
Company of Friends

"You do not yet look so happy as I mean you to be."

*Lucy said, "We're so afraid of being sent away, Aslan. And you have sent us
back into our own world so often."*

"No fear of that," said Aslan. "Have you not guessed?"

Their hearts leaped and a wild hope rose within them.

*"There was a real railway accident," said Aslan softly. "Your father and mother
and all of you are—as you used to call it in the Shadow-Lands—dead. The term
is over: the holidays have begun. The dream is ended: this is the morning."*

*And as He spoke He no longer looked to them like a lion; but the things that
began to happen after that were so great and beautiful that I cannot write them.*

*And for us this is the end of all the stories, and we can most truly say that
they all lived happily ever after. But for them it was only the beginning of the real
story. All their life in this world and all their adventures in Narnia had only
been the cover and the title page: now at last they were beginning Chapter One
of the Great Story, which no one on earth has read: which goes on for ever:
in which every chapter is better than the one before.*

C. S. LEWIS, THE LAST BATTLE

From the starting line in Hopkinton, Massachusetts, to the finish line
in Copley Square in downtown Boston, nearly the entire length of the
Boston Marathon course is annually peopled with onlookers filled with
anticipation and enthusiasm. The running of the Boston Marathon every year is like Boston's version of the Tournament of Roses Parade, ex-

cept without the floats, bands, flags, horses or beauty queens. (OK, so it is not very much like the Rose Parade.) It too is run on a holiday (Patriot's Day, the third Monday in April), and it too gathers hundreds of thousands of spectators to line the streets. They come to see the runners and wheelchair racers, fifteen thousand-plus men and women who run the race officially in addition to the thousands who run the course without a number or an official time.

A few years ago my family walked the half-mile from our home across the Boston University Bridge to Kenmore Square, home of another icon of Boston athletics, Fenway Park, less than a mile from the finish line. The marathon crowd, like a massive queue without movement, was gathered to watch the hours-long event, not simply the few seconds of race that could be seen from any particular vantage point. Watching the race from the side of the roadway is an experience unlike any you get in a sports arena. The crowd itself helped to evoke the feelings of greatness and transcendence as we watched the first runners go by.

As a visual experience, many other sports events would beat it. Even after the first runners came by, there were still several stretches without runners in sight—literally no action to look at. Yet for drama, watching people finish the marathon in Boston cannot be topped. As people run by, they are cheered as if every one of them were a hometown hero or national champion. When older men or women run by, they are given even greater acclaim. When a walker begins to run again, he or she is given honor and vocal encouragement. And with the volume of the cheering, people pick up their pace (or at least succeed in keeping it up) in hope of making it across the line. The more evident struggle a runner displays, the greater the applause.

THE CLOUD OF WITNESSES

Since we are surrounded by so great a cloud of witnesses, let us also lay aside every weight and the sin that clings so closely, and let us run with perseverance the race that is set before us, looking to Jesus the pioneer and perfecter of our faith, who for the sake of the joy that was set before him endured the cross, disregarding its shame, and has taken his seat at the right hand of the throne of God.

Consider him who endured such hostility against himself from sinners, so that you may not grow weary or lose heart.

HEBREWS 12:1-3

The writer of Hebrews called to mind an image similar to athletes running the marathon and called us to "run with perseverance" the race of the life of faith. The author of these words said we are to be so encouraged and empowered to run to the finish line because we have a great cloud of witnesses, people like the hall of famers of faith mentioned in the previous chapter of Hebrews. Adam, Abel, Abraham and Sarah, Moses, Rahab, Samuel, David and the prophets "of whom the world was not worthy" (Hebrews 11:38). "Yet all these, though they were commended for their faith, did not receive what was promised, since God had provided something better so that they would not, apart from us, be made perfect" (verses 39-40).

These worthy souls who have gone on before us are not simply satisfied that they have made it across the finish line. For some reason, they are rooting and cheering for us.

When I was cheering for those men and women in the Boston Marathon, I rarely knew any of them. (Though I often knew people running the marathon, I rarely *saw* them.) They were attempting to accomplish a remarkable feat of human achievement. The running of a marathon, while undoubtedly supported by the encouragement and patience of impacted family members, is truly a remarkable individual feat. However, the marathon described in Hebrews seems somehow different. The writer acknowledged that those who have finished their race are watching from the sidelines, but it almost seems as if they haven't fully entered into their rest, as they await our own crossing the finish line.

It is as if the race being described is a history-long relay race. In a relay race, upon completion of one leg of the race, the runner doesn't leave the field. The finished runner eagerly watches the others on his or her team until every member of the team cheers the final runner as she crosses the finish line, and then they all remain to collect their prize together.

While this image isn't the one we familiarly have in our mind about what heaven is like, it seems the writer of Hebrews had something like this in view. Our running of this race is being eagerly watched and cheered for by the great cloud of witnesses, that company of friends and saints who have finished their legs of the race but know that the entire enterprise is far from over.

So what about our friends? It is one thing to know that a huge crowd is waiting at the finish line; it is quite another to meet your friends there. While I have often heard people say, "We'll all be together again in heaven," it always seemed like "pie in the sky by-and-by." Sure, we'll meet in heaven, but it could be quite different from what we expect. It will be very large, for one thing, and the crowds will be enormous. How can we be certain that it won't take eons to find our friends, by which time they will have forgotten about us?

We know little for certain about heaven, but Jesus did tell us two things. Marriage lasts until death, but no longer (Mark 12:25). Friendships, however, will continue in heaven.

ETERNAL FRIENDS (LUKE 16:1-9)

The story Jesus told in Luke 16 troubles us as we read it. The good guy is cheated and the bad guy is commended!

The manager, serving as an accountant for a wealthy landowner, was accused of wasting his employer's goods, either through faulty accounting or poor decision making. He was fired and told to turn over the written records. It is as if he were told, "Have the records up-to-date and be ready to turn the books over to me by Friday." So he decided to cook the books before turning them over to his master. He made friends by giving away his master's money. In decreasing the amounts of rent people owed, he was making his master poorer and his master's tenants wealthier. He hoped he could later turn these transactions into contacts and friendships he could literally take to the bank. His plan was that these clients would be indebted to him and would welcome him into their homes when he was turned out. It seems to be an encouragement of Machiavellian thinking or of outright dishonesty!

The master was a shrewd businessperson himself. He had fired the manager because the manager was *not* shrewd in his dealings. So, in a moment of desperation, this inept manager developed a plan that was uncharacteristically shrewd. When the master discovered the plan, his own appreciation for shrewd thinking (even though at the same time he was dismayed about it) made him commend his former manager for this unexpected display of brilliance.

At this point in the plot, the parable ended and Jesus spoke to the listeners: "Children of this age are more shrewd in dealing with their own generation than are the children of light" (Luke 16:8). To retranslate, "Businesspeople know how to use money to make friends, but Christians don't." And then Jesus went on to say perhaps the most confusing thing of all: "And I tell you, make friends for yourselves by means of dishonest wealth so that when it is gone, they may welcome you into the eternal homes" (verse 9).

Let us consider what Jesus meant by a few of these phrases. First, "dishonest wealth" could also be translated "worldly wealth." He was not speaking about wealth gained illegally. Jesus went on to contrast "worldly wealth" with true riches, that is, treasure in heaven (v. 11). Second, Jesus spoke about "when it [wealth] is gone" (v. 9). Wealth is gone when life itself is over, and that is when only treasure in heaven matters. For all people and all time, money always fails at the point of death. Finally, Jesus spoke of "eternal homes" (v. 9). Here Jesus was referring to heaven, where his disciples will live eternally with him and with one another.

So what was Jesus trying to tell his disciples? Jesus told them to use money to make friends who would welcome them into heaven. Was Jesus actually telling people to buy friends?

Missionary and martyr Jim Elliot wrote, "He is no fool who gives what he cannot keep to gain what he cannot lose." Jesus appears to have agreed. Money one day will fail, but friendship, it seems, has the potential to be eternal. Jesus told his followers to invest their temporary, worldly wealth in other people who will become friends and welcome them into heaven.

How does this happen? How do we make friends who will welcome us into heaven? We do this by spending our resources so that people will come to know our generous and wealthy God. As we spend our money on people, we communicate that they are valuable. The gospel says that God so loved people that he spent his only begotten Son on the cross in order to save them. God used his resources to make friends who would celebrate with him in heaven. Jesus, in this parable, was telling us to do the same.

Is it appropriate to anticipate heaven for the company we'll enjoy there? Our pursuit over, our quest achieved, what will fill our days? What society will we keep? Certainly we'll drink deeply in fellowship with Jesus and bask in the glory of God. We'll worship with the saints of history and the great men and women of faith of our own time. But it seems it is quite appropriate to seek to prepare for ourselves a company of eternal friends. We are told to order our affairs, set our priorities, even allocate our resources so that our eternal lives will be as friend-filled as our natural lives, if not more so. We are to live out our pursuit of God so that not only we but also those we care about find God as we do, in this life of love and joy.

Jesus' words in Luke 16 tell us that no effort in friendship is wasted. In a society as transient as ours, it is easy to become cynical or complacent, settling for entertainment over intimacy and familiarity over risk. Nothing—no act of friendship, no friendship itself, however brief—is wasted on us, for whom "all things work together for good" (Romans 8:28). So we can love with abandon, knowing our love in faith will abide, even as our friendships change over time.

So, faced with my frequent choice between making a phone call to a friend versus sinking into my solitary reading of *The Economist* magazine, I can be counseled by Jim Elliot. I cannot keep time—it slips through my fingers at an alarming rate of speed—but I can invest it so that I can gain wealth I cannot lose: deeper knowledge of God and friends committed with me to the enjoyment of God forever.

VISUALIZE ETERNITY

Eternity includes time because it is the fifth dimension. A line includes points; a surface includes lines; a solid body includes surfaces; and motion through time includes solid bodies moving. As the fourth dimension includes the third, the fifth dimension includes the fourth.

This is not merely philosophical curiosity but has practical, personal application. It makes eternity interesting, not boring. The square walls of a house are rather boring when flat and detached from the house. But when the two-dimensional walls are part of the three-dimensional house, they come alive. And the three-dimensional house itself comes alive as part of someone's four-dimensional lifetime. Our four-dimensional lifetimes are the walls of our five-dimensional heavenly house.

PETER KREEFT

Peter Kreeft wrote his book *Heaven: The Heart's Deepest Longing* in part to answer the question "Won't heaven be boring?" His answer, given in many pages of articulate argument, includes the previous illustration, which appeals to me because I have long conceived of heaven in precisely the same mathematically textured language. But Kreeft used this image to reinforce the message of Luke 16, indeed the message of this book. If our earthly lives, four-dimensional as they are now (three-dimensional bodies moving through time), are to be compared to the flat walls of our heavenly homes, then the shape and manner of heaven's dwelling places for each of us will be informed and enriched in some way by our efforts in the pursuit of eternal things while in this life. We can make friends who will welcome us into eternal homes and who will join us in our heavenly story. Our enjoyment of heaven, as rich as it will be, will be richer and deeper because of the choices we have made to value heavenly things, eternal things, while on this earth.

I recently read through mv twentieth college reunion directory. I

looked for the name and address of my freshman roommate, fully knowing that I would not find it. I lived with Art for two years, and sometime
after that, he became a follower of Jesus. Our friendship deepened in a
dimension we had not shared during our years of living as roommates.
After we graduated, he worked as an engineer (and soon as a manager)
for Intel; I joined IVCF staff. We toured Silicon Valley delis, lunching
together every few months. This continued for a few years, until I received a phone call telling me of Art's death from injuries sustained
from a thousand-foot fall while ice-climbing Mount Shasta. That night
was seventeen years ago. Art never knew my wife or children; I had
heard he was recently engaged but never had a chance to meet his fian-
cée. Our friendship dates from a distant past, all but inaccessible to my
life today. Yet this friendship is not inaccessible to my life a hundred
years hence. Art will be one of the friends who will welcome me into
the eternal homes. Our friendship will be part of the framing of our
heavenly dwellings, with threads of each of us enriching the fabric of
the earthly tapestries adorning the walls.

I began this book by asserting that our twin desires for God and for
friendship are met in the same process. We find friendship by seeking
God, for it is his resources that make friendship satisfying and literally
make lasting friendships possible. He hosts us into friendships; he administers his healing and wisdom through friendships; and he forgives
us so that we have resources to forgive those closest to us.

Yet we find God in our embrace of friendship as well. Our friends
welcome us back from death to life. They see in our lives what we cannot see. They speak to us gently but clearly, directing us back to God
when we stray.

Friends love us because of God's love for them, and friends' love for
us shows us God's love for us. We are able to believe God's promises are
true because our friends have trusted God and found them so.

As an IVCF staff member, I am supported by a team of people who
believe enough in what I do that they have sent their money to IVCF to
keep me at it. Occasionally my wife and I have welcomed supporters of

ours into our ministry to meet people who have been served or brought into faith by our work with IVCF. That is always a fun experience, but it happens too rarely, and most of our supporters never get to experience this.

Imagine what it will be like when the faith is sight and the skies have been rolled back as a scroll. When we no longer see as through a glass darkly, what will we see? Among other things, the tremendous personal and eternal impact our lives and choices have made on so many, and the ripple effects from those lives similarly spent.

C. S. Lewis told us (and by the final page of the Chronicles of Narnia we are ready to believe it) that our whole earthly lives are like the title page of the never-ending story of the people of God in the realm of God. We are, in this life, compiling the *dramatis personae* of our heavenly tale.

So the pursuit of God in the company of friends ultimately turns into a celebration of God in the company of friends. Friends are with us not just for the journey but also for the party afterward. As we begin to suspect about many things in this life of faith, it is true also of friendship: the best really is yet to be.

FOR REFLECTION

1. Think about friends you'd like to see in heaven but aren't entirely sure, at this point, that you will. How can you spend your resources in such a way that your friends may become open to finding their source of salvation in Jesus?

2. How does the expectation of heaven shape your life now? Your friendships?

Notes

Introduction: The Transforming Power of Discipleship in Community

[1]A. W. Tozer makes this observation at the opening of his book *The Pursuit of God* (Camp Hill, Penn.: Christian Publications, 1982), first published in 1948. Tozer writes, "Christian theology teaches the doctrine of prevenient grace, which, briefly stated, means that before a man can seek God, God must first have sought the man" (p. 11).

Chapter One: Friends in the Pursuit of God

[1]*Nicomachean Ethics* 8. While Aristotle sets these three motives as separable bases for friendship, he also states that when they are combined, they form the height of friendship, its greatest and most enduring instance. Friends that share a joint commitment to virtue find that the relationship is both mutually useful and enjoyable.

[2]Robert N. Bellah et al., *Habits of the Heart: Individualism and Commitment in American Life* (Berkeley: Regents of University of California, 1985), p. 115. Bellah's work is a landmark analysis of the loss of the understanding of the common commitment to the "good" (religion, civic duty, public and private ethics and morality) from our cultural understanding and practice of friendship. For a more recent look at the same set of cultural trends, consider *Bowling Alone: The Collapse and Revival of American Community* by Robert D. Putnam (New York: Simon & Schuster, 2000).

Chapter Two: The Hospitality of God

[1]Geoff Gordon, IVCF staff in Boston at the time, told this story for his friends. We were all impressed. Now he has graciously allowed me to reproduce it here. Geoff and Val were indeed married and now live in Providence, where they serve with IVCF leading the staff team in Rhode Island.

[2]The six other miracles, besides changing water into wine, are as follows: (1) the healing of the royal official's son (John 4:46-54); (2) the healing of the paralytic on the sabbath (5:1-9); (3) the feeding of the five thousand (6:1-14); (4) Jesus walking on the water (6:16-21); (5) the healing of the man born blind (9:1-12); and (6) the raising of Lazarus (11:1-44).

[3]I am going to treat this story of the miracle of the water made wine both as a historical event and as a parable, as I believe John (the author of this story) meant for us to understand this and each of the miracles he recorded.

[4]Henry Cloud and John Townsend, *Boundaries in Marriage* (Grand Rapids, Mich.: Zondervan, 1999).

[5]Henri J. M. Nouwen, *Clowning in Rome* (Garden City, N.Y.: Image, 1979), p. 15.

Chapter Four: Life, Death and Love Among Friends

[1]A good friend, upon hearing this example, remarked that my experience may not be typical or helpful for people with an addiction to pornography. The abstain-binge-shame-abstain cycle isn't necessarily easily broken in this way, and I don't want to be construed as touting simple solutions to deep struggle. However, as with any addiction, our ability to turn to friends who are able to speak into our lives and direct us toward God is a part of what makes victory possible. A helpful resource to aid accountability among friends dealing with Internet pornography temptation is found at <www.covenanteyes.com>.

Chapter Five: Presence and Intimacy in the Company of Friends

[1]Luke 8:1-3 indicates that, although Jesus' twelve apostles were all men, women followed him from the earliest days of his ministry. Women were certainly counted among the 120 followers gathered in the upper room at Pentecost.

[2]The central ideas of this section, and indeed the seminal ideas of this book, extend and build upon Robert Coleman's crucial work, *The Master Plan of Evangelism* (Grand Rapids, Mich.: Revell, 1963). This section builds on his first chapter, "Selection," and this is typical: "Everything that is done with the few is for the salvation of the multitudes" (p. 35).

Chapter Seven: Friends Serve, Lead, See and Speak

[1]*Nicomachean Ethics* 8.3.

[2]I am going to describe servanthood in the ideal. Frankly, I know of only rare examples of servanthood in the ideal, just as I have seen few live with entirely pure motives. The cynical reader will be justified in pointing out that seeing life the way Jesus did is difficult for mere mortals. And yet let me assert that servanthood, as described below, is indeed possible, to a great extent, and reality can indeed attain the standard of perfection of Ivory soap, "99-44/100% pure." With that caveat, please don't be distracted by the description of an ideal.

[3]Robert Greenleaf, *Servant Leadership* (Mahwah, N.J.: Paulist, 1977), pp. 24, 26.

[4]Mark 1:17; 6:7-13; 8:31—9:1, 12, 31; 10:39; 11:2-3; 13:2-31; 14:7-9, 13, 27; Luke 22:31-32; among many other examples.

[5]Paul used the following phrases: "serving the Lord with *all* humility and with tears" (Acts 20:19, emphasis added); "I did not shrink from doing *anything* helpful" (verse 20, emphasis added); "for I did not shrink from declaring to you the *whole purpose of God*" (verse 27, emphasis added); "I *did not cease* night or day *to warn everyone with tears*" (verse 31, emphasis added); "*In all this* I have given you an example" (verse 35, emphasis added).

Chapter Eight: Listening and Gentle Influence

[1]Dietrich Bonhoeffer, *Life Together*, trans. John Doberstein (San Francisco: HarperSanFrancisco, 1954), p. 97.

[2]Robert Bolton, *People Skills* (New York: Simon & Schuster, 1986), pp. 44-45.

[3]It is beyond the scope of this book to detail the nature of narrative evangelism, but an excellent resource is Leighton Ford, *The Power of Story* (Colorado Springs, Colo.: NavPress, 1994).

Chapter Nine: Competition and Comparison Among Friends

[1] I understand that the lack of gender-neutral language here may be distracting for some, as (no doubt) this note will be for others. But the reality is, I am a man, and I find myself occasionally feeling competitive with other men in a different way than how I might feel competitive with women.

[2] An excellent resource on crosscultural sensitivity is Sherwood Lingenfelter and Marvin Mayers, *Ministering Crossculturally* (Grand Rapids, Mich.: Baker, 1986).

[3] Helpful to me was a discussion of the Myers-Briggs Type Indicator (MBTI) from David Keirsey and Marilyn Bates, *Please Understand Me: Character and Temperament Types* (Del Mar, Calif.: Prometheus Nemesis, 1984).

Chapter Ten: Reconciliation and Forgiveness Among Friends

[1] C. S. Lewis, *The Great Divorce* (New York: Macmillan, 1946), p. 8.

[2] Yes, I know that *bazillion* is not a real number. One talent equaled six thousand denarii, or about twenty years' wages. Ten thousand talents would roughly equal two hundred thousand years' wages, which is far larger than the largest income in Palestine at the time—King Herod's. This amount, ten thousand talents, is a fantasy figure, and in today's parlance, the most accurate translation, I believe, would be "$1.5 bazillion."

Chapter Eleven: Jesus' Vision for the Company of Friends

[1] In fact, Aristotle does himself extend his comments to marriage and he speaks at length about the friendship between husband and wife in *Nicomachean Ethics* 8.7. Of course, his topic in this section is the general kind of friendship where there is an inequality between the parties, "that of man to wife and in general that of ruler to subject"! While, of course, I don't share Aristotle's views on the relative inequality beween the genders in marriage, it may be said that his extended comments were relatively enlightened and generous for his time.

[2] The Greek word translated "brothers," as used by Jesus, almost always, and quite obviously from the text, was meant to refer to both men and women in the household of faith and is translated helpfully as "brothers and sisters" in the New Revised Standard Version.

[3] For my study of the "deceitfulness of sin" and the "evil heart of unbelief," I am greatly indebted to Daniel P. Fuller, *The Unity of the Bible* (Grand Rapids, Mich.: Zondervan, 1992), pp. 279-97. Fuller's insights were further applied and elaborated in John Piper, *Future Grace* (Sisters, Ore: Multnomah Press, 1995).

[4] Claudia Black, author of *It Will Never Happen to Me*, in a web-published talk given on September 6, 2001, at the Russell Senate Building in Washington, D.C. This was a Capitol Hill Luncheon sponsored by Al-Anon, celebrating its fifty-year anniversary.

[5] *The Life of Saint Teresa of Ávila by Herself*, trans. J. M. Cohen (New York: Viking Penguin, 1957).

[6] Rebecca Manley Pippert, *Out of the Saltshaker* (Downers Grove, Ill.: InterVarsity Press, 1981).

[7] I am trying to avoid either extreme of the Christ-and-culture debate here without making an extended argument. Of course Christians will be involved in society, including as individuals. But I don't think that is the point of the images of salt and light in Matthew 5.

[8] See John 5:17-23; 8:54-55; 10:29-38; 14:7, 20-24; 15:15; among others.

[9]For the extended list of sinful attitudes of the heart, I am indebted to Tom Pratt, former IVCF staffworker and founder of Servant Partners, a ministry among the poor centered in Pasadena, California.

Chapter Thirteen: The Mission of God in the Company of Friends

[1] Not to belabor the insight too much (or perhaps I'm beyond that already), but Aristotle's claims about friendship are like the Trinity—once you know about them, you see them everywhere. With our terms *practical* (useful), *spiritual* ("the good") and *fun* (enjoyable), we were declaring that we offered a well-rounded experience of a company of friends in the pursuit of God.

[2]This is a simplified version of what Jesus said to them in Mark 8:2, before the feeding of the four thousand. There the disciples respond to him a little better, without any sarcasm but simply a sincere question: "How can one feed these people with bread here in the desert?" They were doing better on that day than the first time around.

Annotated Bibliography

GENERAL RESOURCES

Aelred of Rievaulx. *Spiritual Friendship.* Translated by Mary Eugenia Laker. Kalamazoo, Mich.: Cistercian Publications, 1977. This little treatise is an excellent source of monastic thinking on friendship. Aelred was something of a renegade (as much as an abbot can be) in monastic tradition. Typical monasteries forbade monks to have special friendships—this was thought to impede the general brotherhood of the entire order. And in general, any other devotions were considered a threat to devotion to Christ. Aelred, quite obviously, argued otherwise, saying that friendship is a great source of sharpening and refining love for God.

Anderson, Keith R. *Friendships That Run Deep: Seven Ways to Build Lasting Relationships.* Downers Grove, Ill.: InterVarsity Press, 1997. Anderson describes friendship in terms of hospitality. When inviting people to be friends, we are welcoming them into our lives just as we would invite someone into our homes. In this way, friendship is about learning to become good hosts to our guests. This book also has some helpful material on the seasons of friendship.

Benner, David. *Sacred Companions: The Gift of Spiritual Friendship and Direction.* Downers Grove, Ill.: InterVarsity Press, 2002. This book is worth the purchase price for the annotated bibliography alone. It is an excellent resource for those who are considering seeking spiritual direction or who hunger for more depth in their spiritual friendships.

Harris, Mark. *Companions for Your Spiritual Journey: Discovering the Disciplines of the Saints.* Downers Grove, Ill.: InterVarsity Press, 1999. This book provided me one of my first introductions to Aelred of Rievaulx. Harris introduces the reader to John Bunyan, Julian of Norwich, Bernard of Clairvaux and Origen (among others) in an accessible and practical style.

Lamb, Richard. *Following Jesus in the "Real World": Discipleship for the Post-College Years.* Downers Grove, Ill.: InterVarsity Press, 1995. While I suppose it is tacky to refer to my own book, let me just say that if you are between twenty-one and twenty-eight years of age, then this book was written for you. It addresses many of the themes of this book, with contextualized examples for people who are in the transition phase between attending college and starting a family.

A Spiritual Friendship. New York: Crossroad, 1999. This anonymous book is in the format of letters written by two nuns, M.F. and H., to one another over several years. Their letters are filled with both gentle wisdom and familiar details. A portrait of an unusual spiritual friendship.

Tozer, A. W. *The Pursuit of God.* Camp Hill, Penn.: Christian Publications, 1982. Tozer's classic work combines simple descriptions of "The Human Thirst for the Divine," as the work is subtitled, with clear statements of the need for people in his day to turn back to God. His is the book that put the phrase "the pursuit of God" into common parlance, and any treatment of the topic owes Tozer a debt.

RESOURCES FOR SPECIFIC CHAPTERS

Chapter Three: The Healing Touch of God

Flynn, Mike, and Doug Gregg. *Inner Healing: A Handbook for Helping Yourself and Others.* Downers Grove, Ill.: InterVarsity Press, 1993. This book will give practical help for people hoping to help group members or friends by praying for the healing of their past memories, psychological wounds and inability to forgive.

Chapter Five: Presence and Intimacy in the Company of Friends

Coleman, Robert E. *The Master Plan of Evangelism.* Old Tappan, N.J.: Revell, 1963. This little book, a modern classic, can be read in an hour but will stick with you for life. Its principles have tutored millions to be effective at the relational side of the ministry of the gospel.

Chapter Six: On the Road in the Company of Friends

Stiles, Mack, and Leeann. *Mack and Leeann's Guide to Short-Term Missions.* Downers Grove, Ill.: InterVarsity Press, 2000. This is a practical help for anyone thinking about a mission trip for any length of time. It has a helpful discussion of parenting and kids on mission trips. The stories are funny and well told, combined with lots of practical help and deep, faith-stretching challenges.

Chapter Eight: Listening and Gentle Influence

Adler, Mortimer J. *How to Speak, How to Listen.* New York: Macmillan, 1983. Though this book is more insightful on how to speak and a great tool for anyone who must engage in public speaking, it also contains an engaging discussion of how to listen silently to a speaker and how to have productive discussion and pleasurable conversation. This follow-up to Adler's classic *How to Read a Book* is a great tool for anyone with a desire to develop his or her conversational ability.

Bolton, Robert. *People Skills: How to Assert Yourself, Listen to Others and Resolve Conflicts.* New York: Simon & Schuster, 1986. A primer on active listening, asking questions, resolving conflicts and in general the verbal tools that make for good friendships.

Chapter Nine: Competition and Comparison Among Friends

Keirsey, David, and Marilyn Bates. *Please Understand Me: Character and Temperament Types.* Del Mar, Calif.: Prometheus Nemesis, 1984. The book, giving the theory and typology of the four basic temperaments and sixteen personality types, is accessible in its style and